Rock and Roll, Social Protest, and Authenticity

For the Record: Lexington Studies in Rock and Popular Music

Series Editors:

Scott D. Calhoun, Cedarville University

Christopher Endrinal, Florida Gulf Coast University

For the Record: Lexington Studies in Rock and Popular Music features monographs and edited collections that examine topics relevant to the composition, consumption, and influence of the rock and popular music genres which have arisen starting in the twentiethth century in all nations and cultures. In the series, scholars approach these genres from music studies, cultural studies, and sociological studies frameworks, and may incorporate theories and methods from literary, philosophical, performance, and religious studies, in order to examine the wider significance of particular artists, subgenres, fandoms, or other music-related phenomena. Books in the series use as a starting point the understanding that as both products of our larger culture and driving forces within that wider culture, rock and popular music are worthy of critical study.

Advisory Board

Joshua Duchan, Wayne State University; David Easley, Oklahoma City University; Bryn Hughes, University of Miami; Greg McCandless, Full Sail University; Ann van der Merwe, Miami University; Meg Wilhoite

Titles in the Series

Rock and Roll, Social Protest, and Authenticity

Historical, Philosophical, and Cultural Explorations

Kurt Torell

LEXINGTON BOOKS
Lanham • Boulder • New York • London

Published by Lexington Books
An imprint of The Rowman & Littlefield Publishing Group, Inc.
4501 Forbes Boulevard, Suite 200, Lanham, Maryland 20706
www.rowman.com

6 Tinworth Street, London SE11 5AL, United Kingdom

British Library Cataloguing in Publication Information Available

Library of Congress Cataloging-in-Publication Data

Names: Torell, Kurt, 1962- author.
Title: Rock and roll, social protest, and authenticity : historical, philosophical, and cultural explorations / Kurt Torell.
Description: Lanham : Lexington Books, 2021. | Series: For the record: Lexington studies in rock and popular music | Includes bibliographical references and index. | Summary: "This book investigates the relation of rock and roll to social protest music and authenticity. It examines the nature and commercial origins of rock and roll, why rock and roll was frequently considered subversive, and the nature and significance of authenticity to rock and roll as social protest music"-- Provided by publisher.
Identifiers: LCCN 2021025771 (print) | LCCN 2021025772 (ebook) | ISBN 9781793655639 (cloth) | ISBN 9781793655646 (epub)
Subjects: LCSH: Rock music--Social aspects--United States--History--20th century. | Rock music--Political aspects--United States--History--20th century. | Sound recording industry--United States--History--20th century.
Classification: LCC ML3918.R63 T65 2021 (print) | LCC ML3918.R63 (ebook) | DDC 781.66--dc23
LC record available at https://lccn.loc.gov/2021025771
LC ebook record available at https://lccn.loc.gov/2021025772

♾™ The paper used in this publication meets the minimum requirements of American National Standard for Information Sciences—Permanence of Paper for Printed Library Materials, ANSI/NISO Z39.48-1992.

For my parents,
Barbara and Erven Torell

Contents

Acknowledgments

The work of this volume would not have been possible without my learning from the excellent research and analysis conducted by a number of serious students of music and culture over many decades. Therefore, I believe it is only appropriate to further acknowledge their monumental intellectual contributions and to express my gratitude for what their work has taught me. These students include, but are by no means limited to, R. Serge Denisoff, Archie Green, Fred Hoeptner, Bill C. Malone, Judith McCulloh, Ingrid Monson, Richard A. Peterson, and D. K. Wilgus. Finally, I would be remiss if I did not also thank Jacqueline Edmondson who cheerfully and consistently encouraged me to complete this project.

Introduction

"But the Man Can't Bust Our Music" *(Columbia Records Print Ad, 1968)*

It is often expressed that a surge occurred in the creation and popularity of commercial protest songs during the 1960s,[1] many of which have been typically associated with the musical genre of rock and roll. Moreover, it remains a widespread belief that this surge in commercial protest songs was related to "countercultural" behavior of younger, middle-class and "mainstream" members of society, as well as various forms of social activism directed toward a spectrum of ongoing social injustices which permeated the American demographic landscape. Indeed, despite its widespread condemnation and blacklisting by Top 40 stations and ABC affiliates (Denisoff 1972, 21), the release of the wildly successful song "Eve of Destruction," which Paul Hirsch described as "a trenchant condemnation of war in general and American society in particular" (Hirsch et al. 1972, 87), has frequently been offered as evidence of the apparent surge in popularity of protest music, having rocketed to number one in the charts in 1965 (Denisoff 1972, 22). And yet, perhaps to temper this perception a bit, it has also been noted that it was another, still arguably political, song which received "the most AM airplay in the 1960s," namely "the Pentagon inspired pro-war 'Ballad of the Green Berets'" (Denisoff 1983, 195), a tune that also happened to reach number one in 1965 shortly after its release (Hirsch et al. 1972, 87). In addition, one of the most commercially successful political songs of the early 1970s, having been credited with selling a million copies in just five and a half days, was "The Battle Hymn of Lt. Calley" by the Country and Western company of Shelby Singleton (Denisoff 1972, 25).

Although it should not be overlooked that the so-called "folk-revival" of the early 1960s probably accounts for most of the commercial social protest music of the period, it is also true that rock and roll, before and after the revival, has been historically affiliated with some kind of social resistance toward various dimensions of the social mainstream. From the very advent of rock and roll in the early 1950s, through its development in the 1960s, sociologists, psychologists, historians, popular spokespersons, persons in leadership positions, as well as "concerned" citizens from various corners of society, perceived rock and roll as somehow undermining the important moral fabric of the extant society, and they adamantly questioned or expressed passionate concern or disdain about its effects on the generations coming of age.

By protest music in general, and in particular that of the 1960s, one may imagine, perhaps axiomatically, that the protest in question is directed toward the norms, conventions, and various infrastructural pockets of power and systems of control of mainstream society and culture that serve to maintain the status quo; that is, one may think of the production and performance of such music as a genuinely countercultural enterprise to some degree. That there is something to this assumption is evident from the groundbreaking scholarship produced by a few signature writers on the subject. In his early research on the presence of social protest songs of the 1960s, Paul Hirsch defined "social protest" hits as those that contained "controversial themes surrounding the morality of war, relations between different racial groups, drug usage, and also any songs whose lyrics are critical of widely accepted values or legitimized roles in American society" (Hirsch 1971, 374; cf. Hirsch et al. 1972, 87). In *Sing a Song of Social Significance*, Serge Denisoff defined a protest song as "*a social-political statement designed to create an awareness of social problems and which offers or infers a solution which is viewed as deviant in nature*" (Denisoff 1983, 26), while also adding that "[s]ongs which only point to societal problems without offering solutions may be interpreted as protest songs to the already converted" (Denisoff 1983, note 24, 237). Meanwhile, one definition, labeled as "classical" by Denisoff (1983, 21), and originally offered by John Greenway, construed protest songs as:

> the struggle songs of the people. They are outbursts of bitterness, of hatred for the oppressor, of determination to endure hardships together and to fight for a better life. Whether they are ballads composed on the picket line, they are imbued with the feeling of communality, or togetherness. They are songs of unity, and therefore most are songs of the union (Greenway 1953, 10).[2]

Drawing a distinction between the old protest songs, inspired by the sort of union causes referenced in Greenway's account, and the newer protest songs of the late 1950s and early 1960s, Josh Dunson notes important differences:

> [t]he young song writer today is sparked by disillusionment and anger. Often he has gone through the hardship of rejecting the values of his parents and those he had considered infallible during childhood. His rejection of segregation, war and exploitation often grows into a conviction that none of the older people knew what they were doing when they made or tried to remake the world . . .

> In the songs they wrote, the young people asked questions. The older
> song writers gave in their songs what they believed to be the answers . . .
>   The subjects of the new songs were the conditions that aroused the stu-
> dents' concern and feeling. There was little reference to the labor movement,
> but many dealt with the theme of civil liberties, peace and civil rights (Dunson
> 1965, 47–48).

Be that as it may, if one speculates that music can only exist, ontologically
speaking, in the heads of listeners (be they composers, performers, audience
members),[3] the matter of what qualifies as protest music appears to become
even more complicated (cf. Platoff 2005, 263; Denzin 1970). What happens,
for example, if an author intends a work to be an expression of social protest, but its audience, overwhelmingly, perceives the work to be an affirma-
tion of the status quo? Conversely, what happens when an author intends a
work to align with the status quo, but there is no consensus among various
audiences as to whether it so aligns or is subversive in nature? With regard
to the former question, for example, James R. McDonald underscores the
problematic rather clearly when he explores "the metatextual possibilities" of
Bruce Springsteen's "Born in the U.S.A." By examining both recordings and
performances, the song may be interpreted by some as a kind of ode to the
wonders of being an "American," particularly when one takes note that the
refrain "is repeated to raised fists by both the performer and the audience"
during live performances,

> suggesting a spirited enthusiasm similar to the ending of the national anthem at a
> baseball game. On one level, at least, the text describes pride in America. . . . On
> another level, however, the text can be viewed as highly critical of the American
> government. Portraying the plight of a Vietnam veteran, the song has also been
> heralded by veterans as a realistic assessment of the difficulties some had to face
> upon their return to this country, particularly through lines like the following:
> "Down in the shadow of the penitentiary / Out by the gas fires of the refinery /
> I'm ten years burning down the road / Nowhere to run ain't got nowhere to go"
> (McDonald 1988b, 499–500).

With regard to the latter question, a paradigmatic case of the problematic
may be found in the crafting and reception of the Beatles' two versions of
"Revolution" (that is, "Revolution" and "Revolution 1"), which I will discuss in detail below, or one may consider the various performances of Merle
Haggard's "Okie from Muskogee." In this case, I think it is fair to say that
the meaning of such lyrics as "We don't smoke marijuana in Muskogee, We
don't take no trips on LSD. . . . Caus' we like livin' right and bein' free" could
change depending upon the audience.[4]

Given all of this, I believe it is intellectually fruitful, prima facie at least, to proceed by casting the definitional net rather liberally and construe music as a form of protest if it is justifiably "subversive" in some respect, but typically in relation to so-called "mainstream values" and widely accepted systems of interpersonal modes of conduct (cf. Ferrandino 1969, 266, 289; Cole 1971, 391), including, but certainly not limited to, the advocacy, or at least a favorable opinion of, drug use (Robinson et al. 1976, p. 135). There are certainly a few reasons for casting the net so broadly in this way, at least at the outset, once one also considers the relevance of lyrics and styles of performance in relation to the layered sociocultural contexts in which those elements may be found to be specifically situated. It is hoped that this will become more apparent in what follows.

In this book, I attempt to articulate the respects in which rock and roll can be accurately construed as social protest music. In general, my conclusion will be that the nature of protest in rock and roll is such that it embodies, or, perhaps, is symptomatic of, a sort of "contradiction" that, time and again, has permeated, not just in rock and roll, but a variety of other cultural realities of American society. While rock and roll may have originally emerged possessing certain subversive qualities, due, on occasion, to seemingly "genuine" or "authentic" subversive inclinations, its evolution was also simultaneously shaped by efforts to co-op and further popularize it for profit. For it was launched, for the most part, by elements of the very *status quo* toward which its subversive qualities were directed, namely the economic instruments and interests, as well as the assisting political and cultural ideologies and mechanisms, that constituted that *status quo*'s fabric. Indeed, in like fashion, one can see this sort of "contradiction" often manifested in other cultural products that emerged prior to, contemporaneous with, and following the rise of rock and roll, such as the manufactured film persona of James Dean as putative rebel, Marlon Brando's depiction of Johnny Strabler in the film *The Wild One*, or the commercially refined "muscle cars" of the 1960s that emerged out of the chop-shopped roadsters of the early 1950s (cf. Conroy 1983).

With regard to rock and roll, that apparent contradiction, I think, is particularly well-instantiated in a much-discussed poster, produced in 1968 by Columbia Records, that contained the slogan "But The Man can't bust our music" (cf. M. Lydon 1969, 320). For the irony exemplified in this poster is certainly to be found residing nearly at its surface. On the one hand, it appears to express the concern that the so-called "Establishment," "The Man" that is, was attempting to thwart the spirit and message of the rock music of the day, where that music's spirit and message, perhaps its very raison d'etre, was presumably intended to be a criticism of that very establishment. And yet, on the other hand, the poster itself was, in fact, a message designed and widely telegraphed by a privileged member of that very establishment, namely Columbia Records.

It is probably not surprising that this irony of the poster did not go unnoticed by members of its contemporary audience at the time it first appeared. As Joe Ferrandino asserted upon its appearance, "Columbia records has the audacity to put out a record ad which says 'The man can't bust our music,' when in fact Columbia is *the man*" (Ferrandino 1969, 286). As Ralph Gleason further remarked at the time,

> [t]he implication [of the poster] aligns "us" against "them," and the context of the advertising design and illustration is interracial, hippie, pot-smoking youth. . . . Is Columbia for legalization of marijuana? No. Columbia is for making money. Thus the investment in music aimed at long-haired youth. The music speaks directly to them, it leaps past all barriers and is justified by the sacred principles of the true religion of the United States, making money. (Gleason 1969, 137)

Indeed, the ironic co-optation of the subversive by its target during this time is not only to be found so bluntly represented in this ad, but elsewhere as well, such as in a 1968 full-page ad in the *Wall Street Journal* that read, "in inch-high block letters, 'Let's put the power suckers up against the wall'" (Peterson and Berger 1972, 298).

Understood within this context that the "contradiction" of the poster conveys (a context perhaps further underscored in the ambiguous, if not intentionally duplicitous, quality of such signature rock anthems as the Beatles' "Revolution" and "Revolution 1" or the Rolling Stones "Street Fighting Man"), namely a context where one finds a music industry diligently undertaking measures to appropriate for profit qualities of music which appeared to question and subvert dimensions of the institutions upon which the industry's operation and success depended, I intend to examine in what respects rock and roll still managed to remain "authentic" protest music, from the time of its inception and throughout its development. For despite its issuing from within the bosom of its paradoxical appropriation and commodification for profit, like so many other instances of countercultural paraphernalia, lifestyles and rhetoric, I intend to explore to what degree rock and roll could still manage to retain some trace of an "authentic" social protest quality. In this regard, the theme of this book aligns to some degree with Michael Lydon's take on rock and roll when he asserts that

> [f]rom the start, rock has been commercial in its very essence. An American creation on the level of the hamburger or the billboard, it was never an art form that just happened to make money, nor a commercial undertaking that sometimes became art. Its art was synonymous with its business. The movies

are perhaps closest to rock in their aesthetic involvement with the demands of profitability, but even they once had an arty tradition which scorned the pleasing of the masses. (M. Lydon 1969, 314)

And yet, Michael Lydon also seems to acknowledge that, unlike commodities such as hairspray, rock and roll was still the sort of thing that chafed, at least to some degree, the commercial infrastructure that made possible its existence in the first place:

> [r]ock musicians, like their followers, have always been torn between the obvious pleasures that America held out and the price paid for them. Rock and roll is not revolutionary music because it has never gotten beyond articulation of this paradox. At best it has offered the defiance of withdrawal; its violence never amounted to more than a cry of "Don't bother me." (M. Lydon 1969, 321)

To render this account of rock and roll, I begin by providing a rough sketch of what kind of music it was at its inception, followed by a discussion of various environmental factors of a technological, economic, social, and strictly historical nature that attended and shaped its roots and subsequent development. Given this context, I then apply what I believe is a useful heuristic distinction, which I borrow from Plato, to cursorily identify an often-overlooked aspect of rock and roll within which a noteworthy degree of its protest quality may be said to be situated. This demonstration is, in turn, followed by a discussion of the nature of authenticity and the degree to which social protest music, as such, can survive any commercialization. By appeal to this discussion, I then conclude with a summary of what I take to be the interface between the social protest quality of rock and roll, on the one hand, and the astonishing efficacy, on the other hand, of the wider sociocultural and economic environment within and by which it emerged. While appropriation of everything that makes money was certainly not new to American life prior to nor since the onset of rock and roll, what is peculiar and instructive about the case of such social protest music, and what may be, on that account, additionally illuminating for us about the nature of the culture that gave rise to it, was the appropriation for a buck of something emblematic of resistance to that very cultural tendency.

NOTES

1. Cf. Robinson and Hirsch 1969, 42. According to Denisoff, the first "overtly politically significant song to reach the national Top Ten listing was Pete Seeger's 'Where Have All the Flowers Gone?,'" first released in July of 1960, but "as recorded by the Kingston Trio" in 1962 (Denisoff 1983, 34).

2. It is worth mentioning that there is not unanimity regarding the opinion that protest songs must challenge some mainstream value system or are expressions of discontent regarding the status quo. Referencing songs such as "Please Mr. Professor," "Welfare Cadillac," and "Okie from Muskogee," Jerome Rodnitzky remarked that "[t]hese new protest songs on the right are destroying another folk-protest myth—specifically, the legend that topical songs appealing to the discontented common 'folk' were almost by definition ballads sympathetic to social reform" (Rodnitzky 1971, 46).

3. I propose this claim is true, unless, of course, there is available a plausible ontology that explains how sound waves, in and of themselves (and, thus, as they exist outside and independent of brains), could be music.

4. The Grateful Dead performed "Okie From Muskogee" on at least one occasion, namely April 27, 1971, with members of the Beach Boys and presumably in front of an audience populated primarily of pot smoking, LSD tripping hippies.

Chapter 1

The Nature and Origins
of Rock and Roll

Since its advent, what qualified as rock and roll as a musical genre has not been a straightforward matter by any means. Moreover, as time has passed, there has not even been much consensus about how the term "rock and roll" should be use—that is, to what it may be reasonably expected to refer. On the one hand, it has been commonplace in the literature to see a distinction drawn between the referents of "rock and roll" and "rock" (Denisoff and Levine 1970, 50; Peterson 1990, note 1). On the other hand, Carl Belz opted to use the term "rock" to include reference to rock and roll (Belz 1972, 3; cf. Belz 1967). Perhaps more or less arbitrarily, I will treat the terms "rock and roll" and "rock" as roughly referring to the same thing, but privileging the use of the term "rock and roll" insofar as, whatever distinction may be drawn, I believe that what the two terms generally refer to share the same roots, and I think a case can be made that rock and roll bled into whatever rock is to such an extent that it is probably not very useful to attempt to draw some hard distinction between the two. In addition, I will also construe rock and roll to include the kind of musical genre to which the term "rockabilly" typically refers, a term that the music scholar D. K. Wilgus credited himself with coining (Wilgus et al. 1970, 184), and that Bill Malone characterized as a hybrid musical artist, namely "an individual who possessed characteristics of both the roll-and-roll and the country singer: the rockabilly" (Malone 1968, 246), so that the term "rock and roll" covers the whole genre from its purported inception, sometime in the early 1950s, through the 1970s and arguably beyond.

Having said all that by way of preface, it is certainly by no means any clearer what rock and roll is. In 1971, the sociologist Paul Hirsch suggested that rock and roll was defined as any record selected for airplay by program directors on Top 40 stations (Hirsch 1971, 382), and thus conceived rock and roll as whatever was disseminated through a historically idiosyncratic popular music delivery system. As Hirsch expressed it, "the musical style cannot be defined independently of the radio stations over which the records are broadcast" (Hirsch 1971, 382). In fact, he added, "performers like the Beatles or the Rolling Stones are associated directly with the term 'rock-and-roll' because their records were heard first over Top 40 radio stations" (Hirsch 1971, 381).

Of course, there is certainly something that vaguely lends plausibility to this view. For one thing, it has been commonplace to temporally mark the so-called "birth" of rock and roll as a musical genre by pointing to the commercial success of specific recordings, together with the frequency of their dissemination through the "popular" or mainstream broadcast mechanisms of the day. The advent of rock and roll is often marked by pointing to Bill Haley or Elvis Presley, who, according to Michael Allen, were the first to have #1 hits in 1954 (Michael Allen 2015, 109). "Rock Around the Clock," though released in 1954, became a hit, and was the first so-called "rock and roll" release to reach #1 in 1955 in the United States, and subsequently went to the top of the "English" charts (Belz 1972, 34).[1] Elvis Presley's first released recording, namely the single "That's Alright Mama" and "Blue Moon of Kentucky" that occurred on July 5, 1954, for Sun Records, was actually not a hit, but sold twenty thousand copies (Linden 2012, 53), and has been deemed by some writers to mark "the beginning of rock and roll music" (M. Allen 2015, 111). Meanwhile, Chuck Berry is also often credited with being a, if not *the* founding rock-and-roll performer because of his national hit "Maybellene" in 1955 (M. Allen 2015, 108).[2] In addition, the disc jockey Alan Freed has often been referred to as the "Father of Rock and Roll" (Belz 1972, 50; Chapple and Garofalo 1977, 56), having been credited by some as the first to play rhythm and blues at a station capable of broadcasting nationally, and who also credited himself, and has been credited by others, with being the first person to use the term "rock and roll," which occurred in 1951, in reference to the music he was playing (Belz 1972, 51; cf. Ferrandino 1969, 263; Denisoff 1983, 28; Orman 1984, 3). It should be mentioned, however, that Alan Freed simply used the term "rock and roll" instead of "rhythm and blues" in reference to the records he was playing at the time. Apparently, he did not coin it (Chapple and Garofalo 1977, 56). Originally an expression for sexual intercourse, Marilyn Flood points out, "rock and roll" was used in song titles as early as the song "Rock and Roll" by the Boswell Sisters in 1934, as well as "We're Gonna Rock, We're Gonna Roll" in 1947 by Wild Bill Moore, "Good Rocking Tonight" by Roy Brown, and "Rock All Night Long" by the Ravens in 1948 (Flood 1991, 401, note 15). In addition, the use of the term "rock" in the title and lyrics of a song at least goes back to as early as Uncle Dave Macon's "Rock About, My Saro Jane," which, lore has it, Macon originally learned from black stevedores working in Nashville during the 1880s and is believed, by some, to be of civil war origin.

Now some scholars have defined a piece of music as rock and roll, at least in its early years, as simply "a white cover of a black song" (Chapple and Garofalo 1977, 35). It is also certainly clear, as Joe Ferrandino and others have expressed it, that much of the "music was appropriated from blacks and done by whites primarily for whites" through the recording of "covers" (Ferrandino 1969, 264; Linden 2012, 44).[3] Indeed, there is substantial evidence to support the view that rock and roll came to be through the appropriation of songs originally performed by black artists, particularly when one considers such signature hits as Haley and his Comets' recording of a version of the tune by ("Big") Joe Turner in 1953, namely "Shake, Rattle and Roll" (Denisoff 1983, 29),[4] and "Sh-Boom,"[5] a rhythm and blues tune that was first recorded by the Chords and released on April 24, 1954, and that was subsequently reproduced as a cover by the Crew Cuts to become, according to some accounts, the first rock-and-roll tune to be the best-selling record in the United States (Denisoff 1983, 28–29; cf. Flood 1991, 401).[6] Other noteworthy covers include "Sincerely" performed by the McGuire Sisters, originally issued by the Moonglows; "Wheel of Fortune" performed by Kay Starr, originally recorded by the Cardinals; Elvis Presley's version of "Money Honey," by Clyde McPhatter and the Drifters (Ferrandino 1969, 265); "Rocket 88," an Ike Turner tune performed by Haley; "A Little Bird Told Me," a Paula Watson tune performed by Evelyn Knight (Linden 2012, 45); and "Earth Angel," originally performed by the Penguins and covered by the Crew Cuts (Flood 1991, 401, note. 23). In addition, Pat Boone also capitalized on the cover business with Fats Domino's "Ain't That a Shame," Big Joe Turner's "Honey Hush," and Little Richard's "Tutti Frutti" and "Long Tall Sally" (Maddock 1996, 186). Furthermore, Elvis Presley's first Sun Records recording was a cover of Arthur "Big Boy" Crudup's "That's All Right" (Linden 2012, 53).

All of that said, it should be added that the business of generating profits through covers certainly did not begin in the 1950s, nor was it restricted to the appropriation of the styles and genres of black artists by white artists. One of the earliest "white" versions of a rock tune, for example, has been purportedly based on country music, namely "Crazy Man Crazy," recorded by Bill Haley and his Comets in 1951 (Denisoff 1983, 29). Indeed, the practice of producing covers of tunes originally recorded by other artists was quite widespread early in the record business whenever opportunities to maximize profit presented themselves to record producers. For example, Riley Puckett's recording of "Blue Ridge Mountain Blues" in 1924 was quickly covered by Ernest Stoneman for Okeh Records; Vernon Dalhart for Victor; and Sid Harkreader, Uncle Dave Macon's back-up man, for Vocalion Records (Wolfe 1993, 40).

From what may be a more nuanced perspective, some scholars have suggested that rock and roll actually emerged from the Mississippi River Valley as "biracial music, born from the intermixture of black and white musical forms" (M. Allen 2015, 114–15), namely African American Blues and British American Folk, or "country" music (which some have characterized as an outgrowth of British Folk), with, perhaps, a little Gospel, Jazz, Cajun and Creole French mixed in (M. Allen 2015, 100–101; cf. Ferrandino 1969, 263). Perhaps in line with the spirit of Alan Freed's famous statement in the 1956 film *Rock, Rock, Rock*, rock and roll is thereby conceived as a sort of "river of music which has absorbed many streams, rhythm and blues, jazz, ragtime, cowboy songs, country songs, folk songs. All have contributed greatly to the big beat."

Now there is certainly something to this view. For there has been significant evidence gathered that these musical forms had intermingled extensively during the first half of the twentieth century and, thus, prior to the emergence of rock and roll. According to D. K. Wilgus,

> [t]he "blues" tradition—that is, the influence of Negro and Negro-based materials including jazz and genuine blues—was evident in hillbilly music from the moment it began to be documented. Southeast performers were singing "white blues" and playing hot instrumentals in the 1920s. Jimmie Rodgers popularized both the songs and the style, so that there was no regional limitation to the style in the 1930s. But the tradition flourished most significantly in Louisiana, Texas, and Oklahoma. . . . Whereas in the Southeast the frolic pieces, the blues, and the sentimental songs coexisted in the repertory, usually with stylistic differences in performance, they tended to coalesce in south-western tradition, dominated by a blues-jazz influence. (Wilgus 1970, 167)

Moreover, as early as the 1930s, D. K. Wilgus reports,

> [j]azz musicians sat in with the country string bands and facilitated the development of western swing. Prominent bands like Bob Wills' added horns—trumpets, trombones and saxophones. They played traditional breakdowns and pop tunes; and—most importantly—pseudocowboy or western numbers developed in the Southwest. The repertory ranged from low-down honky-tonk numbers, often with Mexican influence, to rather sophisticated urban songs. (Wilgus 1970, 168)

Along these lines, one way to look at rock and roll in terms of its roots is to conceive of it as simply an extension, albeit in a commercialized form, of "folk" music, broadly construed in the sense of "the music of folks," or "people's music," as opposed to the sort of commercially produced popular music that had been emanating out of the "Tin Pan Alley tradition, or *kitsch* music" (cf. Belz 1972, 15), where "*kitsch*" is understood as "popular art that has the look of traditional fine art" (Belz 1967, 132). According to Carl Belz, the "popular" music that predated rock and roll had a "fine arts orientation" in that it was consciously fashioned or stylized to approximate the so-called fine arts or classical tradition of the "higher" or "upper" classes, even though its route to that end may have passed through the "Broadway musical, operetta, and grand opera" (Belz 1967, 131–32). In contrast, the roots of rock and roll seem to come "up from the people instead of down from the upper classes, the academies, or the drawing rooms" (Belz 1967, 132).

It is, perhaps, from this perspective that other scholars have characterized rock and roll as simply a mixture of the previously extant traditions of so-called "hillbilly,"[7] or "Caucasian country music" (Denisoff 1983, 28),[8] which was later sometimes referred to as "country western music,"[9] and still later formalized as "country,"[10] and rhythm and blues, which was previously labeled as "negro" blues or "race"[11] music (Denisoff 1983, 28; Chappel and Garofalo 1977, 8).[12] As a matter of fact, Elvis Presley's early hits, along with a host of other artists, may be particularly emblematic of this melding of the rhythm and blues and country-western traditions that led to rock and roll as it eventually appeared in the pop market. Elvis Presley was, after all, one of the new artists that emerged from the country and western circuit to receive national exposure at the advent of rock and roll (cf. Belz 1972, 40), having previously been a featured artist in the Louisiana Hayride show that would tour the South. In 1954 he was even voted #8 as "Up and Coming Country and Western Artist" in the *Billboard* DJ poll, and #1 in 1955 (Belz 1972, 41).

So perhaps at least three or more musical genres that were, as Serge Denisoff puts it, "considered deviant and unsavory to supporters of Tin Pan Alley," namely "race music," "hillbilly music," and "folk music," were all "merged into the nebulous idiom of Rock 'n' Roll" (Denisoff 1983, 27). However, in contrast to the more conventional thinking that all the musical genres that eventually fed into rock, such as blues, jazz, and so-called "hillbilly" or, perhaps, "folk," depending on one's definition,[13] merely "borrowed from each other," Peterson suggests, commensurate with Alan Freed's metaphorical characterization above, that it was likely "one caldron" from which various "creative efforts" drew (Peterson 1997, 236–37, note 10). For following the American Civil War, according to Peterson, innovation in musical expression among the "poor and working-class people of the American South" flourished as well as mixed with "the commercial music of the day." By about 1910, "three streams were being distinguished: blues, jazz, and an amalgam that would become country music" (Peterson 1997, 8). To a significant degree, this cross-acculturation of musical genres had been facilitated by a confluence of diasporic events as the social and material landscape of America continued to evolve. Traceable back to the Civil War, according to D. K. Wilgus, they included such things as the materialization of railroad camps along the railroad lines being laid, where the "older white folk tradition" came in contact with "Negro work and social songs, as well as with all sorts of material carried by migrant workers." "Loggers brought in music" to the places they logged, and "circuses and traveling troupes of entertainers," including "traveling medicine shows" (Wilgus 1970, 160), "vaudeville" and "minstrel" shows (Otto and Burns 1974, 412) also contributed to an on-going cultural dissemination of musical genres. Moreover, people relocated to work in Southern mills, in industries in the North, and to oil fields in the West (Wilgus 1970, 168). And, of course, the Spanish-American War, as well as World War I, which Wilgus describes as "the next shock and crisis of cultural contact" (Wilgus 1970, 161), all enhanced the diasporic mingling of musical forms. When poor whites and blacks seeking work moved from rural areas into cities, and to the North or West, and Southwest or West Coast from the Southeast (Wilgus 1970, 169), up through the 1940s, spurred further, as it was, by the industrial efforts of World War II, these individuals, naturally, brought their music with them (Chapple and Garofalo 1977, 8). According to Chapple and Garofalo, "more than three times as many (1,260,000) left the South in the forties as in the decade before" (Chapple and Garofalo 1977, 28). Finally, one should not also overlook that "[s]ervice in the armed forces tended to integrate (not without violence) boys from different areas with different musical tastes" (Wilgus 1970,169).

In many ways, these changing material conditions, which, prima facie, appeared to have nothing to do with music directly, did much to influence the subsequent musical genres and techniques that eventually led to the advent of rock and roll. According to Richard Peterson, for example, one reason why Atlanta, Georgia, was the original center of "commercial country music," rather than Nashville, Tennessee, as it is commonly thought, had to do with the fact that, before the Civil War, Atlanta had served as a "railroad junction" for shipping goods, and later became the center of commercial activities in the region as the use of the Mississippi river for hauling declined. "Dallas, Nashville, Louisville, Charlotte, and Knoxville," in contrast, were "less developed, considerably smaller, or more isolated." As a matter of fact, by the 1920s only Memphis, "which was becoming the center of the blues industry, might have been a serious rival" (Peterson 1997, 25). As one consequence of Atlanta's size, due to this interchange of industrial goods and services, and the intermingling of sometimes desperate persons looking for work, which was likely further fueled by the impact of the boll weevil and the unstable cotton market, in conjunction with the growing industrial opportunities (Peterson 1997, 17), the Atlanta radio station WBS, eventually a magnet for live performances to fill the airtime, became the first "high powered" one of its kind in March of 1922 (Peterson 1997, 27). How and where railroads were built, their importance in the shaping of American music should not be understated.

Moreover, there have been many cases reported of the cross-fertilization of musical genres that occurred through more idiographic channels, such as the exposure to and the sharing of specific musical techniques among individuals. For example, according to Bill Malone,

> Old-time Texas musician Ernest Porter has attested to the fact that he and other young white musicians learned the finger style of guitar playing from Blind Lemon Jefferson and other Negro musicians whom they heard on the streets of Dallas in the late twenties (interview with William Ernest Porter, Dallas, Texas, September 13, 1966). (Malone 1968, 22, note 45)

In another notable case, John Cohen has traced the intermingling of white folk music with black folk music to at least one relationship that developed between the Carter Family, an early but well-known country music band, and Leslie Riddle. Riddle first met A. P. Carter, the presumed leader of the band, on one of his "song catching trips" (Peterson 1997, 42) that Carter was known to frequently undertake to find new songs to adopt that were not already under copyright (Peterson 1997, 35), and subsequently became Carter's human "tape recorder." When writing music down was difficult, Riddle would memorize the music and Carter would write the words. Thereafter, Riddle lived in the Carter home and apparently taught Maybelle Carter, a renowned accompanist, "the blues style of picking melody and the high strings with the index finger" (J. Cohen 1967, 64), while picking rhythm at the same time, a "style for which she became famous" (Peterson 1997, 41). Furthermore, according to Cohen, the song "Cannon-ball," which Maybelle frequently performed on the Grand Ole Opry show, was adopted by her from Riddle (J. Cohen 1967, 64).

Jimmie Rodgers, one of the most successful "country" musicians of the 1920s and credited with twenty million sales of records between 1927 and 1933 (Otto and Burns 1974, 415), was also influenced by his nonmusical background as a railroad worker. Early on, he accompanied his father, Aaron Rodgers, a foreman of an "extra gang" for needed line repairs on the railroad, throughout the South, where, according to Bill Malone, Jimmie was "subjected to almost every conceivable type of musical influence that the South possessed, with the possible exception of gospel music" (Malone 1968, 84). For example, Mrs. Pearl Rodgers,

> the widow of Jimmie's oldest brother Talmadge . . . remembers that, at the age of fourteen, Jimmie and a young friend named Mike Murphy began carrying water for the railroad workers in the Meridian railroad yards. It was in this capacity that he learned songs and fragments of songs from the Negro workers, who also taught him to play the banjo and guitar (Malone 1968, 84).

For fourteen years, Jimmie Rodgers worked on lines throughout the Southwest, typically as a flagman or brakeman, and played with his fellow workers during breaks, and sometimes with "Negro musicians down around Tenth Street in Meridian" (Malone 1968, 85). Over time, according to Malone, Rodgers "became thoroughly conversant with the vocabulary and music of the railroad workers" (Malone1968, 84).

Early in his career, Dave Macon also learned numerous songs from black singers (Wolfe 1993, 40), and one of his first recordings, "Hill Billie Blues," which is, perhaps, the first released recording to include the term "Hillbilly" in its title, was actually, according to Charles Wolfe, "a reworking" of renowned African American artist W. C. Handy's "Hesitation Blues" (Wolfe 1993, 40). Meanwhile, Doc Boggs had worked in the coal mines around Norton, Virginia, as early as 1910 where he interacted with black artists, and even "[a]s a boy, he would occasionally escape from the mines and go to nearby black communities, such as Dorchester, to listen to the kind of string-band music that was played there" (Wolfe 1993, 41). As a result of being a finalist for a Brunswick "talent audition," Boggs also recorded "Down South Blues" in 1927, which, according to Charles Wolfe, "he had adapted from a 1923 Vocalion disc by city blues singer Rosa Henderson" (Wolfe 1993, 42), and in later years, Boggs learned from black artists such as Go Lightning and Jim White. According to Charles Wolfe, Boggs once remarked that "he wished he had been given the gift to play the guitar instead of the banjo, so he could cop the music of his favorite, Mississippi John Hurt" (Wolfe 1993, 42).

As another example, Frank Hutchinson, a coal miner from West Virginia, was also influenced by black artists starting at a very young age. At about seven or eight, according to Charles Wolfe, Hutchinson met a certain Henry Vaughn, who was laying tracks for the mine, and he learned some of Vaughn's blues guitar playing, including the technique of using a knife as a slide. Later on, Hutchinson met Bill Hunt, "a crippled Negro living back in the Hills," from whom it is reported that Hutchinson learned "dozens of songs from his [Bill's] repertoire of nineteenth-century traditional tunes that blacks and whites had shared before the blues became fashionable" (Wolfe 1993, 41). In 1926, Hutchinson recorded the classic "Worried Blues," as well as "The Train That Carried My Girl from Town" for Okeh Records using "his pocket knife as a guitar slide, the instrument tuned to D" (Wolfe 1993, 41).

Furthermore, Hank Williams learned to play from the African American blues artist Rufe "Tee Tot" Payne, who he credited with being "his greatest early influence" (Peterson 1997, 174), and Jesse Jarnow asserts that Woody Guthrie used his own portable turntable to learn "licks and vocal moves from blues 78s" such as those of Blind Lemon Jefferson (Jarnow 2018, 19). Finally, John Otto and Augustus Burns suggest that "bottleneck" or "knife" style of slide on a guitar, sometimes believed to be an adaptation by black artists to guitar from slides on the "one string" or "diddley bow," an instrument believed to be of African origin, may have, in fact, been adopted by both black and white artists from "Hawaiian guitarists who toured the South in tent shows and fairs in the early twentieth century" (Otto and Burns 1974, 409). Charles Wolfe, for example, reports that Jimmie Tarlton, who recorded the wildly successful "Birmingham Jail" with Tom Darby in 1927,[14] met Frank Ferera in 1922, a well-known Hawaiian guitarist, who subsequently taught him how to use "a better slide, a piece of highly polished steel that allowed him to note with more dexterity" (Wolfe 1993, 42).

It might be worth pausing at this juncture to consider how the terms "race" and "hillbilly" originated in relation to music, leaving aside, for the time being, "country," "cowboy,"[15] or "folk," in general, even if doing so only ends up making the matter of clarifying the roots of rock and roll more, rather than less, opaque for the conceptually disciplined. In 1965, for example, Archie Green remarked that

> *hillbilly music*, however defined, has been employed for three decades as a rubric covering a kaleidoscopic variety of sub forms: old time, familiar tunes, Dixie, mountain, sacred, gospel, country, cowboy, western, country-western, hill and range, western swing, Nashville, rockabilly, bluegrass. *Hillbilly* can cover all available (recorded and published) white commercial country music or it can be equated simply with one limited type or recent period; for example, *Time*'s folksong expert reports that *bluegrass* is a polite synonym for *hillbilly*. (Green 1965, 205)[16]

In any event, according to the dominant narrative, it was Ralph Peer, an Okeh Records' producer, dedicated to "specialty records" (Peterson 1997, 18), and who has been credited with producing the first so-called "country" recording in 1927 of Jimmie Rogers and the Carter Family, as well as Mamie Smith's recording of "Crazy Blues" in 1920, which sold 7,500 copies in a single week,[17] who was the first person to use the term "race" and "hillbilly" in the record industry (Chapple and Garofalo 1977, 8).[18] Thereafter, Peer used the term "race records" for those releases that were specifically marketed to the black community (Chapple and Garofalo 1977, 2), and, at some point, the term caught on and became an industry-wide, categorical reference, until 1949, when it was replaced by the expression "rhythm and blues" (Belz 1972, 22).[19]

Prior to the music industry's use of the terms "race" and "hillbilly" as marketing categories, the sorts of recordings that were afterwards so categorized were often labeled with a variety of different terms, and sometimes simply lumped into the category of popular music.[20] For example, according to Peterson, "[t]he historic first release by Fiddlin" John Carson, "The Little Old

Cabin in the Lane," in 1923, was simply placed in Okeh Records' "Popular Music Series," which included records that were identified as "dance band," "sacred," "Hawaiian," "Broadway tunes," "novelties," "instrumentals," and "standards" (Peterson 1997, 194–95). Moreover, with regard to the white, rural music being recorded, other expressions began to be used, starting in 1924, such as "Old Time Tune Records" by Okeh Records, "Old Time Fiddlin' Tunes" by the Victor Talking Machine Company, and "Familiar Tunes on Fiddle, Guitar, Banjo, Harmonica and Accordion" by Columbia Records. In addition, alphanumeric series designations, which grouped recordings together, were soon introduced by record companies and eventually came to be identified with specific styles of music in advertising, even though determinations for inclusion in a series were almost exclusively based on the complexion of the performer rather than the style of the music.[21] For example, those recordings originally listed in conjunction with Columbia's expression mentioned above were grouped together as part of Columbia's 15000-D series, and were performed, almost without exception, by white artists. In contrast, most of the recordings listed within an "equally heterogeneous" 14000-D series were performed by African American artists, the secular instances of which, in contrast to gospel, had previously been called "blues" (Peterson 1997, 196). Victor and other record companies followed suit in grouping record releases based on skin-color (Richardson 1997, 195). In some cases, however, this practice was not consistent. For example, a particular white blues group comprised of the Allen brothers, Lee and Austin, "threatened to sue Columbia for $25,000 because one of their records was placed in both the 14000 series and the 15000 series" in 1927 (Peterson 1997, 196; cf. Otto and Burns 1974, 414).[22] Furthermore, the African American string band, the Mississippi Sheiks, had also been listed in the "Old Time" catalogs (Peterson 1997, 196), and the Grand Ole Opry harmonica player, De Ford Bailey, eventually came to be included in the country series of the Brunswick and Vocalion labels (Otto and Burns 1974, 414). Additional stylistic distinctions characteristic of these groupings, primarily attributed to company policies, have also been noted by Otto and Burns in that emphases were placed on string bands versus solo performances in the case of the white artist groupings, and solo performances in the case of the black artist groupings (Otto and Burns 1974, 409). In any event, by the 1930s, companies incorporated the labels of "race," and "Old Time" and "hillbilly" to aid their customers, but even as late as the 1935 catalog of Vocalion, there were still some examples of crossover, as in the case of the black bluesman, "Funny Papa" Smith (Otto and Burns 1974, 414).

Getting back to the dominant narrative about the origin of the categories, the use of the term "hillbilly" in relation to music, developed because of an initiative to record "white rural music" that was fostered by Ralph Peer and the ambitious business machinations of a certain Polk C. Brockman. Prior to his interaction with Brockman, as it has already been suggested above, Peer had previously experienced some success marketing recordings of what was to be eventually labeled "race" music, such as the profit he enjoyed from Mamie Smith's recording of "Crazy Blues" (cf. Malone 1968, 38). In conjunction with other factors to be further described below, part of that initial success was likely fueled by an overall increased demand for recorded blues that was otherwise not available to persons who had previously migrated to the North in search of defense jobs during World War I (Malone 1968, 80). Meanwhile, shortly before his interaction with Peer, Brockman, who happened to be the grandson of the owner of James K. Polk, Inc., a prominent furniture store in Atlanta, Georgia, and who previously had worked as a travelling sales representative for the Simmons Bedding Company, had agreed to work for his family's business, but only provided he was allowed to establish a phonograph department.

At this time, phonographs were typically sold in furniture stores because they were primarily considered to be furniture, and records were stocked and sold along with them so that potential buyers would be further encouraged to buy the phonographs. The influx of migrants of low to middle-income means to the Atlantic area at the time also enhanced the pool of potential customers for these phonographs since they involved wind-up mechanisms that did not require the purchase of electricity (Peterson 1997, 17–18), unlike the developing technology of radio. Even so, sales of records were initially slow for Brockman, with the exception of the jazz and blues recordings that Okeh Records had previously released, such as Mamie Smith's. Part of the reason for these meager sales, it seemed, had to do with a couple of factors. On the one hand, a good portion of the records available to potential consumers had consisted of the popular, orchestrated music, which tended to appeal to more urban audiences, instead of Brockman's low to middle income migrants. On the other hand, this more mainstream symphonic and popular music had recently begun to be accessible through radio, starting around 1922, while the kind of music that had greater appeal to some of Brockman's customers, such as blues and jazz, was not as accessible through that medium (Peterson 1997, 18). This inaccessibility was partly due, as I will discuss in greater detail below, to copyright and membership issues that were fostered by the American Society of Composers, Authors, and Publishers (ASCAP) and the American Federation of Musicians (AFM).

Despite these challenges, Brockman naturally sought to expand the portfolio of records attractive to his potential buyers of phonographs and managed to acquire the Atlanta dealership of Okeh Records to accomplish that. Having enjoyed some success from stocking Okeh's "race" records, namely blues and jazz, Brockman then approached Okeh Records executives, Otto Heineman and W. S. Fuhri, for the wholesale regional distributorship.[23] This was followed by one auspicious business trip to New York in June of 1923 when Brockman, according to the story, happened to view a newsreel of a Virginia fiddlers' competition at the Palace Theater in Times Square and made a note on a pad which said "Fiddlin John Carson—local talent—let's record," which he subsequently shared with Ralph Peer. As implied by Peterson, Brockman assumed that since blues and jazz records had sold so well in the black community of Atlanta, it was likely that there was also a market among "white farmers and townsfolk" for recorded music "played and sung by one of their own" (Peterson 1997, 19). Meanwhile, Brockman's timing seemed right because Ralph Peer had already been considering additional strategies to boost sales, such as entry into other ethnic music markets (Green 1965, 208), for example, "Cajun" and "Mexican," both because of the success he had experienced recording "race" music (Wilgus 1970, 161–62), and because Peer had to find a way, like everybody else in the record business at the time, to offset losses in record sales due to the advent of radio, as I will further outline below.

And so, motivated entirely by potential sales and profit, and lacking any interest in or concern for the preservation of any particular kind of musical genre (Peterson 1997, 27–28),[24] Brockman, in collaboration with Peer, rented a loft on Nassau Street in Atlanta for Okeh recording engineers, Charles Hibbard and Peter Decker, and rounded up some local talent to record (Green 1965, 208), including Fiddlin' John Carson (Roy 2004, 274), to launch the development of a record series, which they labeled "Old Times Tunes."[25] It was, then, in the process of recording one of the bands for the series, comprised of "middle class urban southerners," and while Peer and company were trying to identify a better marketing expression that would best describe the music, that Peer asked what they wanted to be called. In response, one member of the band said, no doubt, pejoratively, "We're nothing but a bunch of hillbillies. . . . Call us anything" (Roy 2004, 274), which was how they were subsequently labeled, the "Hill Billies," as headliner for Okeh's "Old-Time Tunes" series. After that, so the story goes, the expression was employed as a category label for Okeh Records, and later further adopted by the industry at large (Roy 2004, 274). From then on, according to Bill Malone, "hillbilly" was used as a category in the commercial music industry until the late 1940s, at which point certain country singers, including Eddie Kirk, Cliffie Stone, Ernest Tubb and Red Foley, lobbied the recording companies to have it replaced with "country," since they thought that "hillbilly" was associated by some members of the public with music of a "low-class origin and beneath their dignity." By June of 1949, *Billboard* also began to use "country" and "country and western" in lieu of "hillbilly" (Malone 1968, 216).

That the proposal of "hillbilly" as the name for the band to be called was intended to be pejorative when it was originally suggested, and that it was later adopted by the music industry, in part, because it reflected the latent degree of contempt the industry actually possessed for audiences of this genre of music, would seem to be further born out by the fact that, at this time, at least according to Richard Peterson, "billy" was understood to refer to "a rough, unschooled and simple-minded person" (Peterson 1997, 7). Indeed, in a 1926 issue of the industry magazine *Variety,* individuals so-called were described as "illiterate and ignorant, with the intelligence of morons" (Green 1965, 221; quoted in Peterson 1997, 8).

NOTES

1. According to Paul Linden, Milt Gabler, an executive at Decca, is listed as its co-author, a strategy executives referred to as "ghost writing" and used "to insert themselves into (and thereby dilute) the artist royalty stream" (Linden 2012, 57).

2. According to some, "Maybellene" was co-authored with Alan Freed (Belz 1972, 51; Peterson 1990, 110), but some credit has also been attributed to Leonard Chess of Chess Records, the company that recorded the song. According to Chapple and Garofalo, "Leonard Chess told Berry to give it a 'bigger beat,' and they changed the title to 'Maybellene,' taking the name from a hair crème bottle" (Chapple and Garofalo 1977, 39).

3. A "cover" may be roughly defined as a song performed by a band or performer who is not credited as the original author. With reference to the covers often produced of songs originally performed by black artists, Marilyn Flood also notes that their lyrics were often "sanitized." "For instance, 'Roll with Me, Henry,' released by Etta James in 1955, became 'Dance with Me, Henry' when covered the same year by White singer Georgia Gibbs. . . . Changes in lyrics occurred in 'Shake, Rattle, and Roll' from the original version recorded by Joe Turner in 1954, to the Bill Haley release of that same year . . . Joe Turner sang, 'Well, you wear low dresses, the sun comes shining through / I can't believe my eyes that all this belongs to you.' Haley sang, 'You wear those dresses, our hair done up so nice / You look so warm, but your heart is cold as ice'" (Flood 1991, 402, note 39).

4. John Orman credits "Ivory" Joe Hunter as the original artist of "Shake, Rattle and Roll," when actually the original artist was "Big" Joe Turner (cf. Orman 1984, 3). That said, both artists had signed with Atlantic Records around the same time.

5. It is curious that Belz construes "Gee," a song by the Crows, released in 1954, as a "proto-rock" song in comparison to "Sh-Boom" (Belz 1972, 30).

6. In fact, Shane Maddock believes that the success of "Sh-Boom" was what originally triggered the whole corporate strategy of producing white covers of black tunes in the first place (Maddock 1996, 186; cf. Peterson 1990, 12).

7. Stephen Conroy quotes the March, 1957, publication of *Musical America* (vol. 77, 4) which describes rock music as a "kind of glorified hillbilly music" (Conroy 1983, 127).

8. Although, through an idiosyncratic confluence of events, according to Archie Green, only the term "hillbilly" was eventually associated with the music thereby labeled, other disparaging and pejorative terms that circulated, and were rough "analogs" that were associated with the class of persons from whom the music was presumed to emanate, included *"lubber, peckerwood, cracker, conch, sandhiller, red-neck, Cajun, woolhat, squatter, clayeater, sharecropper, linthead, swamprat, tarheel . . . ridge-runner, appleknocker, cherrypicker,* and *turdkicker"* (Green 1965, 206). In addition, Green mentions that "Ozark speech reveals two dozen additional terms, *acorn-cracker* to *weed-bender*, in Vance Randolph and George Wilson, *Down in the Holler* (Normal, Oklahoma, 1953)" (Green 1965, 223, note 12).

9. Because some flavor of the style frequently appeared in Western movies and television during the 1950s, and had been popularized by Gene Autry and Roy Rogers, according to Belz, "Country and Western songs were usually lumped together in the popular imagination under the heading of 'hillbilly' or 'cowboy' music" (Belz 1972, 23–24). Meanwhile, according to Bill Malone, "honky-tonk" was typically associated with, no less often treated as a synonym for, "Western," because it referred to the sort of "country music" played in "taverns" and "dancehalls" in the Southwest (Malone 1968, 279).

10. Richard Peterson points out that the label "country music" was not often used until the 1940s, and not universally adopted until the term "country and western" fell out of favor (Peterson 1997, 9). In fact, Peterson adds, the term "country" was not technically used to characterize the genre until 1953 (Peterson 1997, 194). Because of this, Peterson asserts, the term "country music" is now understood as referring to a form of commercial music "that began to develop rapidly in the 1920s and is now widely recognized around the world as 'country'" (Peterson 1997, 9).

11. Paul Linden also mentions some other less formal, more derogatory, pejorative, and often significantly racist labels that were sometimes used in reference to the early years of the music such as "sepia tones," "boogie," "jump blues" and "n***** bop" (Linden 2012, 52). In addition, Norman Cohen mentions that in the 1890s "a scattering of danceable pseudo-Negro songs" ("pseudo" presumably because they were developed in the context of minstrel shows and likely delivered in blackface) (cf. N. Cohen 1970, note 8) were "designated in the parlance of the times "coon songs" (N. Cohen 1970, 12). In contrast, and as counterintuitive as it may seem to contemporary ears, the term "race," according to Peterson, was commonly employed during the mid-1920s as a "positive" term in the "African American press." "To say a black man was a 'race man,' for example, was to say he took pride in his African American heritage (Green 1972: 36)" (Peterson 1997, 196).

12. To complicate matters further, according to Malone, "[t]he secular music produced by rural southern Negroes became known as the 'country blues,' and it laid the basis for modern race or rhythm-and-blues music and underlies, in fact, the whole congeries of modern popular music ranging from rock-and-roll and folk rock to England's Mersey Beat" (Malone 1968, 81).

13. As it should become increasingly apparent over the course of this book, definitions of, and understandable disagreements about what "folk music" is, have and continue to litter academic study and ordinary discourse. In contrast to one historical trend, Richard Peterson includes "blues" in "folk," and, in an effort to avoid many of the pitfalls that accompany wide-ranging disagreements about the authenticity of various forms of folk, complicated by the history of the commercialization of folk and the existence of "professional" folk musicians at various stages of "revivals," he defines "folk music" as including "the various kinds of music . . . studied, collected, composed, or performed by those interested in the oral music of any group of people," such as musicians, academics, and employees of government agencies, including the Folklife Division of the National Endowment for the Arts, the Folk Division of the Smithsonian Institution, the Library of Congress, and the National Folklife Endowment (Peterson 1997, 238, note 12). To offer another definition, for which its prima facie simplicity may be its merit, Norman Cohen suggested that a folk song is "any song whose survival is not entirely dependent on commercial media" (N. Cohen 1970, 15).

14. "Birmingham Jail" sold nearly 200,000 copies, and Columbia paid Tom Darby and Jimmie Tarlton $75 for the recording and rights. Tarlton claimed in later years that he wrote the song in 1925 while sitting with his guitar in the Birmingham jail, having been convicted for moonshining. The staff and warden of the jail were so impressed that he was eventually awarded a pardon and was invited to attend the dedication of the new jail in 1937 (Wolfe 1993, 43).

15. According to D. K. Wilgus, "[c]owboy songs were in the repertory of eastern hillbillies before the commercialization of the tradition. Ex-cowboys began recording in 1925. Yet the cowboy contribution, in addition to a relatively few traditional songs, was more image than actuality. Whatever was viable in the music of the cowboy was largely absorbed into hillbilly tradition by 1930. After this time, cowboy singers came under the spell of pop or hillbilly music, and whatever authentic cowboy culture remained now borrowed the hillbilly tradition." That said, Wilgus continues, "the cowboy 'myth' was as influential on hillbilly music as on American mass culture. Although cowboy and hillbilly music were and are often bracketed, there is a connotative difference. The cowboy's image was almost the reverse of the hillbilly's. Furthermore, the culture that gave birth to hillbilly music shared the general regard for the image of the cowboy as representing values that were being lost in the urbanization of America. After all, the hillbilly 'uniform' is more humorous than romantic. So the hillbilly musician adopted the songs and the image of the cowboy; he composed ersatz cowboy songs, and assumed the ersatz dress of the movie cowboy. In style there was little to adopt" (Wilgus 1970, 166).

16. Perhaps in a manner not unlike the way that "hillbilly" came to be a generic term for a genre of music, as we shall see, Bill Malone reported that the term "bluegrass music" originated from the name of Bill Monroe's string band, "the Blue Grass Boys." Beginning in the late 1940s or early 1950s, the term "bluegrass" was used to refer to the music that sounded like that produced by the bands "of Flatt and Scruggs and the Stanley Brothers" or others "associated with Bill Monroe." Furthermore, according to Malone, characteristics of bluegrass music include an unamplified

sound, and at least the presence of a guitar and five-string banjo, although the "standard bluegrass band" also includes a fiddle, mandolin, and string bass (Malone 1968, 306).

17. Incidentally, Mamie Smith is credited, perhaps incorrectly, by Chapple and Garofalo as the first black person to record (Chapple and Garofalo 1977, 2). Perhaps they meant the first black person to record a hit, since W. G. Roy reports that "the major record companies had recorded African-American musicians in the first two decades of the century" (Roy 2004, 272).

18. While Ralph Peer has sometimes been favorably construed as instrumental to fostering the mass exposure of "race" (blues, jazz, rhythm and blues) and "hillbilly" (country) music to the general public, some have characterized him somewhat negatively as an opportunist. As John Ryan notes, "Peer concentrated on finding performers of either original songs in the folk genre or songs so old that their copyrights had expired. Peer would then acquire the copyright and act as publisher for those songs, taking as much as 75 percent of the royalties from record sales" (Ryan 1985, 61). Moreover, in a letter to Assistant Attorney General Thurmond Arnold in 1940, complaining about Peer, Ferdinand "Jelly Roll" Morton of "Wolverine Blues" fame described Peer's tactic of producing a fake telegraph from Melrose Music Company, with which Morton was contracted, stating it would be "okeh" to record with Peer when, in fact, it was anything but "okeh," thereby damaging Morton's relationship with Melrose. That said, it should be added that Melrose's tactics of doing business were not, themselves, always on the up and up, according to Morton (cf. Ryan 1985, 61–62).

19. According to Chapple and Garofalo, "'rhythm and blues' was an umbrella term that covered several styles of black music in different areas of the country. In the most simple sense rhythm and blues was just that: prewar blues styles with a dancing rhythm added, but it included vocal harmony groups as well. . . . Said Don Robey, the founder of Duke-Peacock in Houston, 'Sometimes it's even called folk music.' To the larger music industry and to the white audience, 'rhythm and blues' was simply a euphemism for 'race music,' any music directed to the black audience and designed for it" (Chapple and Garofalo 1977, 30).

20. According to Roy, "[w]hen rural black and white musicians were first recorded, they were cataloged as popular music without racial designation" (Roy 2004, 274).

21. Richard Peterson suggests that these designations were simply an extension of Jim Crow laws that were "pressing segregation into ever smaller towns where contacts between the races had been more informal and their cultural sharing less self-conscious" (Peterson 1997, 196).

22. What may simply be a typographical error, Charles Wolfe quotes the figure of $250,000 for the lawsuit. That said, as Wolfe recounts the story, the origins of the lawsuit about the listing of their recordings "Chattanooga Blues" and "Laughin' and Cryin' Blues" on the 14000 Race series (14266) had less to do with concern over record sales per se. After all, historical precedence, such as in the case of Mamie Smith, would suggest there was not necessarily any reason for concern. Instead, the real concern was that they did not want to be mistaken as black: "'We were trying to

get into vaudeville back then,' recalled Lee Allen. 'It would have hurt us in getting dates if people who didn't know us thought we were black'" (Wolfe 1993, 39).

23. Richard Peterson suggests that it was the other way around. Because of his previous success in marketing their records, Okeh Records approached Brockman in 1921 to become their "regional wholesale distributor" (Peterson 1997, 18).

24. Brockman told Richard Peterson in 1973: "My interest in hillbilly music and black music is strictly financial." Peterson also reports that Brockman, referring to himself and his business contemporaries, told Archie Green and Ed Kahn that he and his contemporaries in the business "were simply looking for something they could sell" (Peterson 1997, 28).

25. According to Richard Peterson, other names used in early attempts to market the music included "Old-time," "Old Time Tunes," "Old Familiar Tunes," "Hearth and Home," and "Hill and Range" (Peterson 1997, 4). In addition, the expression "Hill Country Music" is used in a 1924 Okeh Records advertisement intended to promote Fiddlin' John Carson and Henry Whitter (Peterson 1997, 26, fig. 2.2).

Chapter 2

The Influence of Records

Despite the ambiguity about what sort of musical genre rock and roll might be, what seems pretty clear is that it was significantly prefaced and enhanced by additional cross-acculturation made possible when local, independent radio stations up and down the Mississippi valley broadcasted "hillbilly" or "country" music, and "race" or "rhythm and blues" to otherwise often segregated communities. According to Michael Allen,

> [b]lacks listened to the Opry and Hayride on radio station WSM in Nashville (Malone "Charley Pride" 342–43) [*sic*] and KWKH in Shreveport, Louisiana. Meanwhile, white youths turned their radio dials to the all night "r and b" show on WREC and WDIA (Memphis), and KFFA's (Helena, AR) "King Biscuit Hour," while clear channel WLAC (Nashville) broadcast "r and b" music across much of the eastern half of the Mississippi River Valley (Guralnick, *Last Train*, 59–60). (M. Allen 2015, 106)

It should be noted, however, that this cross-cultural exposure to musical genres and its subsequent influence was significantly engendered by the radio broadcasting of records, rather than of live performances, and other means of exposure.[1]

In fact, it is probably fair to speculate, counterfactually, that without the recording industry and the radio industry working in tandem and within the otherwise highly idiosyncratic American society of the late 1940s and early 1950s, rock and roll would not have even come into existence in the first place, or at least when it did. For, to a great extent, it was through the record in conjunction with the radio that a significant number of white people, and in particular white youth, became exposed to black music through "race" records and "black-directed" radio (Chapple and Garofalo 1977, 28, 30), and black people became exposed to "hillbilly" records through the radio stations that elected to play them.

One notable respect in which the existence of records directly influenced rock and roll, unlike much of the popular musical product that preceded rock and roll, namely that which was conceived by trained professionals and largely controlled by Tin Pan Alley as I will further discuss below, was that a number of artists who made significant contributions to the development of rock and roll's aesthetic style, from Elvis Presley to the Beatles and the Rolling Stones, were not formally trained to any great degree. Rather, they often learned from others by listening to records on phonographs or through radio stations.[2] It is also because of this fact, perhaps, that, unlike most, if not all, other musical genres up to that point, there occurred a sort of strange, conceptual reversal in what artists and audiences alike construed as the "original" medium of rock and roll. Rather than supposing the record to be a mere "copy" of music and a live performance as its "original" form, as had been a typical way of understanding recordings of music before rock and roll; for rock and roll, at least to some extent, the record came to be conceived as the "original" form that budding artists, as well as the recording artists themselves, would attempt to imitate (Belz 1972, 48), while the live performance, strangely enough, came to be treated as a mere copy of the former.[3] As a matter of fact, this bias, which treated the recorded versions of tunes as the original, often became so deeply entrenched in audience attitudes that "early rock artists frequently lost their aesthetic impact when they performed in live concerts situations which could not duplicate the mechanical effects of the recording studio, and which forced them to compete with the mental images that their own records had created" (Belz 1972, 45). Of course, there were exceptions to this attitude.[4] For example, Chuck Berry, Fats Domino, and Elvis Presley, among other performers, managed to create a stage presence or style that compensated for the difference between their recorded music and their live performances (Belz 1972, 45). That said, the overall attitudinal inversion of conceiving a recording as an original and a live performance as a mere copy certainly stood in stark contrast to much earlier efforts to fabricate concert-like atmospheres when stations were limited to only playing records, as was the case for Al Jarvis and Martin Block's original Make Believe Ballroom (cf. Belz 1972, 46).[5]

In any event, D. K. Wilgus traces the existence of some of this musical cross-acculturation due to records to as early as 1927 and the Victor recordings of Jimmie Rodgers and the Carter Family, insofar as Rodgers "prefigure[d] the 'western' tradition of the Southwest" and the Carters "drew on Negro tradition and performed blues" while embodying "the 'country' tradition of the Southeast" (Wilgus 1970, 164). In addition, while many poor African American and white persons moved to the North and West to work in the defense industries during World War II, people from the Midwest and the East also moved to the South "where they were bombarded by some 600 hillbilly stations."[6] Furthermore, because of the existence of records and radio, and in particular the Armed Forces Network, exposure to a mingling of musical tastes was further facilitated for the "sixteen million persons who passed through the armed forces" (Mabry 1990, 417),[7] as I also more vaguely insinuated above. Not only were these people forced to associate because of their circumstances, but, as also occurred through the accompanying defense jobs, they came to possess more money for discretionary spending (Mabry 1990, 417; Wilgus 1970, 169), some of which would likely find its way into the revenue stream of a music industry that specifically focused on the commercial production of a music genre that would be particularly attractive to hitherto rural and financially challenged, but newly urbanized, persons. Thus, no less than the radical physical diaspora brought about by World War II, records, and their transmission through radio, certainly appear instrumental in shaping the development of the musical genres from which rock and roll drew, namely "hillbilly" and "race," and, accordingly, the eventual emergence of rock and roll.

Now records, at the outset of their inception, were certainly big business, at least in the United States. In fact, from the advent of the available technology for producing and playing records around the turn of the twentieth century, through the onset of the film industry and up to the emergence of commercial radio, the purchase of records appears to have exceeded "all other leisure expenditures" (Chapple and Garofalo 1977, 1). By 1921, as a matter of fact, the gross revenue from the sale of records surpassed $106 million. However, this figure was not matched again until 1945 (Peterson 1997, 254, note 1) since, with the advent of commercial radio in 1922 which allowed for music listening at a distance and without having to buy phonographs and records,[8] the record industry's sales plummeted (Chapple and Garofalo 1977, 1; cf. Green 1965, 208; Peterson 1997, 16) to $59 million by 1925 (Peterson 1997, 254, note 1), with about 104 million records sold in 1927 (Malone 1968, 106). Moreover, although sales rebounded a bit to $75 million in 1929 (Peterson 1997, 50), they precipitously fell again, presumably due to the Depression, to a low of $6 million in revenue in 1933, or "less than one tenth of the 1929 figure" according to some reports (Peterson 1997, 50),[9] and 7 percent according to others (Marcus 1995, 39, note 8).

Following the advent of commercial radio, together with the onset of the Depression, the recovery in record sales, dependent as it was on discretionary spending, was initially quite slow. By 1939, it had only rebounded to $44 million (Chapple and Garofalo 1977, 7), primarily because of growth in the jukebox business (Peterson 1997, 50),[10] and not because of sales to private individuals per se. Then, with the outbreak of World War II, other obstacles to the production and marketing of records also materialized. Shellac, one of the essential ingredients needed for producing records at the time, and an insect secretion available primarily in India, became difficult to obtain. Because of this, persons were sometimes even required to turn in old records when they purchased new ones (Chapple and Garofalo 1977, 8). In 1941, total sales of records reached $41 million (Peterson 1997, 188), which, according to Peterson, was somewhat depressed presumably because of a dispute between the American Federation of Musicians (AFM) and the record companies (Peterson 1997, 262, note 3). To make matters worse for the business, there was also a ban on record making from 1942 to 1943 (Peterson 1997, 165).

As World War II ended, however, record sales began to rebound more robustly to a high of $224 million by 1947 (McDonald 1988a, 296; cf. Peterson 1997, 188). Nevertheless, most likely perhaps because of the advent of television, together with a possible lack of interest in the kind of music being produced,[11] the business dropped off again by 17 percent in 1948, followed by another 8 percent in 1949 (Peterson 1997, 188), to $189 million in 1950, when it remained relatively static for a few years,[12] with only a slight growth in 1953.[13] Then, in 1955, record sales increased to a whopping $277 million, a figure based on the list price of the products (Chapple and Garofalo 1977, 13), which was presumably due to sales of rock-and-roll records. From 1955–1959, the revenues from record sales continued to skyrocket up to $511 million by 1959 (Chapple and Garofalo 1977, 25; McDonald 1988a, 296; Peterson and Berger 1975, 13), and between 1963–1969, total record sales doubled again, cresting above the $1 billion mark in 1968, according to *Billboard* (M. Lydon 1969, 316).[14] when it became, once again, the largest gross revenue of all forms of entertainment at the time (Peterson and Berger 1975, 167).

I think it is worth pausing here to consider briefly how much of this mid-to-late 1960s increase in revenue has been attributed, more or less single-handedly, to the recordings of the Beatles. Ralph Gleason, for example, remarked in 1967 that the Beatles had "become the biggest success in the history of show business, the first attraction ever to have a coast-to-coast tour in this country sold out before the first show even opened" (Gleason 1967, 64). Carl Belz also reported that the Beatles recording "I Want to Hold Your Hand" moved from number forty-five to number one in only two weeks of its appearance on the "national chart of best-selling records" and, within ten days of its release, over a million copies had already been ordered. Indeed, by April of 1964, the Beatles had twelve singles in the Top 100, with five singles in the Top 5 spots:

> "Can't Buy Me Love" was number one, while "Twist and Shout," "She Loves You," "I Want To Hold Your Hand," and "Please Please Me" occupied the next four positions. Overwhelmed by this activity, the music industry estimated that

the Beatles' records actually accounted for 60 per cent of the entire singles business during the first three months of 1964. (Belz 1972, 130)

Furthermore, after its release in January of 1965, the LP *Beatles 65* moved
from number ninety-eight to number one in just one week, and *Hard Days
Night* sold enough copies to pay for the film of the same name before it was
even premiered (Belz 1972, 131).

Be that as it may, the growth in the recording business did not end with the
1960s. By 1972, for example, record and tape sales were grossing nearly two
billion in the United States. (Fox and Williams 1974, 353) and, although a
slowdown in industry growth was noted between 1976–1977, with increases
in profit being credited merely to an increase in price per unit rather than
to the number of units sold (*Fortune* 1979, 60), Steve Chapple and Reebee
Garofalo reported in 1977 that the music industry in the United States was
substantially greater than the $600 million in revenue of professional sports
and the $1.6 billion generated by the film industry in 1974.[15] By 1979 *Fortune*
magazine reported that gross retail of records and tapes in the United States
had doubled again, reaching $4.2 billion, which was five times that of 1964,
when the Beatles first became popular. In contrast, gross box office film revenue was $2.7 billion in 1978 and spectator sports was $3 billion. Finally, it
is certainly important not to ignore the fact that the U.S. market represented
only a third of the total world market, with rock music accounting for most
of the revenue growth (*Fortune* 1979, 59). Indeed, in 1983, George Lewis
claimed that the "popular music industry" was "the largest entertainment
industry in the world—bigger than film or television" (Lewis 1983, 136).

Prima facie, part of the commercial interest in selling music from the
advent of its commodification, like some other cultural products before and
since, was its potential for a massive profit margin given a relatively small
investment. And, in fact, it is probably fair to say that this has remained
largely the case since the inception of the commercial music industry in
the United States. Unlike some other industries, that massive profit margin
potential was likely partly due to the fact that there was not really much
"physical" product that was manufactured for sale, nor an expansive physical infrastructure needed to manufacture it, in contrast to commodities such
as cars, refrigerators, or oil, and the corresponding infrastructures needed to
produce them. At first, "music" was sold as sheet music, keeping in mind that
the paper and ink was only the medium used to physically realize the actual
commodity, which was, in effect, the information communicated through that
medium. Accordingly, the physical infrastructure needed to "produce" the
commodity was a printing press, a place to shelter it presumably, and various
sundry tools likely needed for the press's maintenance. As time passed, and
"recorded" music became the commodity, the infrastructure and materials

needed to produce, and to reproduce that commodity on records remained relatively modest and, in fact, often became increasingly inexpensive as new technologies were developed and implemented. Here, the "product" itself, at least in one sense, consisted merely of grooves cut into vinyl that could, subsequently, be mass produced endlessly with little physical infrastructure. Once the master recording was created with recording devices, and the physical infrastructure for producing records was dedicated, it became relatively inexpensive to produce endless copies of recordings for sale. In contrast, expansive production infrastructures that demand continuous maintenance are needed for producing commodities such as oil, steel, refrigerators, and cars. Furthermore, unlike other commodities such as dog food, door hinges, and oil, records did not face the same kind of market limitations on the rate that they were likely to be consumed or replaced, and, therefore, purchased, discretionary spending limitations aside. Unlike the commodity of music, that is, one can expect some quasi-physical restrictions exist that limit the amount of demand that might exist at any particular moment for dog food, door hinges, and refrigerators, barring unexpected booms that might occur in their markets, like unforeseen fads of owning packs of dogs, or natural disasters of varying sorts. In fact, the market for cultural commodities such as records, books or, more recently, computer games, was, and is, in principle, endless, limited only by such things as interest coupled with the amount of disposable income that may exist at any given time.

Of course, conditions for generating even larger profits from producing records than had hitherto been enjoyed, and particularly those of rock and roll, became increasingly favorable in the United States, especially after World War II. First, while the expense to produce records had been relatively modest to begin with, it became even less expensive with the advent of various technological innovations, such as more portable tape machines designed by the Germans during the war (Mabry 1990, 417). According to some estimates, the cost to record a song for distribution on a 45 rpm record by the late 1950s was only a few hundred dollars,[16] while in some cases it might sell as many as a million copies at fifty cents a unit, gross.[17] Secondly, as implied to some extent above, disposable income had increased within certain segments of society, both during and after the war. Labor shortages brought about by World War II had created new opportunities for hitherto marginalized segments of society to have higher paying defense jobs (Chapple and Garofalo 1977, 28), which specifically helped to support the growing market of "race" records (Chapple and Garofalo 1977, 8) and "hillbilly" music, since such music was particularly attractive to the beneficiaries of these higher paying jobs. After the war, the trickle-down effects of the post-war economy also eventually reached the younger members of society. For example, Hirsch estimated that the "teen market" of disposable income was about $10 billion by 1959 (Hirsch 1963, 69) while about 60 percent of all 45 singles sold in 1962–1963 were purchased by teenagers, and 80 percent by persons under twenty-five (Hirsch 1963, 68, footnote 77). Finally, it is important not to forget the fact that sales of records for use in jukeboxes also added to the profits of specific records if they were hits. By 1940, 350,000 to 400,000 jukeboxes were operating in the United States,[18] each containing records purchased for about thirty-five cents a unit, and individual selections costing consumers a nickel to play (Chapple and Garofalo 1977, 6).

Still, despite the modest expense to produce a record and the existence of a market of consumers favorable to the product, it was typically difficult to turn a profit on any given record, since, as *Fortune* magazine further noted in 1979, there was no clear correlation between the amount of product produced and the profit thereby generated, and no clear formula to follow to ensure that a record was successful (*Fortune* 1979, 59).[19] Indeed, just prior to the boom in record revenues that was precipitated by the advent of rock and roll, only about one of thirty-six singles made the Top 20 of *Billboard* (Chapple and Garofalo 1977, 13–14) and by the 1950s, at least 90 percent of records produced lost money (Mabry 1990, 443), with 80 percent of those released resulting in losses, both for the record companies and their distributors (Mabry 1990, 444). Moreover, this trend was consistent in the industry. To note a couple more figures, seven thousand 45s and four thousand albums were released in 1970, with 74 percent of singles and 61 percent of the "pop" LPs not producing enough sales to even cover expenses (Denisoff and Levine 1972a, 240), and in 1979, *Fortune* reported that "more than two-thirds of all records are dismal flops" (*Fortune* 1979, 60).

Now, just before the advent of rock and roll's popularity, the record business itself comprised what some scholars have characterized as an "oligopoly," where control of the record market was concentrated into the hands of very few businesses.[20] In 1950, there were six "major" record companies, as they were typically labeled,[21] namely Columbia (a division of CBS), RCA-Victor, American Decca (which was eventually absorbed by MCA) (Peterson and Berger 1975, 160), Capitol (what was a division of EMI at the time), MGM, and Mercury,[22] with Columbia and RCA leading the pack in terms of their overall influence on the industry (Chapple and Garofalo 1977, 15; Belz 1972, 17–18). Even though Joeri Mol and Nachoem Wijnberg have probably overstated it, considering what we will learn below about the intersection of the radio broadcast business, copyright protection agencies, such as the American Society of Composers, Authors and Publishers (ASCAP), and other constituencies, these "majors," more or less, "controlled the whole value system from the artist upstream to distribution downstream" (Mol and Wijnberg 2007, 708).

Four of these "white-owned" (Linden 2012, 49) companies, namely RCA-Victor, Columbia, Capitol, and American Decca, controlled 78 percent of all record sales in 1950, leaving the balance to other so-called "independents" (Linden 2012, 52). Shortly prior to that, in 1948, they "had released 81 percent of all the records that reached the weekly top-ten hit list any time during the year," and "[t]he top eight firms together released 95 per cent of all the hits and only three other firms had any hits at all!" (Peterson 1990, 104). Indeed, according to Hirsch et al., "[u]ntil 1955, over eighty percent of all top hit songs were manufactured and distributed by only five record companies: RCA/Victor, Columbia, Mercury, Decca, and Capitol" (Hirsch et al. 1972, 85–86; cf. Linden 2012, 49). Put another way, the scope of this oligarchical control over the entire market is exemplified by the fact that only five records that sold at least a million copies, out of a total of 162 million-selling records released between 1946–1952, were produce by independent record companies, with the rest being produced by the majors (Chapple and Garofalo 1977, 44).

Such concentration of market share into the hands of a few record producers, however, was certainly not absolute prior to 1950. During the 1920s, for example, there existed a multitude of the "independent" companies, so-called in contrast to the majors, many of which, together with the majors, produced records for a number of specialty markets, including black, gospel, and country. However, when the Depression occurred, the smaller firms were eventually wiped out, and the majors absorbed their portion of those markets (Chapple and Garofalo 1977, 29; Peterson and Berger 1972, 287). Nevertheless, this trend was once again reversed with the advent of World War II, when shellac became difficult to obtain. When that happened, the majors withdrew from the specialty markets to concentrate on more mainstream popular music, leaving new independent companies an opportunity to establish themselves (Chapple and Garofalo 1977, 8). As a result, and in conjunction with the assistance of new, "cost effective" technologies to produce records (Mol and Wijnberg 2007, 708), about four hundred new independent companies became established during the 1940s, according to Nat Shapiro, roughly a hundred of which survived until 1952 (Chapple and Garofalo 1977, 29).[23] Among those independents that proved particularly successful were Atlantic Records, Chess Records, and Sun Records.

Atlantic Records was founded in October 1947 by Ahmet Ertegun, the son of a Turkish ambassador to the United States and lover of jazz and blues, and Herb Abramson, a trained dentist and former A&R man from National Records who had signed Joe Turner and the Ravens while at National (Chapple and Garofalo 1977, 31). Under their management, Atlantic Records was responsible for "Sh-Boom" by the Chords, Joe Turner's recording of "Shake, Rattle, and Roll," as well as other recordings by such notable artists as Aretha Franklin, Ray Charles, and Bobby Darin (Chapple and Garofalo 1977, 32–34).

Chess Records was established in 1949 by two Polish immigrants named Leonard and Phil Chess. Chess's first hit, selling about seventy thousand copies, was "Rolling Stone" by Muddy Waters (Chapple and Garofalo 1977, 37). They also produced "Sincerely" by the Moonglows before it was covered by the McGuire Sisters on Decca's subsidiary, Coral Records (Chapple and Garofalo 1977, 38). They also signed Howlin' Wolf (Chapple and Garofalo 1977, 38). Muddy Waters also recommended to Chuck Berry that he should check out Chess, with whom Berry eventually recorded "Maybellene" (Chapple and Garofalo 1977, 39) as I mentioned above, and they enlisted Alan Freed to help them promote their records (Chapple and Garofalo 1977, 38).

Sam Phillips, an ex-radio engineer from Alabama (Chapple and Garofalo 1977, 40) established Sun Records in Memphis, Tennessee (M. Allen 2015, 109), in 1950 (Chapple and Garofalo 1977, 40). Sam Phillips's first records included the artists B.B. King, Howlin' Wolf, and Walter Horton, and later Carl Perkins with "Blues Suede Shoes" in 1956 and Jerry Lee Lewis with "Whole lotta Shakin' Goin' On" in 1957 (Chapple and Garofalo 1977, 42). Meanwhile, it took Elvis Presley going to Sun Studio, which happened to be located fifteen blocks from Presley's home, for about a year and a half until Sam Phillips finally called him one day and asked him to record a country tune which apparently did not go so well. Nevertheless, Sam called him back in one day to try some blues songs, which resulted in "That's All Right." After "That's All Right," followed by five other records, Phillips eventually sold Presley to RCA for $35,000, according to RCA's figure (Chapple and Garofalo 1977, 42), which resulted in Presley's first recording with RCA, namely "Heartbreak Hotel" (Chapple and Garofalo 1977, 42–43).

For a variety of reasons, to be elaborated below, that concern a confluence of changes in technology and copyright dynamics within the record industry, these independents had gained nearly total control of the rhythm and blues market, with twenty-three of the Top 30 hits, by the end of 1954 (Chapple and Garofalo 1977, 35), and by 1956, just over 50 percent of all Top 10 records were produced by independents, despite the fact that Elvis Presley and Bill Haley had, by that time, switched to the majors. Moreover, by 1957, the independents produced half of all pop record successes as well, with the four "giants," namely Columbia, RCA/Victor, Capitol, and Decca, controlling only 50 percent of the entire market in the United States (*Fortune* 1979, 61), and by 1959 the independents were responsible for two-thirds of all hits (Chapple and Garofalo 1977, 43–44),[24] with the "Big 5" producing only 47 percent of the Top 3 singles.[25] In fact, between 1955 and 1962, the market share ratio between the majors and the independents had significantly reversed itself with the share of the majors, collectively speaking, dropping from 74 percent to, roughly, 25 percent (Mol and Wijnberg 2007, 710), while the independents increased their market share from about 20 percent in the early 1950s to 76 percent by the late 1950s (Linden 2012, 52).

Various technological innovations in record production, together with control of their attending patents, also affected market share and, thus, the music to which the general public was subsequently exposed. In 1948, for example, under the direction of Edward Wallerstein, then president of Columbia Records, and by way of the work of Peter Goldmark and his team, Columbia produced the first high fidelity, 33 1/3 rpm microgroove "LP"[26] (Mabry 1990, 417; Chapple and Garofalo 1977, 20; Grendysa 1986) in combination with a player produced by Philco, which Columbia then made available to all record companies through a licensing arrangement (Grendysa 1986). It should be noted, however, that RCA had previously experimented with a 33 1/3 rpm groove in the 1930s, but abandoned the idea because the public rejected it for a number of reasons, not the least of which was the need for a new player during a time when disposable income was scarce (Peterson 1990, 100).[27] Be that as it may, when Columbia released its LP in 1949, RCA quickly responded with the release of the 45 rpm record, in combination with an inexpensive 45 rpm player, which it sold at a loss and gave away through various promotions (Mabry 1990, 417; Belz 1972, 53; Chapple and Garofalo 1977, 22).[28] Both formats, in any event, were initially intended for classical music, since previously that genre had been difficult to record on the short-playing shellac 78 format (Peterson and Berger 1972, 294–95).

As things unfolded from there, Columbia's LP initially gained a market advantage over RCA's 45 because Columbia had also developed a conversion kit for the 78 players that everyone already had in their homes so that the new LPs could be played on them, whereas the 45 required people to purchase a whole new system. Nevertheless, RCA eventually managed to sell ten million 45 players in 1953 (Chapple and Garofalo 1977, 22) and, in fact, at least surpassed the 78s in pop market sales by 1954. At the outset, however, RCA resisted any releases of its own on LPs until 1950, substituting box sets of singles to overcome the long-playing advantages of the LP, even though Columbia quickly implemented a strategy of releasing seven-inch singles with a small hole that played at 33 1/3 rpms (Grendysa 1986). For one thing, 45s had an advantage for record companies, particularly the independents, from a production standpoint, "due to the development of automatic injection and compression systems in record production which obviated the older hand compression molds still in use for many 78s in 1954" (Belz 1972, 54). The 45s were also light, easy to package and handle, physically resilient compared to the 78s (Belz 1972, 54), and they were a nice platform for short playing tunes on jukeboxes.

Finally, during 1960 and 1961, there was also consideration of a 33 1/3, seven-inch single to standardize record speeds, and the "major companies—including RCA, Columbia, and Capital—planned to issue singles in this new format" (Belz 1972, 55). However, the project was eventually dropped, in part because of resistance from juke box operators who were ambivalent about having to retrofit the players (Belz 1972, 55) and, perhaps, Belz speculates, because the format did not have a musical genre that accompanied it, unlike what 45s had managed to cultivate (Belz 1972, 56). For one initial and likely unintended consequence of the advent of the new record formats was that rock and roll came to be associated with the 45, while the 33 1/3 came to be associate with "adult" and "good music" (Belz 1972, 54). As "the publisher of *Billboard*, Hal Cook" noted in 1963 "'the general public identifies the 33 as 'good music,' while it classifies the 45 with the black leather jacket and motorcycle set' *(Billboard*, July 20, 1963, p. 3)" (Belz 1972, 55), which Paul Ackerman further confirmed, more or less, during the payola hearings, when he said that "singles" were "a product which today is aimed essentially at the teenage market" (Belz 1972, 114). As a matter of fact, the later shift in rock and roll away from the 45 to the 33 1/3 format came to be represented, for some, its graduation to a status of being a more serious musical genre (Belz 1972, 56).

Meanwhile, although radio stations were at first ambivalent about the 45 format, RCA eventually forced them to adopt it by sending them only 45s (Chapple and Garofalo 1977, 22; Belz 1972, 53). By 1957, 45s had completely replaced 78s in all fields of popular music (Belz 1972, 55), with the exception of a strategic lag implemented in the case of rhythm and blues, which record companies continued to produce as 78s, partly because, according to Belz, the genre's principle audience, namely the black community, was slow to enjoy the benefits from the growth in the economy (Belz 1972, 53).

NOTES

1. It is important, however, not to overstate the significance of recordings and radio as the only means to which the wider public became exposed to so-called "hillbilly" music during the 1930s. During this time, as Wilgus remarks, "musicians were still oriented toward personal appearance, and . . . anxious to use the commercial media for publicity. They recorded for flat fees and performed their radio shows for little or nothing in order to promote their appearances or to vend songbooks and merchandise on percentage. Media executives, on the other hand, were often slow to recognize the total tie-in of radio, recording, and personal appearances with merchandising" (Wilgus 1970, 165). Personal appearances, in particular, were nonetheless quite popular and lucrative for some performers through the 1940s. For example, in reference

to Roy Acuff, Bill Malone reports that Acuff filled Constitution Hall in Washington at $6.60 a head; attracted an audience of 13,000 for two performances with Ernest Tubb at Cincinnati's Music Hall; and "drew the largest crowd that had ever gone to a Foreman Phillips promotion [at Venice Pier, California]. There were 11,130 paid admissions, and it seemed that the pier was going to fall from the weight" (Malone 1968, 205).

2. For example, recalling his youth, Elvis Presley remarked: "I'd play along with the radio or phonograph, and taught myself the chord positions" (Chapple and Garofalo 1977, 41).

3. Indeed, unlike in the case of other musical genres, it has been commonplace for some scholars to conceive of recordings as the "original" form of rock and roll, and live performances, as the "reproduction" of the music (cf. Belz 1972, 42). Michael Roberts, for example, asserts that "[r]ock and roll . . . developed as a record culture. . . . The record not only had an impact on the culture of rock and roll consumers. . . . Records made it possible for working-class youth—like John Lennon—to teach themselves how to play music. Many rock and roll musicians became skilled at their craft without learning how to read music" (Roberts 2010, 13). As a matter of fact, this reversal might have been part of what spurred an "anti-record" bias, if not also an "anti-rock" aesthetic, that seemed to have emerged and been vocally expressed by certain members and officers of the AFM (American Federation of Musicians) who demanded the maintenance of a "professional" demeanor for musicians, who saw the skill of reading music as essential to the profession of music making, and who, accordingly, believed it should be sustained as a requirement for professional musicianship and so AFM membership. Because of this, as Roberts further notes, "the AFM required potential members to pass a music reading test—an audition—as part of the process for gaining access to union membership. Many rock-and-roll bands were excluded from the AFM on the basis of failing the audition, one of the more infamous cases being the Beach Boys who were initially refused membership to the AFM because they failed their audition" (Roberts 2010, 13).

As an aside, this practice of the AFM of exercising significant control over the kinds of music that were afforded an opportunity to become popular by no means merely began with rock and roll, as I will discuss in greater detail below. Rather, it was another permutation of what had transpired during the early days of country music, when performers of the genre, who could typically not "sight-read" sheet music and were precluded from gaining membership in the AFM often on that pretense, were blocked from securing contracts in the large venues of urban environments, "except in the South and Southwest, where the union was weak" (Peterson 1997, 13). Many of these artists were thus driven to remain mere amateurs or semi-professional, delivering performances for meager remuneration at "barn dances, music contests, store openings, festive occasions, political rallies, church functions, and the like" (Peterson 1997, 13). Although such exclusions from membership in the AFM and securing well-paying gigs also occurred as well for certain black artists who performed blues, these latter artists were likely excluded often for specifically racist reasons, as should become increasingly apparent below.

4. As one such example of an exception to this view, Belz referenced a personal interview with promoter Bill Graham that occurred in April 1966. Paraphrasing Graham, Belz remarked "[h]e feels that younger, more sympathetic producers will gradually close the aesthetic gap between records and concerts. In other words, Graham envisions records as having an imitative function" (Belz 1972, 49).

5. Although they suggest that the original idea of the Make Believe Ballroom was stolen from the L.A.-based Al Jarvis, Chapple and Garofalo trace its actual inauguration to Martin Block when, in 1935, he played a number of recordings on WNEW by bandleader Clyde McCoy, during a break in the Lindbergh kidnapping trial broadcast, and accompanied them with a feigned conversation with Clyde (Chapple and Garofalo 1977, 54). But this practice of producing "simulated" live performances appears to have quickly extended beyond Block, as Wilgus reports its implementation in relation to so-called "hillbilly music" by CKLW, in Windsor, Ontario, and "XERA and other Mexican stations" during the late 1930s (Wilgus 1970, 165–66).

6. Moreover, according to Chapple and Garofalo, "Detroit jukebox operators reported in 1943 that hillbilly records were the most popular" (Chapple and Garofalo 1977, 8).

7. This seemed particularly true for country music. "In Europe the American Armed Forces Radio Network voted Roy Acuff, a Nashville Grand Ole Opry start with a fiddle, to be more popular than Frank Sinatra" (Chapple and Garofalo 1977, 8; cf. Mabry 1990, 417). Perhaps surprisingly, according to Bill Malone, "[a] two-week popularity contest held on the Armed Forces Network's 'Munich Morning Report' gave Roy Acuff, out of 3,700 votes cast, a lead of 600 votes over popular crooner Frank Sinatra" (Malone 1968, 206). Moreover, for obvious reasons, the recruit "could not always silence a company radio tuned to the armed forces network; nor could he always silence the guitar of the boy on the next bunk. The training campus of the South and the Southwest exposed the recruit to a heavy dose of country music, on the radio and in the honky tonks" (Wilgus 1970, 169).

8. Richard Peterson also reminds us that, in addition to being free, "live music broadcast over radio sounded better than did music heard on the acoustically recorded phonograph records of the time" (Peterson 1997, 16).

9. Bill Malone reports that only six million records sold in 1932 (Malone 1968, 106).

10. The name "jukebox" was presumably given to the "automatic music vending machines" that were placed in small bars and clubs in the Southeast that quickly proliferated after the repeal of Prohibition in December 1933, and which came to be called "Juke Joints" (Peterson 1997, 164), a term originally applied to establishments frequented by African-American patrons of working-class means, and devoted to "jooking," which referred to "fast couple dancing" (Peterson 1997, 259, 4). According to Peterson, they were not unlike those establishments that popped up in the Southwest and that were called "honky tonks" (Peterson 1997, 164), namely small roadside clubs located on the edges of cities and county lines where police oversight was limited, and which were so named because, due to the primary business being drinking, they tended to be loud places with frequent fights (Peterson 1997, 162).

11. According to Peterson, industry experts attempted to analyze the causes of the slump and to identify new musical products to offset it (Peterson 1997, 188).

12. It is worth mentioning that despite very little market growth overall, the rhythm and blues market grew to $15 million by 1952 (Chapple and Garofalo 1977, 34).

13. For example, Victor was up about 20 percent. The head of Victor at the time, Mannie Sachs, attributed the company's growth in revenue to the introduction of multi-speed turntables and high-fidelity sound, according to Chapple and Garofalo (1977, 25).

14. *Billboard* reported over $1.124 billion of record revenues in 1969–1970, with albums yielding $949 million and singles $175 million, with Columbia Records single-handedly responsible for nearly 20 percent of the total figure (Denisoff and Levine 1972a, 245).

15. With "rock music" "account[ing] for more than 80 percent of all records and tapes sold" (Chapple and Garofalo 1977, xi).

16. The figures seem to vary widely in the literature. Chapple and Garofalo have reported that records were produced for about $150 between the years of 1937–1941 (Chapple and Garofalo 1977, 7). Meanwhile, Hirsch reported that a single would cost a few hundred dollars to record and manufacture (Hirsch 1971, 383). Finally, to provide some greater detail of the cost of producing recordings, Donald Mabry reports that, "[i]n late 1959, Cosimo billed Ace for one and one-half hours of studio time at $20 an hour and for three 1,200-foot tapes at $2.50 each, for a total of $37.50. Huey 'Piano' Smith signed a contract in December of that year, which guaranteed him $10 for each song he recorded ($40 for a full, four-song session) plus union scale as a musician on the session. . . . In August 1960 the American Federation of Musicians Local #174 charged Vin Records $1,070 for a four-song recording session; the band leader received $135, thirteen other musicians received $67.50 each, and one received $57.50. For a three-song session in October 1960, however, the local union charged $618 ($103 for the band leader and $51.50 each for the nine other musicians). If these two sessions are representative, musician' wages for a record (two songs) cost about $480. . . . In addition, the record company paid for food and drink before, during and after the recording session. If a participating musician did not live in the New Orleans area, the company also paid for housing" (Mabry 1990, 441). Other costs include album covers and record sleeves. "In 1962, Lithographing of New York charged Ace $581 for 5,200 album covers, or 11.2 cents each" (Mabry 1990, 441).

17. During the prewar period, Decca, the third major company to begin producing records, in addition to Columbia and Victor, entered the competitive fray for Depression plagued customers by implementing the business plan of making records more affordable by undercutting "Victor's and Columbia's prevailing price of 75 cents a record to 34 cents or three for a dollar" (Chapple and Garofalo 1977, 6). Bill Malone actually reports Decca's price to have been thirty-five cents (Malone 1968, 107). In the late 1940s, Modern Records sold its blues singles for $1.05, and the major record companies sold their pop singles for seventy-eight cents. According to Chapple and Garofalo, "Blacks were willing to pay more for their music" (Chapple and Garofalo 1977, 30). Looking to the "independent" company, Ace, Mabry reports that "Ace's gross profit on a 45 RPM record was thirteen cents; the production costs

averaged thirty-three cents; the record was sold to a distributor for forty-six cents. The net profit was considerably lower" (Mabry 1990, 442).

18. While Chapple and Garofalo report the figure of 350,000 jukeboxes by 1940 (Chapple and Garofalo 1977, 6), Peterson cites the higher figure of over 400,000 jukeboxes in use by the late 1930s by appealing to a *Billboard* supplement article by Walter Hurd, dated September 28, 1940 (Peterson 1997, 165).

19. As Paul Ackerman, Music Editor of *Billboard*, also remarked during the 1960 payola hearings, "[a]bout 130 single records and about 100 long-playing records are released weekly. Competition for exposure is extreme, for, without wide public exposure, the potential buyer would never hear of most of these records" (Belz 1972, 113). That said, however, the industry's output actually rose "to over 300 new singles *per week*" at the height of the industry growth of rock and roll, according to Hirsch (1971, 383).

20. As Peterson defined it, "[i]ndustry structure is oligopolistic when a few firms effectively control the style, amount and price of products produced. Perfect competition is when the actions of no firms significantly influence any of these factors," and a perfect oligopoly is, in effect, a monopoly (Peterson 1990, 103). In reference to the record industry, "oligopolistic concentration . . . was maintained by control of the total production flow from raw materials to wholesale sales . . . [what] economists call 'vertical integration'" (Peterson and Berger 1975, 161).

21. Although slight fluctuation occurs in the literature as to which record companies qualified as "majors," in contrast to those deemed "independent," by the late 1940s and early 1950s, Chapple and Garofalo suggest, record companies came to be so qualified when "they owned their own manufacturing plants and directly controlled their distribution outlets in addition to simply producing records" (Chapple and Garofalo 1977, 15). That said, by the 1960s the term "major" had become extended to include other companies which were merely successful in selling records (Chapple and Garofalo 1977, 15).

22. According to Peterson and Berger, "Mercury Records, a Chicago-based company formed in 1947, was the only independent firm to garner a significant share of the market in this era. It is reputed to have used the channels of organized crime to market its product and force its records on juke box operators" (Peterson and Berger 1975, 162). To explain the lack of citation for this claim, Peterson and Berger remarked that "[f]or understandable reasons, the three individuals who independently supplied this information have asked not to be cited by name" (Peterson and Berger 1975, 162, footnote 2).

23. Mol and Wijnberg report that "[w]hereas there were as little as half a dozen active record companies in 1941, this number grew to 1,500–2,000 in the 1950s because of the diffusion of new cost-effective technologies" (Mol and Wijnberg 2007, 708).

24. According to Peterson, "[t]he four firms that had 81 per cent of the popular music hits in 1948 gradually lost market share until it reached 74 per cent in 1955. Then things changed rapidly. Their market share was down to 66 per cent in 1956 and sank rapidly over the next few years reaching just 34 per cent by 1959!" (Peterson 1990, 106).

25. By 1969, this trend in the hit market had continued with the majors producing only 37 percent of the Top 3 singles (Hirsch 1972, 86).

26. The expression "LP" was actually a Columbia Records trademark (Grendysa 1986).

27. "In 1931 RCA-Victor, then under the leadership of Edward Wallerstein, produced a series of long-playing records offering a maximum of 10 minutes playing time per 12-inch side. They revolved at 33 1/3 rpm, the groove width was slightly smaller than that of the standard 78 rpm discs, and they were made of a plastic substance called 'Vitrolac'. . . . This enterprising innovation turned into a debacle. For some strange reason, many of the long-playing records were merely dubbed from 78 rpm discs, with the resultant loss of sound quality. Adding to Victor's woes, the thinner groove wall could not stand up to the lethal combination of metal needles and massive tonearms then in use . . . the sound quality got even worse towards the center of the discs. And you couldn't play them at all unless you bought a special player or attachment . . . the line was discontinued sometime in 1933" (Grendysa 1986).

28. That said, according to Peterson and Berger, because companies initially priced the new format records well above the cost of production to ensure their profitability, the higher standard retail prices allowed the smaller independent producers to get into the business of pressing records, sometimes out of their garage, because some profit could still be generated from selling fewer copies (Peterson and Berger 1972, 295).

Chapter 3

The Nature and Influence
of Commercial Radio

Like the record industry, and in conjunction with it, the radio industry had a significant impact on how the commercialization of music in general unfolded in the United States, and how it further served to facilitate some cross-fertilization of musical genres, as I have already implied above. For, as R. H. Coase asserts what may seem to some to be a mere truism, "[t]o sell music on a large scale, it is necessary that people hear it" (Coase 1979, 316) and, as Donald Mabry further elaborates, "people bought records they heard" and "no record could become a hit unless it was played on the radio" (Mabry 1990, 445; cf. 446).

Even so, it may be worth mentioning that the meaning and implications of claims such as these are by no means as obvious as they might seem and, accordingly, perhaps warrant at least some scant inquiry before being accepted at face value. William Fox and James Williams, for example, certainly thought so when they undertook a study at the University of Iowa in 1973 to investigate, according to the title of their subsequent publication in the *Public Opinion Quarterly*, the "Political Orientation and Music Preferences among College Students." What they found, surprisingly, was that while 40 percent of students identified as "liberal" bought at least six records during the previous six months, in contrast to only 25 percent of students identified as "conservative" (Fox and Williams 1974, 362–63), those frequencies of buying records did not appear to align with the extent to which each group actually listened to radio. For whereas 30 percent of "conservative" students reported "high radio listening," only 14 percent of "liberal" and 23 percent of "moderate" students did (Fox and Williams 1974, 363),[1] In fact, the study seemed to indicate (a) that radio listening did not correlate to record listening, (b) that radio listening correlated negatively with concert attendance and record purchases (Fox and Williams 1974, 360, footnote 33), and (c) that higher radio involvement corresponded to "more conservative political orientations" (Fox and Williams 1974, 363). As Fox and Williams expressed some of the implications of their study, "[t]he data we have examined thus far indicate that students with different political orientations tend to listen to music from different media [either records or radio, that is]" (Fox and Williams 1974, 367). Moreover, "[a]ssuming that radio listening primarily involves listening to music, these data suggest that commercial broadcasting provides programming most compatible with the musical tastes of more conservative students" (Fox and Williams 1974, 363).

From having only a military purpose by the end of WWI, radios were soon adopted thereafter by the general public in the United States, as the commercial radio broadcast industry evolved. By 1922, sales of commercial radios ballooned to $60 million by 1922 and $842,548,000 by 1929. Furthermore, while one million sets were reported to have been in use in 1922 (Sanjek 1991, 10), "[a]ccording to federal census of 1930, 12,078,345 families owned radio sets" by that time (Malone 1968, 34). That said, it should be noted that ownership was not always uniform across the geography and demographics of the United States. For example, while roughly 45 percent of "mid-western farm families had radio sets" by 1930, only about 10 percent of white Southern farmers had one (Peterson 1997, 100).

Be that as it may, radio was particularly instrumental to enhancing public exposure to otherwise "non-popular," or hitherto "specialty" genres, such as "hillbilly" and "race" music. For example, on March 16, 1922, WSB in Atlanta, Georgia, went on the air as the first powerful radio station covering the southern United States (Peterson 1997, 20) and shortly thereafter, on November 29, 1922, broadcasted what was advertised as a live "Old-fashioned Concert," which was "probably the first 'all-country' radio program to air anywhere" (Peterson 1997, 20), followed, perhaps, by the "Radio Barn Dance," which was first aired in Chicago on April 19, 1924, by WLS (Peterson 1997, 99). Since the reach of WSB was also enhanced in the evening, when "hillbilly" or "country" music was most likely to be broadcasted (Peterson 1997, 25), a wider audience was afforded access to musical genres such as these.

Initially, however, one of the incentives to hiring "hillbilly" or "country" performers for broadcasting purposes likely had little to do with attraction to the music by the station's management, let alone the urban residents of Atlanta, Georgia. Instead, the reason the management of radio stations tended to hire hillbilly performers, on average, had to do with the basic fact that they were inexpensive to broadcast. Unlike performers of the more mainstream popular music, that is, they did not require "complex or expensive studio arrangements," "they could be called upon to play at a moment's notice," and they could play "as long (or short) a time as was required" (Peterson 1997, 27).

Now, mirroring the five or so majors in the record business that dominated the marketplace until the end of the 1940s, the commercial radio business quickly concentrated into four national networks, together with their affiliated stations, alongside a handful "of newly licensed independent commercial stations" (Peterson 1990, 103). Appearing by the late 1920s, and involving such monolithic companies as General Electric, Westinghouse, RCA, and AT&T (Ryan 1985, 32), these "networks" were presumably first established as one mechanism by which otherwise individual stations could pool their programming resources (cf. Peterson 1997, 120). Although by 1930 there were roughly six hundred radio stations in the United States, and by 1940, almost eight hundred; from the 1930s to the 1940s the percentage of stations with network affiliation increased from about 20 percent to nearly 60 percent (Peterson 1997, 120). In some cases, to be expected, the record companies also had close business ties to these national networks that helped to facilitate exposure to their product. For example, Columbia Records promoted its records over its own radio network CBS, and RCA promoted its records over its radio network NBC (Mabry 1990, 413). It is also worth noting that Decca Records was affiliated with the major media outlet, MCA, while Capitol Records was associated with Paramount Pictures (Mol and Wijnberg 2007, 707).

Part of the reason for this concentration in the commercial radio broadcast industry appears due to the fact that, despite the submission of many applications for licenses to new stations, the established networks vigorously and successfully lobbied the Federal Communications Commission (FCC) against granting additional broadcasting licenses. This occurred principally from about 1930 until the beginning of World War II (Peterson 1990, 101), at which point the FCC then deferred all such requests (Peterson 1990, 101). One of the primary justifications forwarded by the FCC for denying the licenses prior to World War II appealed to the notion of what was "in the public interest" (which is to say, it was not "in the public interest" to have more radio stations). Thereafter, during the war, the reason for the denials was that "scarce electronic material could not be spared from the war effort to build transmitters" (Peterson 1990, 101).

Presumably to circumvent the difficulties some investors had experienced in seeking new broadcasting licenses from the FCC, a number of stations, typically established by "American" businessmen, and beginning with Dr. J. R. Brinkley's XER station in 1930 (which, in 1935 was changed to XERA), established themselves along the Mexican Border, where they "aimed their transmitters towards the United States," and broadcasted with wattage upwards of 100,000–150,000 watts, two or three times the 50,000 watt limit imposed on Northern stations. In one case, in fact, it was reported that the wattage of one of these "superstations" had been boosted to 500,000. The

Mexican government, in turn, presumably allowed the establishment of these stations, according to Bill Malone, "because of a prior snubbing of Mexico by her northern neighbors" when the U.S. and Canadian governments divided "between themselves the entire long-wave broadcast band, leaving neither Cuba nor Mexico any clear channels at all" (Malone 1968, 112).

In any event, because of previous affiliations that owners such as J. R. Brinkley had with "hillbilly" music, the power of these stations made it possible to override many of the "northern" radio broadcasts, including those of the networks and their affiliates, and blast "hillbilly" music, such as that of the Carter Family, throughout the central United States (Peterson 1997, 134). This occurred not only during prime time, but particularly during the early morning hours when the audience was typically saturated with farmers and truckers (Malone 1968, 113).

Sometimes the studios for these "border" stations were located on the U.S. side of the border, while the transmitters themselves were located on the Mexico side of the border where the FCC did not have jurisdiction over the broadcast itself. This was done to circumvent possible interruptions to station operations and the broadcast of live performers, since, on occasion, either the Mexican or U.S. government might restrict "the flow of artists, advertising material, or telephone connections across the boarder" (sic) (Peterson 1997, 134).[2] To further circumvent this eventuality, some stations even invested in transcription equipment, prerecorded their musical programs without mention of date, time, or place, and made additional copies on 33 1/3 rpm 16-inch disks available to other stations which, in turn, tailored them to their own occasions and circumstances (Peterson 1997, 134–35).

Starting in 1947, however, the networks began to remove their objection to the granting of new radio broadcasting licenses, and many were then approved for new stations. Part of the reason for this, it is speculated, had to do with the advent of television, since there had been concern in the radio industry at the time that TV would eventually replace radio (Peterson and Berger 1972, 293). Indeed, "[m]any experts, reasoning that no one would listen to a box when they could listen to a box that also showed moving pictures, thought that TV would completely replace radio" (Peterson 1990, 102).

It is certainly true that, beginning in 1949, the move away from investment in radio to investment in television was dramatic. While in 1948 there were less than 172,000 families with TV sets, and 85 percent of all households had radios (Chapple and Garofalo 1977, 12; cf. Peterson and Berger 1972, 293), or seventy million to be more precise (Mol and Wijnberg 2007, 707), there were about ten million TV sets in homes by 1950 (Peterson and Berger 1972, 293), twenty million by 1952 (Peterson and Berger 1975, 165), and by 1955, 65 percent of households had acquired a TV set (Peterson 1990, 102). By 1957 roughly 80 percent of households had a TV set, roughly thirty-nine million sets (Chapple and Garofalo 1977, 12) and, in 1958, fifty million TV sets existed in homes (Peter and Berger 1972, 293).

Of course, with the advent of television, and at roughly the same time that new radio broadcasting licenses began to be granted and purchased, the commercial radio networks began to divest their interest in radio stations (Mabry 1990, 418) which, in turn, flooded the market with additional radio stations for sale and caused station franchises to be sold at a loss (Peterson and Berger 1972, 293). However, for some people, including some southern black investors who had managed to prosper to some degree during the war, the drop in the market price for radio stations, in conjunction with the availability of new licenses, presented attractive opportunities to invest in commercial radio and, perhaps counterintuitively, the number of stations actually doubled during the next four years.[3] Still, advertisers who had previously contracted with radio stations also began to divert their advertising dollars to the new medium of television to market their products (Peterson and Berger 1975, 165), just as the multitude of newly licensed radio stations began to materialize, and this, in turn, caused radio stations, in general, to face increasing competition for a shrinking slice of a limited audience market (Peterson 1990, 102). From 1948 to 1952, for example, the revenue of radio stations dropped by 38 percent (Mol and Wijnberg 2007, 707; Peterson and Berger 1975, 165). Moreover, as the advertising dollars and network budgets transitioned to television, a substantial portion of the programming that had previously appeared on radio followed, such as live comedy shows and drama, together the budgets that had previously supported live musical broadcasts (Peterson 1990, 105).

In particular, the budgets that previously supported live musical performances on radio had been substantial. For as long as the major radio networks controlled the lion's share of the airwaves, live performances, rather than the playing of records, or the use of other recorded shows, had been the prevailing practice in programming. In fact, citing Erik Barnouw, Peterson asserts that "there was an absolute ban against using any recorded programming (other than sound effects) on network programming through the 1940s" (Peterson 1997, 256, note 12). Instead, referencing 1948 specifically, Peterson remarks that the radio networks typically broadcasted "major dance bands" during the weekend evenings from dance halls and hotels, as well as popular hits performed by studio orchestras on various programs throughout the day (Peterson 1990, 103).[4] Of course, the use of live performances had not merely been restricted to the networks, nor to strictly mainstream popular content, as I previously suggested above. For as Bill Malone asserts, "[b]y 1949, at least 650 radio stations used live hillbilly talent" (Malone 1968, 210).

In any event, faced with the success of television shows like Dick Clark's *American Bandstand*, the major record companies started to believe that television was the medium through which to market their records (cf. Mol and

Wijnberg 2007, 708), and it was only until about 1957 that the majors began to sour on the prospect. By that time, however, independent radio stations had already begun to absorb whatever programming vacuum had been created from the former divestment of radio by the networks and their affiliates, and they had even established, by working in tandem with the growing pool of independent record companies, somewhat of a further foothold in various niche markets which they had been working to cultivate in the meantime, confronted as they were by the growing peer competition for an audience.

The development of these niche markets, that is, was triggered to a large degree by the factors described above. First, because many of the existing and newly established radio stations became increasingly underfunded from the migration of advertising dollars, many could not budget for the kind of live programming that had been the staple of the major networks up to that point. Accordingly, these stations had to rely more and more on a less expensive format of broadcasting, such as the playing of records (Peterson 1990, 101; Mol and Wijnberg 2007, 708).[5] Secondly, since a migration of some programming material also followed the migration of advertising dollars, radio stations, including the networks and affiliates, had to identify what to broadcast in lieu of the programs that had been taken up by television. To do so, many radio stations turned to an all-music program format to fill it and so relied on playing even more records to do so (Mabry 1990, 418). However, "rather than four networks duplicating each other's programming hour by hour, but changing the fare over the course of the day, each of the local stations in a city . . . evolved a distinct format which it broadcasted with little change throughout the day" (Peterson and Berger 1975, 165) so as not to compete with each other (Mol and Winjberg 2007, 707). Pressed as they were, that is, with the need to ensure some segment of the available radio audience to boost their otherwise declining advertising revenues, many stations began to search for a program "niche" in the market (Mol and Wijnberg 2007, 708; Peterson 1990, 105), and this in turn led, for the first time since the advent of radio, to a greater receptiveness to broadcasting a range of musical genres that, hitherto, had experienced substantially less opportunity for mass exposure. Thus, "diverse sorts of musical styles from pop tunes to soul, country, gospel, latin, classical, and jazz received unprecedented merchandising over the air (Hirsch, 1971)" (Peterson and Berger 1975, 165; Hirsch 1971, 381). Indeed, by 1954, according to Maddock, "270 radio stations targeted their programming at African Americans, playing mostly blues, spirituals, and pop music" (Maddock 1996, 182). Moreover, faced with the need for more of this niche material to broadcast, radio stations had to scramble to find newly recorded specialty genres to broadcast to their respective niche audiences (Mabry 1990, 418) at the very same time that the many new independent record companies were seeking out inexpensive avenues by which to gain exposure for their product, given that the high advertising costs of television were certainly out of reach for them.

Thus, the self-interests of both aspects of the music industry, radio, on the one hand, and records on the other, serendipitously overlapped and intertwined, particularly in terms of the "independents," and this helped to further foster the promotion and airplay of new genres, such as rhythm and blues and, eventually, rock and roll, on a wider scale (Mol and Wijnberg 2007, 708). Further still, since a significant share of the networks' budgets were situated elsewhere in television and, together with those budgets, presumably the specific interest, attention, and oversight of network owners, radio station managers, particularly those of the networks and affiliates, were more ignored, and so came to enjoy a greater degree of freedom to program as they saw fit, provided it remained profitable (Mabry 1990, 418), of course. Meanwhile still, because many of the newer, underfunded stations were often also operating on a shoestring budget, with a correspondingly limited employee roster, this program freedom was further extended to those who had, inadvertently, become the screeners of what music was to be broadcasted, namely the record equipment operators, or what came to be known as "disc jockeys."

One other thing that seems unlikely that the major networks could have predicted in their race to invest in television and divest of radio was that the radio business would rebound significantly, in part because of a little device that would make radio broadcasts more conveniently portable for the first time: the transistor. Though the transistor was originally developed by Bell Laboratories in mid-1950s as a prestige item, Japanese industries managed to preempt dissemination in the U.S. by incorporating them into lightweight transistor radios so that, unlike a television, or the radio sets of previous years, these radios, and subsequently the music they were capable of broadcasting, could be taken anywhere with greater ease (Peterson 1990, 102). So, even while there was an ever-increasing use of TV sets and a corresponding decline in the use of radios in the home, that was quickly offset by the use of transistor radios outside the home, particularly by members of the youth market (Chapple and Garofalo 1977, 12) who also, contemporaneously, happened to be enjoying a greater degree of discretionary spending power due to the post-war boom experienced by the middle-class. In fact, between 1955 and 1960, there was an increase of 30 percent in radio set use (Peterson and Berger 1975, 165),[6] and by 1964, there were more radios in the United States than there were people (Peterson and Berger 1972, 293). Thus, the significance of the commercial advent of a little device such as the transistor by no means should be understated. For it helped to give rise to a generation, as Ralph Gleason remarked, "the first in America raised with music constantly in its ear, weaned on a transistor radio, involved with songs from its earliest moment of memory" (Gleason 1967, 62). Further still, it indirectly helped the record business by reducing the cost and enhancing the portability of record players (Mol and Wijnberg 2007, 708).

Finally, before leaving our discussion of radio it seems appropriate to address, at least to a slight degree, the advent of the Top 40 programming format and the emergence of commercial FM radio before we move on to examine the role of publishing and copyright in the music industry. First of all, according to Chapple and Garofalo, the Top 40 format did not exist in the late 1940s, but eventually emerged as a result of the need for radio to adapt to the impact of television (Chapple and Garofalo 1977, 19), when it replaced the "big band crooner style" of music that had previously dominated the popular record and broadcasting market, controlled, as it had been, by the major players that comprised the extant oligopolistic market-structure and distribution systems to date (Peterson 1990, 113). That is, it is likely that the transition to the Top 40 format was partly due to the decentralization of the radio industry that resulted from the advent of television, and the subsequent need for new and underfunded radio stations to find alternative audiences and niche markets, as we just discussed (cf. also Chapple and Garofalo 1977, 57–59).

Be that as it may, it has been reported that the idea of the Top 40 format originated with Todd Storz, a businessman who had previously bought up a string of independent radio stations in the Midwest and the South and formed them into a chain. Legend has it that Storz acquired the idea of Top 40 in 1954 when he was drinking in a bar in Omaha with his program director, Bill Stewart, and became irritated that the same song was repeatedly played on the jukebox by a waitress (Chapple and Garofalo 1977, 59; cf. Peterson 1990, 112). Faced with falling broadcast ratings, together with the assumption that the song was being replayed by the waitress because that was likely how she wanted to spend her money, and imagining that there were more people like her, Storz conceived the idea of taking a limited list of mainstream pop singles and playing them repeatedly, interspersed with station identifications, hourly news, jingles, and contests for the audience (Chapple and Garofalo 1977, 59; Peterson 1990, 112–13) to, in essence, turn "a radio station into something like a jukebox with forty selections" (Peterson 1990, 113).[7] Subsequently, it seems, Gordon McLendon, another owner of a broadcast chain, then added "instant news" to Storz's Top 40 concept (Chapple and Garofalo 1977, 59). In any event, the Top 40 format was soon adopted by radio stations throughout the broadcast industry and, according to Peterson, "[b]y 1958 industry executives had developed the view of the radio market as a set of distinct segments (teen-oriented Top Forty, soul music, country music, classical music, jazz, religious music, middle-of-the road, etc.), each with jukebox-like radio stations catering to its distinct music preferences" (Peterson 1990, 113).

Meanwhile, as a further extension of the diversification of programming for distinct audiences, FM radio stations, sometimes referred to as "underground," eventually began to offer an alternative to this Top 40 format, and this is where many songs about drugs and sex, and those expressing disapproval about the war, were first broadcasted during the 1960s (Robinson and Hirsch 1969, 45; Mol and Wijnberg 2007; Peterson 1990, 101–2). Perhaps this was due, in part, to the fact that the FCC had previously pressed FM stations in 1966 into a single-format programming, since it had demanded that FM stations broadcast programming which was different "from their AM affiliates for at least 50 percent of their air time. After brief experiments with public service programming, many stations eventually found a lucrative market for topically oriented 'underground' rock" (Peterson and Berger 1972, 294).

It should be noted that FM (Modulating Frequency) had clear advantages over AM (Amplitude Modulation) in that it had less static, required less power (and thus less expensive equipment), and occupied less of the electromagnetic band to broadcast. Unfortunately, however, FM would not bend to the curvature of the Earth, unlike AM (Chapple and Garofalo 1977, 9), which meant that the range of an FM broadcast was ultimately more limited than AM. FM also worked best in the Very High Frequency (VHF) end of the electromagnetic spectrum, rather than the Ultra High Frequency (UHF) in that the signal could travel twice the distance with less static on VHF than on UHF (Chapple and Garofalo 1977, 10).

Nevertheless, and despite these advantages over AM at least in terms of local broadcasting, FM radio's appearance on the broadcasting scene was not without obstacles. First, in 1936, the FCC had sided with David Sarnoff of RCA to block a petition submitted by the inventor of FM, Edwin Armstrong, to use part of the VHF band for FM so that it could be reserved for the unfolding TV industry (Chapple and Garofalo 1977, 10), even though, perhaps surprisingly, RCA had previously facilitated Armstrong's development of the FM technology by affording him use of some of RCA's space at the top of the Empire State Building for broadcast experiments (Chapple and Garofalo 1977, 8). Then, in 1939, the FCC's decision was modified, and the part of the VHF band that had previously been reserved for TV was made available for use by FM (Chapple and Garofalo 1977, 10). However, after the war, the FCC ruled again to limit use of FM to the UHF range as investors diverted funds into TV. As a matter of fact, only eighty thousand FM radios were produced in the first three quarters of 1946, in contrast to 6.5 million AM sets. Meanwhile still, RCA adopted the use of some of Armstrong's patented technologies for FM in its TVs and without his consent, which triggered Armstrong to bring a lawsuit against RCA that was, unsurprisingly, repeatedly delayed through the maneuverings of a battery of RCA lawyers. Finally, distraught over the obstacles to realizing his life-long project, Armstrong threw himself out the window of his 13th floor apartment in midtown Manhattan, and his widow settled with RCA for $1 million (Chapple and Garofalo 1977, 10–11).

NOTES

1. Fox and Williams did note, however, that class year in the sample was "positively related to liberalism and negatively associated with both radio and record listening," which might have affected other numbers (Fox and Williams 1974, 364).

2. For example, some advertisers, such as the Crazy Water Crystals Company that was under pressure from the American Medical Association and the federal government "for marketing a useless but habit-forming purgative (*Business Week* 1935)" made arrangements to advertise on these border stations, such as XEAW (Peterson 1997, 125).

3. Despite the advent of television, for reasons further addressed below, this trend also continued. Between 1955–1960, the number of AM radio stations increased by 27 percent (Peterson and Berger 1975, 165) and, overall, the number of AM stations doubled, and the number of FM stations tripled, between 1950 and 1967 (Peterson and Berger 1972, 294).

4. Moreover, as far as Peterson was able to determine "there never was a national network programme in the 1940s that played phonograph records on the air. There were, however, several music programmes broadcast locally by network affiliates that *did* use phonograph records" (Peterson 1990, 104, 105).

5. Although broadcasting the playing of records in lieu of live performances did appear to help boost the record business, the sales of "which had been in decline in 1948 and 1949" (Peterson 1990, 105), it also managed to further upset the otherwise beleaguered American Federation of Musicians (AFM), the members of which had previously suffered a significant blow to their employment opportunities from the introduction of recording technologies that led to "talkie" movies (cf. Roberts 2010, 13). Indeed, the tensions between the music business in general and the AFM had been ongoing and continued to persist. For example, according to Michael Roberts, the AFM was able to mount a successful general strike against the music industry in 1942 and negotiated an agreement with the majors to create "a fund to be used to support unemployed members of the AFM, who presumably lost their jobs as a result of the application of records" (Roberts 2010, 13). On the effort of the AFM to lobby the U.S. Government to block the 1964 Beatles tour, and on an agreement that was eventually reached between the AFM and the British Musicians' Union (BMU) to restrict rock tours in the U.S. and the U.K., see Michael Roberts 2010, 4.

6. As a result, the broadcasting income grew by 4 percent, "despite a three million dollar loss by the radio networks" (Peterson and Berger 1975, 165).

7. It should be mentioned, however, that this idea may not have been entirely new. According to Chapple and Garofalo, Lucky Strike had previously sponsored a weekly program in roughly the same vein, playing top hits, since the early 1940s through the mid-1950s. Accordingly, what Storz simply did was to extend this format to a daily program (Chapple and Garofalo 1979, 59).

Chapter 4

Copyright, ASCAP, BMI, and Payola

As the industrialization of the music business originally unfolded, particularly in the United States, the nature and circumstances of copyright possession and the mechanisms that emerged for collecting royalties also significantly influenced the mass dissemination of music in general, and later rock and roll, specifically as they affected the extent to which various genres of music could, and ultimately did, enjoy public exposure. As we shall see, the reasons for this are complicated.

Beginning in the late 1800s, a cluster of songwriting and publishing businesses first established themselves around Union Square in New York City as it became apparent that songs could be manufactured and marketed "like any other commodity" (N. Cohen 1970, 11). The initial reason that the cluster of publishers emerged specifically around Union Square had to do with the fact that a number of entertainment establishments that relied on the playing of music and, therefore, that were in need of a musical product had previously located there, such as burlesque shows, dance and music halls, and theaters. As these entertainment establishments then moved toward 28th street, so did the publishers, and the street and surrounding area eventually came to be known as "Tin Pan Alley," a term originally coined in 1903, presumably, by the "journalist-songwriter Monroe Rosenfeld" (N. Cohen 1970, 11).[1]

Although initially Tin Pan Alley focused on publishing sheet music that would specifically serve the needs of the adjacent businesses, its market soon expanded to include the sale of sheet music to the general public for private use, as pianos became more popular in American homes around the 1880s. However, these "participatory" and private uses of sheet music soon waned, as interest in pianos in the home declined, while the "non-participatory" and public forms of musical entertainment continued to flourish, first in the more urban environments and eventually extending to more rural communities, particular through traveling shows, and later radio (cf. Ryan 1985, 15). Thus, although the business opportunities of Tin Pan Alley continued to multiply, the primary source of revenue for these publishers eventually shifted away from the sale of sheet music itself to royalties and other forms of media for the transmission of music. For example, Tin Pan Alley soon became a hub for the sale of music on piano rolls for player pianos, cylinder records, 78s, and later on, 45s, LPs and cassette tapes, as the technologies of music delivery continued to develop.

At first there were few, if any, mechanisms to enforce copyright protections for published songs through the collection of royalties, and even the length of copyright protection was originally quite limited.[2] Even so, the business of publishing sheet music could be very lucrative, especially if a song was a hit.[3] Nevertheless, with the advent of the 1909 Copyright Act, additional opportunities to generate revenue through the publishing of music were afforded to the businesses of Tin Pan Alley. For by construing the music "itself" as a piece of property that could be bought and sold like any other commodity, in contrast to the mere media form for its transmission, the 1909 Copyright Act explicitly prohibited, for the first time (cf. Peterson 1990, 99), the use of musical compositions during live, public performances, or the public playing of music through the use of piano rolls, and eventually records, without the consent of their authors, and thus provided, at least, the legal ground to collect royalties for the dissemination of music in these respects. According to the relevant provision in the Copyright Act of 1909, persons owning a copyright shall "have the *exclusive* right to perform the copyrighted work for profit" [my italics] (Ryan 1985, 13).[4]

Now while it was generally assumed by Congress that the author of a copyrighted work gave consent to perform the work publicly for profit when they simply sold the sheet music itself, and therefore saw the provision as a "mere formalization of a secondary informal right that had already existed for some time" (Ryan 1985, 14), it was this provision that presumably afforded copyright holders of musical compositions the right to seek royalties for the public performances (which is to say "uses") of their "property" for profit, in addition to having received the original payment for the sheet music itself.[5] Even so, the 1909 copyright law did not entail the existence of any mechanism or body to actually enforce the collection of royalties, and "there was no way for each writer or publisher to monitor the individual use of his/her music by the multitude of commercial establishments" (Ryan 1985, 17). So, faced with this predicament, according to one narrative, a "band" of prominent composers and publishers, led by Victor Herbert, a well-known composer responsible for such tunes as "Ah, Sweet Mystery of Life" and "Kiss Me Again," collaborated in 1914 to form the American Society of Composers, Authors, and Publishers (ASCAP)[6] to enforce copyrights by selling licenses to use the compositions of its members for commercial purposes (cf. Peterson

1990, 99; Hugunin 1979, 8). Herbert, it is said, was motivated to find a way to control the performance of copyrighted music when he heard an "atrociously" crooned version of his "Kiss Me Again" in front of a group of diners and felt that "[t]his mangling of a man's work, this piracy, must stop!" (Ryan 1985, 16). However, according to Marc Hugunin, who appeals to Bennie L. DeWhitt's unpublished dissertation entitled "The American Society of Composers Authors and Publishers, 1914–1938," that is not exactly what happened. Instead, by calling this attribution of credit for the founding of ASCAP to renowned composers "the founding myth,"[7] designed specifically for public relations purposes, Hugunin, in line with DeWhitt and Ryan, suggests that ASCAP was actually founded by "Nathan Burke, a Tammany Hall politician and noted copyright lawyer, George Maxwell, an Englishman with a background in European performing rights groups," and, of course, Victor Herbert, who "acted as a figurehead for the society during its early years" (Hugunin 1979, 8) along with "the aid of many associates," none of whom were actually songwriters (Hugunin 1979, footnote 1; cf. Ryan 1985, 16).

Be that as it may, once ASCAP was established, its first order of business was to collect royalties for the use of its members' copyrighted music from various "music users" in the immediate proximity of New York City. To accomplish this goal, ASCAP began by informing hotels and restaurants of its "intent to collect payment for the public performance for profit of songs in its catalog" in September of 1914. Surprisingly perhaps, this action immediately upset the American Federation of Musicians (AFM) since, in response to ASCAP's demands, the hotels and restaurants threatened to terminate the musicians they employed if they were forced to purchase "licenses" from ASCAP to play the music of ASCAP members. Thereafter, in its efforts to further legitimate itself, ASCAP also began to demand royalties from cabarets and eventually the film industry (Ryan 1985, 18), and various legal challenges followed, eventually leading to a decision by the Supreme Court on January 22, 1917, that favored ASCAP's right to collect royalties from any businesses that used the music of its members (Ryan 1985, 20).[8]

Although ASCAP's efforts to collect royalties never extended to vaudeville, despite the fact that vaudeville agreed to only use the copyrighted music of ASCAP members,[9] ASCAP began to inform commercial radio stations, nearly from their inception, that they also needed to pay for permission to broadcast the music of its members. In 1922, Nathan Burke sent a letter to radio stations on behalf of ASCAP "expressing his legal opinion that a radio broadcast was a public performance for profit" (Ryan 1985, 31), and ASCAP stipulated the deadline of September 10, 1922, for radio stations to secure a license to broadcast items in its catalog (Ryan 1985, 32). Finally, WEAF in New York capitulated to ASCAP's demands and became ASCAP's first radio station licensee in 1923.

In response to ASCAP's demands, many radio stations initially banded together in 1924 to form the National Association of Broadcasting (NAB) to handle any negotiations with ASCAP (Chapple and Garofalo 1977, 64) and, by 1926, there were only a few radio stations that persisted to resist ASCAP's fees. Finally, an industry-wide agreement was reached in 1932 (Hugunin 1979, 9), which required radio stations to pay ASCAP 3 percent of their total annual revenue in 1933, 4 percent in 1934, and 5 percent in 1935, with a further renewal at a rate of 5 percent for the following five years. In fact, by the 1930s ASCAP was able to control nearly all the commercial exposure of new music, to the general public, by effectively imposing a mandate that only ASCAP-licensed music could be used in relation to the showing of films and the performance of Broadway musicals, in addition to whatever music was broadcasted on radio (Peterson 1990, 99; Hugunin 1979, 13).[10]

Perhaps it should be noted that ASCAP's move against the film industry certainly did not occur without some resistance. According to Ryan, in "1917, the Motion Picture Exhibitors League of America (MPELA) asked its members to contribute three dollars each to an anti-ASCAP fund and called for a boycott of ASCAP music" (Ryan 1985, 21–22) and in "1922, the Motion Picture Theatre Owners Association (MPTOA) . . . announced that it was forming its own musical department for the purpose of promoting and distributing non-ASCAP music" (Ryan 1985, 23). In addition, MPTOA attempted to "enlist the aid of movie producers and distributors in establishing a general boycott of ASCAP music" (Ryan 1985, 23). That said, the relationship between the film industry and ASCAP should not be overly simplified, as some film companies were eventually able to exert control over ASCAP by purchasing controlling shares of its various publisher members. For example, "[i]n 1928, MGM bought 51 percent of the Robbins Music Corporation . . . [and] Paramount and Harms, Inc. . . . formed the Famous Music Corporation" (Ryan 1985, 25). "In 1929, Warner Brothers purchased a partnership interest in M. Witmark and Sons" (Ryan 1985, 25) and "Fox films developed a working arrangement with the publishing firm of DeSylva, Brown and Henderson" (Ryan 1985, 26). By the late 1930s, Ryan further reports McDougald's analysis that "eight of the Society's highest ranking publishing companies were either owned outright or controlled by the motion-picture industry" (Ryan 1985, 26).

While all this was going on, however, ASCAP and its member publishers also began to lose revenue on sheet music sales. For example, during the 1920s, "songs considered to be 'good sellers' sold 500,000 copies of sheet music compared to 50,000 in the late 1930s. So called 'smash hits' often sold 2 million copies in the 1920s compared to 300,00 copies in the 1930s (MacDougald, 1941, 71)" (Ryan 1985, 36). This general decline in revenue associated with sheet music was due to a variety of reasons, not the least of which was probably because people listened to more radio rather than making music of their own, an argument often touted by ASCAP in various legal cases against the radio industry as to how the latter financially damaged the interests of the former (Ryan 1985, 32), and because, surprisingly perhaps, popular songs came to have a shorter shelf life (Chapple and Garofalo 1977, 64), presumably due to their repeated radio play, so that songs were often out of vogue even before the sheet music could be distributed (Hugunin 1979, 9).[11] In addition, as William Randle explains, rising costs in "wages, paper, rent, printing, and contract costs, resulting from post-war inflation, forced the publishers to desert the traditional ten cent sheet music . . . and radically increase the price to thirty cents retail, a 300 percent increase overnight to the consumer" (Randle 1966, 390, cited in Ryan 1985, 28). This increase in price, in turn, motivated Woolworth department stores, the "single largest retail outlet for sheet music" (Ryan 1985, 28) to close their music departments, followed by other retail distributors, thus apparently shutting off ASCAP's publishing members from access to a host of potential consumers. At the same time, however, perhaps because it was of interest to their audiences, more of the rural, non-network and, thus, "independent" commercial radio stations began to play music not licensed by ASCAP (Hugunin 1979, 9), music about which a number of ASCAP's core members had typically expressed some aesthetic disdain (Peterson 1990, 99–100; Hugunin 1979, 9) and music whose composers or performers had generally been precluded from gaining ASCAP membership. We will return to consider further the implications of these factors.

Meanwhile, over time and through the conditions for membership that it stipulated, its internal membership structure, the subsequent control its board was afforded to exercise over the organization as a whole, and the pressure it placed on "music users," such as hotels, restaurants, theaters, the motion-picture industry, and radio broadcasters, to obtain licenses to use the musical material of its members, ASCAP still managed to leverage significant influence over the degree of access to music the general public had an opportunity to enjoy. First of all, consider that prior to 1941 a condition for publisher membership in ASCAP required that the candidate "regularly engage for a period of not less than one year in the music publishing business (ASCAP Articles of Association, Article III:2)" (Ryan 1985, 53). A composer, on the other hand, needed to be a person who "regularly practices the profession of writing music and/or texts of musical works and who shall have had not less than five works of his composition or writing regularly published (ASCAP Articles of Association, Article III: 2)" (Ryan 1985, 53),[12] and both publishers and composers needed the sponsorship of "at least two members of the board" as well as "approval of the membership committee" to become members (Ryan 1985, 53). Furthermore, embedded in these conditions, another condition for membership required that the works of publishers or composers had to be "in vogue" "or, in other words, sufficiently popular to bring income to the Society" (Ryan 1985, 53). What these conditions meant collectively is that the Society provided itself with sufficient latitude in determining nearly any membership, and thus, in determining the commercial exposure of music to the general public. As expressed in one letter from a publisher to Assistant Attorney General Thurmond Arnold:

> ASCAP states that you must have five successful songs and a generally successful business. They must surely know that for one to have a hit song or even a fairly good seller he must have plugs in the theatre, on the networks, recordings, and if they (ASCAP) are in complete control, how is such a thing possible? People who use music for public performance for profit know only one thing and that is they must have a license and that they must pay a fee for the use of this music to ASCAP. They know no other organization, they have never heard of any other, why then should they pay anyone else for the use of their music. What hope then has the independent publisher from (of) ever receiving any compensation of any nature? (Letter to [Assistant Attorney General] Thurmond Arnold from Ben M. Gershman, President Continental Music Company, July 22, 1940, File 60–22–5) [*sic*]. (Ryan 1985, 54; my emphasis in brackets)

Second, the Board of ASCAP, comprised of twenty-four "self-perpetuating" directors (Ryan 1985, 54)—twelve publisher members, six author (lyrics) members, and six composer members—whose successors were nominated by the directors whose terms had not yet expired, and who enjoyed the support of two-thirds of the board, was responsible, according to Article V, for the "absolute management and control" of the organization, with "no rights being retained by the membership" (Ryan 1985, 54). What this meant was that "[a]ll officers, employees and members were appointed by the board and their decision was final" (Ryan 1985, 54). Moreover, all members were required "to grant the Society the *exclusive* right to license *their* nondramatic works for public performance" (Ryan 1985, 55; my emphasis in italics), which is to say *any* nondramatic work, the copyright of which the member possessed at the time of becoming a member, through the entire time of being a member, which naturally precluded any member from licensing any work the copyright for which they possessed to any agency other than ASCAP while being a member.

What all of this means is that the Board of ASCAP was able to maintain stringent control over who was a member, along with their property, while it positioned itself to exercise considerable influence over the music-using conduits that served to expose music to the general public, such as theaters, hotels, motion-picture studios, and radio stations. As a result, exposure of various musical genres to the public was, ipso facto, significantly limited to the specific artistic styles and talents possessed by its members. Accordingly, if the artists of specific genres were, on average, excluded from being members of ASCAP, then ASCAP, in turn, was able to exclude, on average, those genres from exposure to the public, at least to some degree. This is what seems to have happened during the early years of ASCAP.

First, there is certainly evidence that a number of black composers, writers (lyrics) and performers were excluded from the membership ranks of ASCAP. For example, Ryan reports that "[a]mong the 170 composers and 22 publishers who were charter members of the Society were one black musician and one black writer" and "[d]uring the next 12 years . . . only eight other blacks became members" (Ryan 1985, 65). In fact, some more well-known black artists, such as "Jelly Roll" Morton and Louis Armstrong, became members late in their career or, like Scott Joplin, only after they were dead.

Moreover, obstacles to becoming members extended to the country or "hillbilly" genres as well (Peterson 1997, 13). This practice even extended to some of the more well-known, if not also wildly successful, stars of the country or hillbilly variety, who struggled to gain membership in ASCAP and, in some cases, were also only able to secure it after they were dead. For example, Jimmie Rodgers, arguably the first true superstar of the country genre only eventually became a member in 1937, which was four years after he had died in 1933 (Ryan 1985, 69).[13] In addition, Gene Autry, another "hillbilly" superstar, struggled to become a member of ASCAP for eight years, beginning with his application in 1930, and was only awarded the status of a "nonparticipating" member after he was voted, in Autry's own words, "the biggest boxoffice attraction in motion pictures, and that included at the time Clark Gable, Shirley Temple, and others" (Ryan 1985, 64).[14] Incidentally, what this eventual "non-participating membership" status in the organization meant for Autry is that although ASCAP collected fees on his songs, he was not entitled to receive any portion of them from ASCAP (Peterson 1997, 186). Finally, that a membership bias that excluded country or "hillbilly" performers existed within the ASCAP organization is certainly suggested by a review of *ASCAP Biographical Dictionary* of 1948, wherein, out of the two thousand entries, only twenty-two "writers were even remotely connected to the 'hillbilly' genre" (Ryan 1985, 69).

Even more personal to the artists themselves, one might surmise, is that by excluding membership of artists of certain genres, ASCAP was able to adversely affect the ability of those artists to make a living from practicing their art. For example, by excluding most composers and performers of blues, jazz, and country from the ASCAP membership ranks, artists whose repertoires focused primarily on these genres were often precluded from live performances in urban centers since, to recall the implications from above,

ASCAP had agreements with all the main venues in major cities (Peterson 1997, 13).

But even if one was fortunate enough to be admitted to ASCAP as a member, that certainly did not guarantee certain artists equal treatment in the distribution of the royalties ASCAP collected, as an additional *internal* system of stratification or membership ranking also existed that financially benefited some members over others.[15] Here, the general idea was that all royalties that ASCAP collected were "placed in a common fund and then divided according to each member's ranking" (Ryan 1985, 55). For example, Donald Mabry reports that ASCAP distributed "only 20 percent of the royalties in a given year to the people whose songs created those royalties; the remainder were distributed to persons whose songs had been popular in the past but were no longer" (Mabry 1990, 416). Moreover, rankings were apparently determined by such things as the length and success of their career to date, as constituted, in part, by the number and the nature of the venues for their performances. The problem with this for some members was that

> ASCAP sampled only live, prime-time radio performances in determining its membership rankings. Yet the music of most "race" musicians and composers was found primarily in recorded form, and on nonprime-time, nonnetwork radio. . . . Thus, the rankings of those black composers who were ASCAP members were probably so low as to preclude making a living simply from performance-rights income. (Ryan 1985, 66)

In conjunction with the common practice of publishers buying songs outright from composers, Ryan speculates that this may also help to explain why there existed a dominance of performers over composers among the black membership of ASCAP (Ryan 1985, 66).

In any event, as the original agreement between the commercial radio broadcast industry and ASCAP, brokered by NAB in 1932, was nearing its conclusion on December 31, 1940, ASCAP's opening volley for a new agreement consisted of a substantial increase from 5 percent of total radio station revenue to 15 percent, although ASCAP subsequently revised the figure down to 9 percent, and then eventually back to 5 percent.[16] In the meantime, however, in part perhaps to generate additional leverage for any upcoming negotiations with ASCAP to extend its licenses to radio broadcasters, if not also to try to undermine ASCAP's general monopolistic hold on the broadcasting of music, NAB invested $2 million to establish an alternative organization to license music to radio stations, which was not copyrighted by ASCAP.[17] This organization was Broadcast Music, Incorporated, or "BMI" (Hugunin 1979, 9–10; Peterson 1990, 100). However, since ASCAP already possessed most of the copyrights of music published in the United States from 1884 forward, with the exception of what it had previously excluded, namely rhythm and blues, jazz, "hillbilly" or country (cf. Malone 1968, 31), and Latin (Peterson 1990, 99), and since BMI, despite its rigorous effort, enjoyed only modest success encouraging existing ASCAP publishers and composers to defect to its own ranks,[18] BMI needed to adopt a strategy to develop a sufficient catalog of copyrighted material to license to radio stations in order to present a viable alternative to ASCAP. Consequently, it turned to the copyright of songs that had so far remained in the public domain,[19] combined with what had sometimes been labeled "bad" music and previously excluded by ASCAP (Peterson 1990, 100; Peterson and Berger 1972, 293), most notably blues, jazz, and country. In fact, this is, presumably, partly why BMI was sometimes disparagingly referred to as "Bad Music Incorporated" by persons in the industry.[20] Furthermore, BMI absorbed roughly thirty thousand Argentinian numbers, twenty thousand Mexican works, as well as some Jewish, Italian, and Native American compositions (Ryan 1985, 109).[21]

As negotiations for a new contract between ASCAP and NAB remained largely at an impasse, and the old contract expiring on December 31, 1940, a number of radio stations still without an ASCAP license[22] participated in a boycott against airing ASCAP-licensed songs,[23] formally beginning on January 1, 1941, and eventually ending on September 31, 1941 (Mabry 1990, 415).[24] Despite ASCAP's standing in the industry, this boycott seems to have had a significant impact. For example, the Top 20 songs in 1941, in terms of sheet music sales, were licensed by BMI, and only one of the Top 15 songs of the year, according to *Variety*, was an ASCAP song, and it appeared only after an agreement was reached between ASCAP and BMI and the boycott had been lifted (Hugunin 1979, 10).[25] Indeed, whereas ASCAP had controlled 100 percent of the "No. 1 Sheet Music Leaders" in 1939 according to *Billboard*, BMI ended up controlling 84.6 percent in 1941 (Ryan 1985, 107), as well as 100 percent of "Songs with the Most Radio Plugs" (cf. Ryan 1985, 108).

It should also be mentioned that while the boycott and struggle between ASCAP and BMI persisted, the Justice Department revived an investigation that it had initially begun in the mid-1920s on the suspicion that ASCAP was acting in violation of the Sherman Anti-trust Act. However, unlike the initial investigation, this one resulted in criminal charges not just against ASCAP, surprisingly, but also "against BMI, NBC and CBS" on December 26, 1940 (Ryan 1985, 95). In contrast, the initial investigation that occurred during the mid-1920s had previously concluded that ASCAP "was not an organization acting in restrain of the Sherman Anti-trust Act" in its dealings with "places of amusement," although a decision was not specifically rendered in terms of ASCAP's relationship with the radio broadcast industry (Ryan 1985, 93). It is perhaps a coincidence that the lead investigator in this original investigation of the Justice Department, namely John A. Brann, later happened to become appointed as an ASCAP officer.[26] Furthermore, while another separate investigation had emerged during the mid-1930s because of complaints presented to the Federal Communications Commission by various broadcasters, and a formal complaint had been issued by the Justice Department to ASCAP in August of 1934, pursuit of that particular action was eventually suspended when "the Warner's Group of publishers withdrew from the Society in 1936 over an internal dispute, and with the signing of a five-year contract between the Society and broadcasters" (Ryan 1985, 94), since the Justice Department had, at least at that juncture, concluded that ASCAP was not operating as a monopoly (Ryan 1985, 94).

As far as the charges brought against ASCAP, BMI, CBS, and NBC, in December of 1940, they included:

1. The illegal pooling of most of the desirable copyright music available for radio broadcasting in order to eliminate competition and to monopolize the supply.
2. Illegal discrimination against users of copyright music.
3. Illegal discrimination against composers who were not members of ASCAP.
4. Withholding music from publication in order to exact fees not permitted under copyright law.
5. Illegal price fixing.
6. Restraining composers in their rights to bargain for the sale of their own music.
7. Requiring users of music to pay for music on shows in which no music was played.
8. Mutual boycotts by ASCAP and by the broadcasting chains (through BMI) in an attempt by each of these conflicting groups to obtain for themselves control . . . (and thereby) threaten to restrain and obstruct the rendition over radio of about 90 percent of the desirable modern copyright music (*Variety*, Jan. 1, 1941: 20) (Ryan 1985, 95–96).

Still in its fledgling state, and perhaps in order to reduce the pressure it experienced from the Justice Department, BMI was quick to sign a consent decree with the Justice Department on January 28, 1941, the essence of which demonstrated its intent not to violate the Sherman Anti-trust Act by affording equal access to its music (e.g., early on in its inception, ASCAP had extended preferential treatment to newspapers presumably in return for good press), providing music-users the option of blanket or piece-meal licenses, making the relationship between the BMI, music users, and publishers non-exclusive, and not requiring affiliates to pay for licenses for product licensed and distributed through the networks (cf. Ryan 1985, 97–99). In return, the Justice

Department agreed to drop its legal action against the networks, and on February 26, 1941, ASCAP signed its own consent decree with the Justice Department, the significant features of which included provisions that members could now license their works through ASCAP or directly to music-users on their own terms (Ryan 1985, 98), that revenues would be distributed equitably among the members of ASCAP, and that the self-perpetuating Board of ASCAP be replaced with one that was elected by the membership as a whole (Ryan 1985, 99).

All of this aside, once the broadcasters' boycott of ASCAP material had been lifted, ASCAP's control over popular music appeared to rebound rather quickly, and by 1942 it looked as if ASCAP had managed to regain its absolute control over the music industry, with almost an immediate mirror reversal of percentages of plugs, and sheet music leaders. As a matter of fact, it certainly should not be understated that the inroads into the popular music industry took quite some time for BMI to permanently pave after the initial success it experienced from the boycott. While fifteen publishers had controlled 90 percent of all popular music through the 1930s, eight of which were either owned or controlled by film producers (MacDougald 1941; cf. Ryan 1985, 71, 26),[27] only eighteen publishers continued to determine the sorts of songs that reached the public through the available mainstream media forms until the 1950s, which happened to be ones that primarily involved "abstract love themes, strong melodies, and muted jazz rhythms and harmonies" (Peterson 1990, 99), that is, "music from movie productions" (Ryan 1985, 71) or the product of Tin Pan Alley with which ASCAP had principally maintained a mutually rewarding relationship.

Even so, BMI, which had only begun to sign recording agreements once the ban was implemented, was apparently still able to quickly increase its market share of record sales by 30 percent (Hugunin 1979, 10). Moreover, because of its inclusion of genres that had hitherto been excluded from airplay, due to their aesthetically antagonistic relationship with the member-leadership of ASCAP, BMI had provided a copyright licensing venue for new publishers, writers, and composers who eventually made significant contributions to the advent of rock and roll. Between 1944 and 1954, BMI licensed 77 percent of the songs on the charts, and in 1952, 74 percent of the songs that reached number one, and 62 percent of the songs that reached positions 2 and 3 (Ryan 1985, 112). By the mid-1950s, "most of the classic rhythm and blues/rock and roll cross overs—songs like 'Crying In the Chapel' (Valley Publishers, Inc.), 'Sh-Boom' (Progressive Music Publishing Co., Inc, and St. Louis Music Corp), Fat's Domino's 'Ain't It A Shame' (Travis Music Co.) and the Platters' 'Only You' (Taunton Music)—were BMI-licensed Songs" (Hugunin 1979, 12), and BMI eventually controlled much of the repertoires of Chuck Berry, B.B. King, Muddy Waters, and Little Richard (Hugunin 1979, 12). By the end of 1957, BMI had licensed thirty-six of the fifty "most popular pop songs," forty of the fifty "most popular rhythm and blues songs," and forty-five of the fifty "most popular country songs" (Ryan 1985, 113).

As the foregoing probably illustrates, however, it would be quite an over-simplification to suggest that BMI "caused" the popularity of rock and roll despite the fact that this was a frequent charge made against BMI by ASCAP during the various legal actions and congressional hearings that followed. According to Ryan:

> Much of the testimony at the hearings to amend the Federal Communications Act of 1934 was by ASCAP supporters claiming that a conspiracy existed between BMI and the radio industry to exclude ASCAP music in favor of rock 'n' roll and country music. Many of the witnesses felt that there was no real demand for these genres except that created artificially by constant radio airplay. (Ryan 1985, 115)

That said, it seems evident that the advent of BMI certainly served to significantly enhance the degree of commercial exposure a variety of genres subsequently enjoyed, and it is probably not such an overstatement to suggest, counterfactually, that rock and roll probably would not have developed when it did were it not for BMI.

It also seems to be true that despite the agreement that was eventually struck in 1941 between ASCAP and BMI, ASCAP continued to dedicate substantial effort to regain the portion of the popular market it had originally lost to BMI. In 1953, ASCAP sued BMI "for $150 million for conspiracy to dominate and control the market for the use and exploitation of music companies." In 1956, ASCAP "persuaded the Antitrust Subcommittee of the House Judiciary Committee to look into BMI's activities." In 1958, ASCAP supposedly motivated a bill prohibiting music publishing businesses from possessing broadcast licenses,[28] and in 1959 it "claimed with some pride to have persuaded the same committee to shift the focus of its investigations into the electronic media from the rigging of television quiz shows to the practice of payola in the popular music industry" (Hugunin 1979, 11; cf. Maddock 1996, 198).[29]

As a matter of fact, with the unexpected rebound of the radio audience in the wake of the introduction of television, as we discussed above, together with the lack of close network oversight over radio programming the introduction entailed, conditions for "payola" to flourish in the radio business had become increasingly favorable, even though "payola" certainly had been a regular practice in the music business, and the entertainment industry more broadly considered, nearly since their inception in the United States. Indeed, "payola,"[30] or more technically referred to as "consideration payments" by the Financial Accounting Standards Board (FASB) (Rennhoff 2010, 133), was quite pervasive within the music industry since the nineteenth century, and particularly during the rise to dominance of Tin Pan Alley, when professional songwriters would churn out songs according to preestablished formulas.[31] In those days, the practice of what was then called "plugging"[32] was widespread, where singers were paid to sing songs, sometimes seemingly spontaneously, in places where a crowd was gathered. For example, pluggers might sing songs in stores, railway stations, and parks, or during intermission during various live theatrical and musical performances. Waiters might sing along with a performer on stage, or audience members might be paid to clap (Peterson and Berger 1972, 286; Mabry 1990, 445; Mol and Wijnberg 2007, 706). For that matter, the practice of plugging had become so endemic during the early years of the commercial music business in the United States that publishers and composers perceived the advent of ASCAP with some trepidation as they worried the organization might upset the relationships they had worked for years to cultivate with the primary conduits available to them to expose their product to the general public, namely restaurants, hotels, and theaters (Ryan 1985, 27), and, thereby, to boost their sales of sheet music.

In other cases, payola would involve the payment of well-known singers or bandleaders by providing them with a percentage of royalties, a practice that apparently continued into the 1950s. For example, according to Mabry, Johnny Vincent, founder of Ace Records, "gave part of the copyright to 'Don't You Just Know It' [by Huey P. Smith] to Kincord Corporation, one of Dick Clark's publishing companies, and sent Clark a royalty check for $2,000" (Mabry 1990, 446). In fact, in the early days, payola manifested itself in a variety of forms, from "free copies of sheet music, orchestral arrangements, and rehearsal rooms" to cash payments (Coase 1979, 272). In one case, it is reported that Lottie Gilson was offered a diamond ring valued at $500 at the time, and one publisher presumably gave Al Jolson a race horse (Coase 1979, 273).

By 1916, the practice of payola, by then referred to as "the payment system" (Coase 1979, 275), was so pervasive that *Variety* reported some publishers were threatening legal action against performers for not fulfilling their agreements to sing the songs for which they had been paid (Coase 1979, 273), and by 1939, "pluggers" had become such an established constituency within the music industry itself that, as employees of publishers,[33] they formed the "Music Publishers' Contact Employees Union," an affiliate of the American Federation of Labor (Coase 1979, 285). However, the practice of paying payola directly to disc jockeys did not flourish so much in the radio business until the 1950s, even though it certainly began to appear in radio as early as the 1930s (Rennhoff 2010, 134; Belz 1972, 113), primarily because, as has been mentioned, the practice of playing records on radio stations remained relatively limited until that time, and, also perhaps, because there was a general belief often held by record producers that exposure of their product on radio stations could adversely affect retail sales (Coase 1979, 286). Instead, the practice of payola during the early years of radio occurred principally between the members of dance bands that were broadcasted live and the songwriters and publishers who supplied them with material (Belz 1972, 112; Coase 1979, 286).

By the time of the congressional payola hearings in 1959, however, it should be added that the practice of payola was not simply restricted in its occurrence to payments made by record companies directly to disc jockeys. For example, Johnny Vincent of Ace Records admitted to paying "adolescent girls" to write postcards requesting songs on radios, which he would mail during his business trips, and to paying "adolescents to go into stores and ask for his records. In other cases, he would go into record stores and buy some of his own records, and he would pay people to play Ace records on jukeboxes to encourage their purchase by jukebox operators" (Mabry 1990, 443). In addition, there are reports that sometimes, particularly in the South and Midwest, some of the smaller independent record companies would simply purchase airtime to promote their records (Peterson 1990, 104). Furthermore, as Paul Ackerman, music editor of *Billboard*, remarked during the payola hearings, payola also manifested itself at the retail level in the form of free records to "dealers" (Belz 1972, 113). However, this strategy was one undertaken more readily by the small independent record companies, rather than the majors, since, according to Mabry,

> [t]he major recording companies had their own distribution systems and the power to encourage other distributors to stock their products. The scores of independent record companies, however, had to build a national network of distributors if they wanted to have national hits. Distributors wanted only records that sold. Since records produced by the independent companies were often of unknown marketability, distributors demanded concessions before they would stock such records. . . . Ace gave distributors three hundred of the first one thousand copies the distributor took on consignment from the company. The distributor could always sell those records, even when the record was a "stiff," a record that could not be sold in the general market. (Mabry 1990, 444)

That it was the independent record companies, and not the majors, that engaged in the practice of payola at the "retail level" perhaps also helps to shed some light on who probably benefited the most, and who probably was most harmed, by the practice of payola as it specifically occurred between disc jockey and record producers, and who, accordingly, its elimination would best serve.

Regardless of the established tradition of its use in the commercial music industry, payola, with a few exceptions, was mostly practiced unbeknownst to the wider public until 1959, when government agencies and officials begin to investigate and express public opinions about it specifically in regard to the radio business (Rennhoff 2010, 134). Even so, within the industry itself, there certainly had been concerns over payola and what to do about it that stretch as far back as the mid-1890s, when a group of music publishers first agreed to stop the practice, only to immediately, and secretly, violate that agreement (Coase 1979, 273). Then, in 1917,[34] by appealing to the claim that payola interfered with fair competition, and so, the ability for music to become popular merely because of its merit, another attempt to eliminate payola, orchestrated by John J. O'Conner,[35] then manager of *Variety*, was made through the formulation of the Music Publishers' Protective Association (MPPA) (Coase 1979, 275–76).[36] Although news of the MPPA's progress was subsequently, and repeatedly, published in *Variety* as successful, payola continued nonetheless while MPPA's membership also increased, particularly when a threat was made by the manager of the then powerful Keith-Albee-Orpheum "vaudeville" circuit that they would not allow music to be performed if the publishers were not members of MPPA (Coase 1979, 277).

However, one might wonder why O'Conner, the manager of *Variety*, took an interest in formulating the MPPA in the first place. Was it because he had a "philanthropic" motivation to clean up the publishing business? One reason offered by Hazel Meyer, according to Coase, was that his motives were merely business as usual, since O'Conner and others perceived an unfavorable relationship between *Variety*'s advertising revenue and the "payment system," as payola was construed by them as another way for publishers to gain expose for their music without having to appeal to trade publications such as *Variety* (Coase 1979, 278). Another reason, in contrast to the stipulated and seemingly noble reason of cleaning up payola, is suggested by Ryan who, by appeal to a Justice Department report, suggests that "[a] more important function, although hidden, of the MPPA was to increase the publishers profits from the manufacture of electrical transcriptions" by working in tandem with ASCAP.[37]

Be that as it may, the efforts of the MPPA to curb payola in the industry predictably deteriorated, and payola continued largely unfettered until the National Recovery Administration (NRA) was established in June of 1933 through an act that allowed industries to develop trade rules or codes that would be binding for an entire industry. At that time, the MPPA drafted and submitted to the NRA a code the lion's share of which was intended to prohibit payola in the interest of protecting, as Mr. John C. Paine, chairman of MPPA's board, explained during the corresponding hearing, "the small publisher" and, therefore, so that competition was "solely on the basis of the merit of the composition and not on any extraneous inducements" (Coase 1979, 280). Unfortunately, and despite the fact that the code was approved by the NRA on March 4, 1935, the act that established the NRA itself was declared unconstitutional on May 27, 1935, and the NRA was, accordingly, disbanded. Nonetheless, the MPPA then turned to the Federal Trade Commission (FTC) on September 20, 1935, which was empowered to approve rules for fair trade practice that were either (1) legally binding for an industry, or (2) merely advisory, and submitted a new draft of its code for consideration in relation to the music publishing industry (Coase 1979, 281). However, approval of the MPPA's application was, by that time, faced with a myriad of obstacles. For one thing, the code the MPPA proposed required that payola be deemed illegal irrespective of whether it involved the consent of the employer, and yet, (a) the only existing law that payola might be construed to violate was commercial bribery, where instances of commercial bribery, according to the existing statutes, required that gifts or money be accepted without the consent of employers, while (b) most, if not all, cases of payola had the consent, if not also the support, of employers (Coase 1979, 282). Muddying the waters further, the memorandum concerning the matter that was drafted by the FTC's Trade Practices Board made reference to an objection from one independent publisher that the proposed rules would actually inflict great harm on independent publishers, who had, incidentally, "signed the petition unwillingly because of threats that their songs would be boycotted by orchestra leaders and artists under the control of the dominant music publishers" (Coase 1979, 283). Indeed, according to that publisher, the independent publishers were at a disadvantage vis-à-vis the major publishers in their ability to expose the public to their musical products because the latter had, at their disposal, other businesses with which they were affiliated, such as theater chains and other entertainment products like movies, through which to expose their music to the public, and so did not need to resort to song plugging, whereas the independents did not have these alternative avenues (Coase 1979, 283). Considering all of that, the investigating attorney of the FTC concluded that implementing the proposed rules "would mean the elimination of the independent publisher" (Coase 1979, 284). Moreover, in part perhaps because of an impending anti-trust lawsuit against ASCAP and members of MPPA, the FTC finally decided, on May 25, 1938, to deny the proposed trade practice rules and advised that the MPPA could make a new application when "all pending charges against the members of this industry have been disposed of" and if its sponsors could "come before the Commission with absolutely clean hands and unquestioned honesty of purpose and intent" (Coase 1979, 285).

Against the backdrop of the foregoing, multiple explanations have been offered as to why the investigation into payola in the record and radio businesses began in the first place. Prima facie, what seemed to explain the sudden interest in payola in broadcasting, according to *Variety*, was actually the result of the congressional hearings concerning apparent fraud and deception on television quiz shows, as I have already suggested above in passing (cf. Rennhoff 2010, 135; Coase 1979; Belz 1972, 109).[38] According to an article in the November 11, 1959, issue of *Variety*, Mr. Burton Lane, then president of the American Guild of Authors and Composers, and composer of the musical score of "Finian's Rainbow," had entered a letter into the record of these congressional hearings which stated:

> practices of audience deception in broadcasting which have been revealed in the testimony adduced before your committee, is by no means limited to quiz programs. It has a counterpart in the promotion of music, and in music products. There is no doubt that commercial bribery has become a prime factor in determining what music is played on many broadcast programs and what musical records the public is surreptitiously induced to buy. (Coase 1979, 291; Investigation of Television Quiz Shows: Hearings before a Subcomm. of the House Comm. On Interstate and Foreign Commerce, 86h, 1st Sess. At 1142–47, p. 42)

In fact, although the congressional hearings of the quiz shows had initially begun with the question of whether they were rigged, the topic of the hearings soon migrated to concerns about payola as a general business practice, when it was announced, through the testimony of a department store owner from Allentown, Pennsylvania, namely a Mr. Hess, that he had paid $10,000 so that one of his employees could appear on the $64,000 Question and plug the store when the employee was introduced. When asked whether plugging was commercial bribery, Hess responded that he thought it was a "common practice" and a "recognized business," and added that his store had also made payments to other shows, such as Steve Allen's "Tonight" show and "Name that Tune," that one of the store trucks had also appeared in a TV film, and that payments had been made to various newspaper columnists for favorable mentions (Coase 1979, 289–90).[39]

In striking contrast to this account produced by *Variety*, however, Carl Belz has suggested that the real motivation of the hearings was

> related to an assumption that rock was "bad" music, that it encouraged juvenile delinquency, and that it could only have been forced on the public by illegal business activities. . . . For the payola hearings would never have taken place if rock had been aesthetically pleasing to the popular music audience or, to put it another way, if rock had been popular art instead of authentic folk art. (Belz 1972, 109)

Furthermore, while Belz maintained that it was "unrealistic" to construe the "evil" of payola as somehow situated principally in the disc jockey of rock and roll as such, even though the content of the hearings often seemed to imply that, Belz, nevertheless, attributed some of the disapprobation expressed toward payola at this historical juncture to the aesthetic style that disc jockeys began to cultivate on the air while broadcasting rock and roll, and that was, in Belz's words, "as profound and revolutionary as the response provoked by rock music" (Belz 1972, 115).

Perhaps further amplifying Belz's appeal to a general repugnance toward rock and roll, if no less the aesthetic style of the disc jockey responsible for airing it, as the primary trigger for the payola hearings, Paul Linden has suggested that there were racial motivations that caused their manifestation. According to Linden, "the payola hearings of the late 1950s were a straw-man issue used by the government to oppress any surge towards black entry into mainstream popular culture" (Linden 2012, 55). In a similar vein, Shane Maddock has proposed that "[m]any critics of the mass media began to indulge in a conspiracy theory in which the lower class was corrupting middle-class teenagers with the aid of the corporations marketing records, movies, and other media" (Maddock 1996, 199).

Whether it was because some people thought rock was "bad music," or that the government was attempting to push back on black influences into mainstream culture, or that there was a conspiracy on the part of corporations to corrupt middle-class youth, the foregoing explanations for the payola hearings share one assumption in common, which is underscored by elements of the congressional record, as well as media reports. This common assumption was that payola somehow explained why rock and roll was broadcasted at all. In other words, if it were not for payola, rock and roll would not be heard on the airwaves, and the general public would not be so exposed to it. Indeed, according to Coase, "the idea that the demand for 'rock and roll' music was created by broadcasters through playing records of such music on disc jockey programs and that this was in some way connected with payola" generally shaped congressional attitudes (Coase 1979, 288). And, as a matter of fact, the first witness in the hearings on payola in radio was a disc jockey for WBZ in Boston, namely Norman Prescott, who suggested that rock and roll would "[n]ever get on the air" if it weren't for payola.[40] As Donald Mabry further articulates:

> the thrust of the hearings . . . was the argument that R&B and rock 'n' roll (both usually licensed by BMI) would never be played by radio stations if DJs were not bribed and that payola had driven good music off the airways. Opponents of rock 'n' roll (and thus of the independents) were asserting that the independent record companies and BMI had conspired to corrupt the United States by

inundating the airways with bad music, full of sex and disrespect for authority. (Mabry 1990, 446)

Therefore, judging from the media reports and the congressional record, it seems reasonable to imagine that the prevalence of an attitude of aesthetic repugnance toward rock and roll, together with an assumed connection between the existence of payola in the broadcasting industry and the accessibility of rock and roll, certainly helped to precipitate the hearings.

But one wonders whether factors such as these are sufficient to explain why the hearings eventually transpired. For one thing, Linden proposes, payola payments were more or less "under the table" and so the government was not getting their share of the action. As he asserts:

we would never have heard about any of this [payola] if the DJs had only paid taxes on this common expense called radio promotion. The main vehicles that brought this situation into the light—the federal payola hearings of 1960 and the anti-payola laws from five years earlier—are both functions of the fact that the U.S. government was not getting its piece of the action: the DJs were evading taxes, not claiming this as part of their income. (Linden 2012, 57)

Meanwhile still, Mol and Wijnberg tie the concern with payola to attempts of the major record companies to regain market share from the independents, noting that, on the eve of the hearings, and simultaneous with their own efforts to

accommodate the needs of DJs, including the provision of prostitutes . . . they pursued another strategic option: undermining the power of the local DJs who had manifested themselves as supporters of the indies and their new music . . . . The prime objective was to destroy the DJ's claims of authenticity as representatives of the Rock and Roll movement and as representatives of rebellious youth. The prime tool to achieve this objective was to persuade the lawmakers and politicians to look into the subject of payola. (Mol and Wijnberg 2007, 710)

And so, by the time of the hearings, "[t]he major record companies embarked on an extensive lobbying campaign claiming that payola severely limited their chances of commercial success" (Mol and Wijnberg 2007, 710).

Finally, although not entirely unrelated to the foregoing, given the intricate financial affiliations between publishers and record producers, Mabry believes that the real impetus for the payola hearings had to do with another attempt by ASCAP to undermine BMI's market share of copyright fees since "the argument throughout the hearings was that [as mentioned above] R&B and rock 'n' roll would never be played on radio (and thus records sold) were it not for bribery on the part of the independents" (Mabry 1990, 416; my emphasis in brackets).

To some degree, I suggest that all the foregoing elements probably had something to do with why the payola hearings occurred when they did. The belief in rock and roll as bad music would certainly help to serve as a convenient cover for the underlying motive, given rock and roll's aesthetic disfavor among various constituencies of the general public, as I will further addressed below. Meanwhile, the underlying motive was that the hearings were simply another tool wielded by ASCAP and its allies, the major record companies, to regain control of the dominant technological medium to expose their product to the public, namely radio, and to squash their competitors, the independent record companies and BMI, and thus, in general, to increase their copyright royalties and the profits from record sales. Indeed, from 1948 to 1955, ASCAP had controlled 68 percent of the number one hits, according to *Billboard*. But this percentage precipitously dropped to 23 percent in 1956, for the reasons I described above, only to slightly regain some of its market loss in 1957 and 1958 (25 percent) up to 31 percent by the time of the hearings in 1959 (Coase 1979, 315).

To further elaborate this opinion, I think it is helpful to parse out who seemed to benefit most from the payola that was paid to disc jockeys, and who seemed to benefit most from the subsequent 1960 amendment to the Communications Act that made such payola illegal (Coase 1979, 307–8). To this end, consider first that the congressional hearings on payola specifically targeted the commercial radio broadcast industry, while the subsequent Act articulated elaborate exemptions for the movie industry and feature films (Coase 1979) that, otherwise, had close financial ties with ASCAP. Consider further that the presence of payola indirectly helped radio stations, particularly the independent ones, lower the salaries they were pressured to pay to attract disc jockeys (Coase 1979, 308) which, in turn, helped to reduce their overall operating costs, and thereby, increase their profits. So, on the surface of it, it is hard to imagine how payola was not advantageous for the radio stations, and specifically for the smaller ones. However, it is also important to remember that the ultimate goal of radio stations was always to increase the size of their audience so as to justify potential increases in advertising revenues, their primary source of income. Naturally, then, it seems plausible to suppose that radio stations would want to broadcast product that helped to increase, rather than decrease, their audience and ratings so as to justify their demands for higher prices of advertisements. Accordingly, as Belz suggests, it seems plausible to suppose that payola actually accomplished very little to enhance the overall popularity and attractiveness of rock and roll. Instead, it seems more likely that rock and roll somehow brought about an increase in payola.[41]

In any event, it seems reasonable to assume that disc jockeys also had an interest in playing records that increased their own audience and ratings, since that would, in turn, presumably lead to an increase in their own marketability as disc jockeys and, thus, presumably their salary (Coase 1979, 308). And, in fact, disc jockeys looked forward to being the first to play a hit record and would screen their candidates for such potential accordingly. In addition, record companies in general, and particularly the smaller, independent ones, certainly had an interest in paying disc jockeys to play their records, but only provided that the increase in profits from the subsequent exposure their records enjoyed justified such an expenditure (Coase 1979, 308). Given all of this, what constituency then would have an interest in eliminating payola?

To answer this question, it is helpful to underscore that payola mostly benefited the smaller independent record companies who had, as the foregoing indicates, been able to capitalize most significantly on the increased popularity of rock and roll, the advent of which they had, after all, nearly single-handedly helped to foster, thanks, in part, to the work of BMI. Indeed, it was principally because of rock and roll that the independents had managed to absorb the lion's share of the record industry's entire popular market from the former oligopoly, comprised of the majors, that had previously controlled it, as I described above. For payola allowed the independents to maintain an even playing field with the majors for the promotion of their product. As Coase further remarks, "[t]hese [independent] companies lacked the name-stars and the strong marketing organization of the major companies, and payola enabled them to launch their new records in a local market and, if success there was achieved, to expand their sales by making similar efforts in other markets" (Coase 1979, 316). In contrast to what Congressman Oren Harris said in his introductory remarks to the payola hearings, that is, namely that "'we are told' that payola tends 'to drive out of business small firms who lack the means to survive this unfair competition'" Coase asserts, "[t]here is no reason to suppose that a ban on payola would, in general, have helped the small music publishers or has helped the small record companies" (Coase 1979, 316–17). Rather, paying disc jockeys to spin their product was a mechanism, perhaps the only or at least most effective one, available to the small independent record companies to compete directly with the large, affluent majors, for exposure of their music to the general public. So, making payola illegal would appear to have primarily benefited the majors because it precluded the independents from being able to use one of their most productive promotional instruments to compete. As Coase puts it, "the aim of the business interests which sought to curb payola seems to have been not so much to secure a general benefit for the industry as to hobble their competitors" (Coase 1979, 316). Moreover, once payola was illegal, the majors were then able to divert the advertising dollars they had previously paid to the disc jockeys, under the duress and competition they had experienced from the independents engaged in the practice, to the other promotional avenues for record exposure otherwise available to them, at least up to the degree that whatever profit was thereby generated exceeded their total record promotion expenditures (Coase 1979, 317).[42]

In any case, a number of predictable consequences quickly followed the 1960 amendment to the Communications Act that made payola illegal in the commercial music industry. First, radio stations were required to hire program directors or to reassign current employees to develop playlists for disc jockeys so that disc jockeys no longer had the discretion to do so, and the major record companies began to place greater reliance on the "promotion man" to get exposure for their product (Coase 1979, 306). Furthermore, since many of the independents did not have much of a promotional apparatus to speak of other than the paying of disc jockeys directly to generate exposure for their products, the competitive advantage of the majors over the smaller independents was soon restored. Whereas "[t]he large corporations . . . which owned radio and television networks and, in some cases, motion picture studios, could get their records played in major markets or nationally" (Mabry 1990, 446), the smaller independents did not have those commercial affiliations to which they could appeal to make up the difference. Thus, according to Mabry, "[b]y closing some of the gateways to the marketplace provided by the kind of payola used before 1960, the major companies reasserted their control of the market. The new law helped kill many of the companies that had fostered rock 'n' roll" (Mabry 1990, 446). In other words, as Maddock further remarks, "[t]he payola scandal helped to tame the wide-open rock industry. The large record companies now dominated the genre and restricted the types of performers that had access to the recording studios and airwaves" (Maddock 1996, 199). And so, the outcome of the payola scandal, characterized as it was to be a matter of "corruption" in the industry, ended up assisting the majors to regain at least some control over the music exposure system by closing, so to speak, the only backdoor which the independents had been previously able to use to promote their releases, leaving the majors to further capitalized on the other distribution systems already available to them, or with which they were, otherwise, affiliated.[43]

Not surprisingly perhaps, there was no genuine interest during the payola hearings to find any alternative avenue to preserving a legal form of payola, rather than merely affirming the putative claim that payola was intrinsically a deceptive practice, and that a law, accordingly, was required to ban it in toto. There was, however, much motivation to draft elaborate exemptions to include in the Act for other media forms, such as television and film. As Coase reports, "no attempt was made before the 1960 amendments were adopted, to estimate the gains and losses which would flow from the change in law" and "no attempt was made to discover whether it might be possible to devise a form of announcement which would alert listeners to the fact that payments were made by record companies whose records were played (so that 'deception' could be prevented)" (Coase 1979, 319). Still, one might have hoped that, during the morass of testimony that proceeded, some genuine and sustained effort would have been dedicated to inquiring into why such payola payments were made in the first place "and what would in fact happen in the world as it exists if they were made illegal" (Coase 1979, 319). But, perhaps not so surprisingly, that did not happen. One wonders whether it was because those with a vested interest in having payola eliminated had already determined what the downstream effects were likely to be from the elimination of payola, since the expectation that those effects would transpire was, in essence, precisely what likely motivated the hearings in the first place.

Alan Freed, so-called father of rock and roll, was, not so surprisingly, either one of the first targets of the payola hearings, and the career of the West Coast rhythm and blues disc jockey Hunter Hancock was eventually ended by them (Linden 2012, 56). The remainder of the hearings were focused on Dick Clark, who, subsequently, may have been forced by the proceedings to divest himself of his financial interests in various companies related to the music industry, such as recording, publishing and record-pressing businesses (Coase 1979, 293; Mabry 1990, 447), and who may have avoided being formally charged with accepting payola by doing so (cf. M. Allen 2015, 116–17). As is often the case in other similar dealings, Freed was already a bit of an easy target, in part, perhaps, because of his free-wheeling associations with rock-and-roll artists, not to mention much of the "delinquency" that the mainstream, adult public had typically associated with it. For example, in the summer of 1959, Freed promoted a Jerry Lee Lewis concert that ended with Freed being charged for inciting a riot (Chapple and Garofalo 1977, 61) a charge that Freed's station, WINS, did not help him to fight, and which eventually led him to quitting. Then, Freed went to work at WABC but was dismissed when he refused to sign a statement saying he had never received money or gifts to promote records. Following that, Freed went to work for KDAY in Los Angeles, during which time he was eventually indicted, fined, and given a suspended sentence for accepting $30,000 in payola in 1960, in response to which he publicly asserted "[w]hat they call payola in the disc jockey business, they call lobbying in Washington" (Orman 1984, 4), a statement which, no doubt, merely confirmed his non-good-ol-boy, non-team-corporate-player character. Finally, in 1964, Freed was further indicted for tax evasion and, perhaps somewhat predictably, died the next year (Chapple and Garofalo 1977, 61) at a relatively young age and, word has it, from alcoholism. All of that said, as reported by Mabry from conversations with Johnny Vincent of Ace Records, "Alan Freed never wanted money from him but did expect Ace to pick up the tab when Vincent and Freed 'bar-hopped.' The tab could be as high as $2,000, for Freed like to buy drinks for everyone" (Mabry 1990, 445). In contrast, according to Chapple and Garofalo, Dick Clark seemed much more to be the music industry's "good" child in that he appeared to weather the payola hearings quite well (Chapple and Garofalo 1977, 63).[44]

Finally, in the wake of the payola hearings, the Top 40 format may have gained further traction by providing additional cover to radio stations and the major record companies moving forward. For the ranking of tunes according to retail sales, which the Top 40 format employed, "seemed to promise a 'scientific' and seemingly impartial, and thus payola-free manner in which records were selected (Hirsch 1969)" (Mol and Wijnberg 2007, 710), while it nevertheless afforded the majors an opportunity to exercise their promotional and distribution muscle in ways otherwise unnoticeable to the general public (Mol and Wijnberg 2007, 710).

NOTES

1. There are divergent accounts of how this naming actually came to pass (cf. N. Cohen 1970, note 7).

2. The first U.S. copyright statute, which also presumably covers patents, is to be found in the U.S. Constitution, Art. 1, Sec. 8: "The Congress shall have the power. . . . to promote the progress of science and useful arts, by securing for a limited time to authors and inventors the exclusive right to their respective writings and discoveries" (cf. Ryan 1985, 14).

3. For example, "[b]etween 1900 and 1910 almost 100 songs sold over a million copies each" (Peterson and Berger 1972, 286).

4. The following serves as the citation for the provision in the Copyright Act of 1909: Act of March 4, 1909, Ch. 320, 35 *U.S. Stat.* 1075, sec. 1 (e) (cf. Ryan 1985, 13, note 2). Moreover, it should be mentioned that while there is apparently no evidence of any lobbying of Congress on the part of publishers, or record of any public debate for this provision, according to John Ryan, Charles K. Harris, "composer of 'After the Ball' and charter member of ASCAP, does describe some sort of behind-the-scenes lobbying effort on the part of composers and publishers." In addition, Harris also "describes a forty-minute meeting that he had with President Roosevelt concerning copyright legislation" at the conclusion of which Roosevelt said "'Mr. Harris, I am with you to the finish. Good Luck!' (Harris, 1926, p. 279)" (Ryan 1985, 14).

5. I say "presumably," because, as Ryan further remarks, it was this provision that was "the source of often bitter controversy for decades to come" (Ryan 1985, 14). By this, I take it, it is implied that the scope of this provision, based on an interpretation of its meaning, was continually a subject of dispute, as the numerous lawsuits that followed would seem to attest.

6. Donald Mabry identifies the date as 1912 (Mabry 1990, 416). This confusion of dates for the establishment of ASCAP might be due to the fact that, according

to Ryan, the actual discussion about establishing a royalties gathering organization began in Luchow's restaurant in New York City in October of 1913, with the actual drafting of the articles of the association occurring in February 1914 (Ryan 1985, 17).

7. According to DeWhitt, as quoted in Ryan, "[i]t was the image of Herbert as the leader of a group of downtrodden artists whose rights were being violated which was primarily responsible for the perpetuation of the founding myth. The myth, as useful as it was attractive, was consciously publicized by the Society until it became an unquestioned part of ASCAP's 'history'" (Ryan 1985, 17).

8. According to Ryan, it was the Court's opinion that music contributed to the profit-making ability of an establishment and, therefore, constituted a performance for profit, even if no special admission was charged (Ryan 1985, 20).

9. Ryan offers a theory developed in an unpublished dissertation by William Randle for why ASCAP gave an exemption to vaudeville. According to Ryan's summary of Randle's theory "ASCAP exempted vaudeville from license fees in return for using vaudeville's large number of field personnel to collect fees from other music users" (Ryan 1985, 21).

10. Drawing from Ryan's research in *The Production of Culture in the Music Industry* (1985), Peterson notes that fifteen publishing companies jointly controlled 90 percent of all the copyrights of popular music during the late 1930s (Peterson 1997, 262, note 10). Since ASCAP was the only agency within the industry dedicated to collecting and distributing royalties at that time, I assume that these fifteen companies were members. This, accordingly, underscores how powerful a grip ASCAP had on the industry at the time in determining the music that was publicly played and heard.

11. Referencing Duncan MacDougald's research, Ryan asserts that "before commercial radio broadcasting a best-selling song might be popular for as long as 18 months. After radio, he [McDougald] argues, because of saturation airplay, this period was reduced to an average of three months" (Ryan 1985, 36). Of course, that also meant that "there was a need for increased creative output from composers and publishers" (Ryan 1985, 36).

12. Although Ryan notes that "regularly published" remained undefined, he adds that it "meant in practice 'published by an ASCAP member'" (Ryan 1985, 53).

13. Perhaps as an interesting example of rewriting history, although Rodgers's induction into ASCAP is listed in the "first edition of *The ASCAP Biographical Dictionary* (1948)" as occurring in 1937, four years after Rodgers's death, it is listed as occurring during the year of Rodgers's death, namely 1933, in the "fourth edition (1980)" (Ryan 1985, 69–70, note 8).

14. From Hearings before the Senate Subcommittee on Communications of the Committee on Interstate and Foreign Commerce, United States, Eighty-fifth Congress, Second Session, on S. 2834, March 11 through July 23, 1958: 449.

15. Ryan notes, however, that the "actual formula for determining particular classification is not a matter of public record" (Ryan 1985, 55).

16. Ryan suggests that ASCAP's initial proposal was somewhat different. By 1939, the current agreement had entailed a fee of "about two and three-quarters percent

of radio's total billing (*Variety*, October 4, 1939)" whereas the new proposal would "raise radio's rates by 100 percent" (Ryan 1985, 85).

17. According to Ryan, this was not the first attempt to establish an alternative copyright licensing organization for music. "NBC had sponsored Radio Music Inc., in 1932, and the NAB had formed the Radio Program Foundation in 1936. Both organizations were short-lived because of a general lack of industry support (Warner, 1953)" (Ryan 1985, 83–84, note 5).

18. According to Hugunin, some "established houses . . . abandoned ASCAP to join BMI. . . . Among the first was composer publisher Joe Davis, who co-wrote several tunes with Fats Waller including 'Ain't Misbehavin,' and his Georgia Music Corporation, which specialized in race music. Edward B. Marks Music Corporation, one of the two oldest continuous music publishing operations in the United States, jumped to BMI in July 1940. Recording pioneer Ralph Peer's Peer International Corporation moved an extensive catalog, mostly country music, to BMI in 1941" (Hugunin 1979, 12). According to Ryan, the defection of Marks to BMI was particularly significant as it provided BMI with a catalog of about 15,000 songs (Ryan 1985, 85, note 7).

19. According to Hugunin, "[s]ongs in the public domain were arranged by BMI's fifty staff arrangers, published and copyrighted. These songs, particularly those of Stephen Foster, made up most of BMI's early catalog items" [*sic*] (Hugunin 1979, 11).

20. Mabry reports that "Bill Rose, an ASCAP member, eloquently expressed the attitudes of many members of his organization in 1956 testimony before a congressional investigating committee: 'Not only are most of the BMI [Broadcast Music, Inc.] songs junk, but in many cases they are obscene junk pretty much on the level with dirty comic magazines. . . . It is the current climate on radio and TV which makes Elvis Presley and his animal posturings possible. . . . When ASCAP's songwriters were permitted to be heard, Al Jolson, Nora Bayes, and Eddie Cantor were all big salesmen of songs. Today it is a set of untalented twitchers and twisters whose appeal is largely due to the zootsuiter and the juvenile delinquent" (Mabry 1990, 415).

21. Ryan provides an explanation that is probably worth mentioning as to why BMI did not venture too far into the business of licensing classical music. According to Ryan, "there were some structural reasons why this genre was not considered suitable for airplay. For example, most radios stations could not afford to pay large orchestras for live performances. At the same time, the length of these pieces, coupled with the low fidelity of recording technology, made them difficult and expensive to record" (Ryan 1985, 117).

22. Hugunin reports that "[a]s of January 1, 1941, ASCAP had licenses with about 200 of about 750 stations, while BMI had about 700 radio licensees" (Hugunin 1979, 16, footnote 15). Referencing *Variety*, Ryan reports the figure of 175–200 "mostly small, independent stations" that had signed with ASCAP by January 1, 1941, some of which also had signed with BMI, while BMI "had licensed approximately 664 commercial radio stations, including the largest and most powerful stations in the country (*Variety* Jan 15, 1941)" (Ryan 1985, 89).

23. It should be noted that the trend away from using ASCAP songs in broadcasting actually began before the formal boycott, at least according to Ryan. For example,

Variety reported in their April 10, 1940, issue that "CBS and NBC had instructed their music departments to avoid using ASCAP music whenever possible on sustaining programs originating from network sources" and that "[p]reference was to be given to songs licensed through BMI or in the public domain" (Ryan 1985, 87). Other efforts included a weaning off, by NBC and later CBS, of using ASCAP's products by instructing bandleaders to begin to incorporate BMI songs in their performances. This started by directing bandleaders to use one non-ASCAP song per performance, and then three non-ASCAP songs, and eventually involved broadcasters excluding all medleys from being performed for fear that they might include some reference to an ASCAP composition (cf. *Variety* July 24, 1940, November 27, 1940; Ryan 1985, 88). In fact, it was reported in *Variety* that CBS went so far as to soundproof the broadcasting booth for the Orange Bowl in January of 1941 for fear some ephemeral ASCAP content might bleed into the broadcast. Bands that had previously been arranged were also cancelled, and the only band selected to perform was required to submit its numbers for review in advance (*Variety*, December 11, 1940).

24. There were, of course, exceptions to this. According to an article in the January 27, 1941, issue of *Time Magazine*, "[o]ver three independent Manhattan stations (WNEW, WMCA, WHN) ASCAP last week aired a batch of Cole Porter Music on a Tums *Pot o' Gold* program. On hand was Porter himself who made a speech defending ASCAP's position in its war with B. M. I. One purpose of the show: to find out whether the lure of ASCAP music would attract more listeners in Manhattan that the networks (vowed to B. M. I tunes) could entice. This week ASCAP will continue its test, guest-starring Oscar Hammerstein 2nd. On the national front, meanwhile, ASCAP will put on a weekly hour-long coast-to-coast program of ASCAP songs over some 110 independent stations" (*Time* 1941, 48). Other deprecating ditties about BMI circulating at this time by ASCAP included "When the swallows come back to ASCAP-istrano" and "Little Jack Horner sat in a corner his radio tuned up high. He listened aghast, then turned it off fast, and said, 'What a bad B.M.I.'" (*Time* 1941, 48).

25. As an aside, but perhaps not unlike so many other seemingly duplicitous initiatives within the music industry, Chapple and Garofalo note that some persons believe the real struggle between ASCAP and NAB was not for percentages of revenue for royalty payments. Rather, it was a battle between the film and publishing industries and the developing radio industry over control of the entertainment industry as such (Chapple and Garofalo 1977, 64–65).

26. Ryan's evidence for John A. Brann's appointment as an officer of ASCAP is a memorandum to Judge Stephens, dated July 25, 1934, File 60–22–5 (Ryan 1985, 93).

27. Ryan reports these eight music producers as M. Witmark & Sons; Remick Music Corp.; Robbins Music Corp.; Leo Feist, Inc.; Miller Music Corp.; Famous Music Corp.; and Paramount Music Corp (Ryan 1985, 71, note 10).

28. According to Coase, "Broadcasting stations and the networks (who also owned recording companies) were stockholders in BMI. It was alleged that broadcasting organizations favoured the playing by disc jockeys of records in which they had an interest" (Coase 1979, 287).

29. According to Hugunin, ASCAP also "tried to use BMI's affiliation with black music to its own advantage in the early 1950s by sparking a public debate over the

suggestive lyrics of BMI's rock-and-roll listings. See Arnold Passman, *The Deejays* (New York, Macmillan Company, 1971, pp. 189–90). As [Pete] Grendysa notes, no one complained about Bill Haley and the Comets' notorious 'Rock Around the Clock.' It was an ASCAP song" (Hugunin 1979, 16, endnote 28).

30. According to Mol and Wijnberg, the term "payola" "originates from the vaudeville era, when music publishers started paying popular performers or bandleaders to perform a song in theaters and music halls in the hope of increasing the demand for sheet music" (Mol and Wijnberg 2007, 706).

31. From as early as 1900, "songs were literally manufactured according to a number of fixed formulas and promoted in standard ways. In 1908 a pamphlet appeared on how to write hit tunes by formula (Ewen, 1964), and a number of similar pamphlets and books were written through the Tin Pan Alley era (Silver and Bruce, 1939; Korb, 1949)" (Peterson and Berger 1972, 287). Throughout this period, according to Peterson, "[r]ather than writing from personal experience or from inspiration, they wrote well-crafted songs much like those that were hits at the time or were tailored to satisfy the demands of the person commissioning the song. As one of the most famous writers of the time is reported to have said when asked when he generally got the inspiration for a song, 'When I get the check for writing the song'" (Peterson 1990, 110–11). Indeed, "[t]he showmen songwriters like Bob Dylan who crafted songs primarily out of their own experience did not become important in popular music until the 1960s" (Peterson 1990, 111).

32. Later on the practice of "plugging" in radio was so commonplace that the expressions "plugged" and "plugs" had become trade terms for performances broadcasted "over the air" (Erdelyi 1940, 696).

33. Defined by Isaac Goldberg in 1930, "[t]he Plugger . . . is the publisher's lobbyist wherever music is played. He is who, by all the arts of persuasion, intrigue, bribery, mayhem, malfeasance, cajolery, entreaty, threat, insulation, persistence and whatever else he has, sees to it that his employer's music shall be heard" (Coase 1979, 272).

34. John Ryan offers the year of 1918 (Ryan 1985, 41).

35. According to one story that circulated at the time, O'Conner took "an executive of the Keith-Albee-Orpheum circuit to a show in which the same song ('I didn't Raise My Boy to be a Soldier,' an antiwar song of the day) was used in a whole series of acts: the melody served as background music for the opening animal act, accompanied a dramatic sketch, was sung first by a duo and later by a quartet, was used in a 'pepped-up' version to introduce the comic, while the melody was used to accompany (in waltz time) the acrobatic troup which closed the show" (Coase 1979, 278).

36. According to an advertisement published in *Variety*, the primary purpose of the MPPA was "to promote and foster clean and free competition among music publishers by eradicating the evil custom of paying tribute or gratuities to singers or musicians . . . to induce them to sing or render music, which custom has worked to the detriment of the theatre management and the public through its rendition of music, not because its merits, but because those singing or rendering it received gratuities" (Coase 1979, 276).

37. According to a Justice Department report, quoted in Ryan, "[t]he principal purpose for which the Association has been used by the publishers is (as) a medium

through which to extract from companies manufacturing records by electrical tran-scription . . . as much royalty for the use of the copyrighted items as could be extracted by the concerted action of the Protective Association [MPPA] and the Society [ASCAP] (Memorandum to Judge Stephens, July 25, 1934:13, File 60–22–5)" (Ryan 1985, 41, my clarification in brackets). Quoting from Baskerville, Ryan notes "[t]he terms 'transcriptions' and 'electrical transcriptions' have been used for many years in reference to special oversized discs used by radio broadcasters. These discs were licensed only for radio use and were not available to the public. Transcriptions today are now found more often on tape, and the term is applied more broadly to include syndicated programs, library services, and 'wired music services' such as Muzak (Baskerville, 1979: 166)" (Ryan 1985, 40–41, note 4).

38. It should, perhaps, also be noted that concerns of corruption in the broadcast industry had previously extended to the FCC itself when one of its commissioners, who subsequently resigned and was indicted, presumably was paid to support the granting of a television license to a particular applicant (Coase 1979, 287).

39. It is interesting to note that after Hess mentioned the payments to newspaper columnists and provided some names, and Mr. Levine, Hess's public relations man-ager at the store, followed up with additional details about the "transactions," which included some additional names of columnists, like Hal Boyle and Earl Wilson, "Congressman Bennett started to question Mr. Levine about the columnists, [at which point] the chairman (Mr. Oren Harris) intervened to say 'that gets into the newspa-per business' and Mr. Bennett said 'I withdraw the question about the newspapers because I guess that is out of our field'" (Coase 1979, 290).

40. Coase 1979, 293; Responsibilities of Broadcasting Licensees and Station Personnel: Hearings before a Subcomm. of the House Comm. on Interstate and Foreign Commerce on Payola and Other Deceptive Practices in the Broadcasting Field, 86th Cong., 2d Sess. [1960], 39.

41. "Because rock stimulated a phenomenal increase in competition for record sales, it undoubtedly heightened payola practices. But this conclusion implies that rock brought about an increase in payola, not that payola created the popularity of rock" (Belz 1972, 115).

42. The downstream effects of promotional dollars saved through the elimination of payola might also have led to an expansion of a record company's product line, subjected, of course, to the same limiting conditions. For example, as Coase further explains, an increase in profits generated by the saving of payola dollars "would lead to an increase in the supply of new records. Previously, record companies would have been deterred from expanding their output of new titles because they thought that the probable additional receipts would not warrant increasing the additional cost. But in the new situation, the probable net income from producing a record would have risen. The effect would be for the output of new titles to expand. And this would lead to a decrease in the probable receipts from any given new title. When these prob-able receipts have fallen sufficiently to make it no longer worthwhile to incur the cost of producing additional records, the expansion in output would cease" (Coase 1979, 318).

43. That this is what eventually transpired is further supported by what was reported in 1979 by *Fortune* magazine. Quoting the April 23, 1979, issue, Coase asserts: "[i]t notes that record companies are 'vastly increasing promotion expenses, while the most powerful form of advertising—radio play—remains free.' At the same time the smaller companies have lost ground: 'small record companies, and small divisions of big companies have been making deals with, or selling out to, their big competitors—principally because the majors have built up distribution systems so powerful that smaller companies using wholesale middlemen have lost their ability to compete in the retail marketplace. . . . Six major companies—CBS, Capitol, MCA, Polygram, RCA, and Warner Communications—now control more than 85% of the U.S. market'" (Coase 1979, 317).

44. Chapple and Garofalo do not have a positive view of Dick Clark: in response to the investigating committee chairman's characterization of Dick Clark as "a fine young man," Chapple and Garofalo uncharacteristically editorialize by asserting that "[t]here is something hateful and pure [*sic*] about the man. An eternal teenage, he somehow epitomizes the clean cut, money-making, straight-shooting, ultimately corrupt, and ultimately pardoned side of America. He is a good example of how go-getters get into high places, and how money makers are protected" (Chapple and Garofalo 1977, 63). In contrast, Johnny Vincent of Ace Records "asserts that he told the subcommittee that Clark was honest and believes that he [Vincent] was instrumental in turning the tide in favor of Clark" (Mabry 1990, 447).

Chapter 5

The Folk "Revival"

By the end of the 1950s, the popular interest in rock and roll seemed to be waning, and would not revive again until about 1964, when it rebounded, according to some accounts, because of the success of the so-called "British Invasion." There are a cluster of reasons which have been suggested for its intermediate period of dormancy. For one thing, a number of events had unfavorably impacted or unfortunately curtailed the personal lives of some of the major artists of the genre as the 1950s came to a close. Elvis Presley was drafted and served in the United States Army for about a year and a half. Buddy Holly and Richie Valens had died in a plane crash. Jerry Lee Lewis had married his thirteen-year-old cousin, which, for obvious reasons, had damaged his public image. Chuck Berry had also been arrested and was in jail for crossing the border with an underage female (Chapple and Garofalo 1977, 49; cf. Peterson and Berger 1975, 166). In addition, some writers have proposed that the public opinion of the rock-and-roll business may have been adversely affected because of the payola hearings. Finally, one might surmise, the adolescents, "teenie boppers" or "bubble-gum crowd," whose interest had apparently contributed to much of the original popularity of rock and roll, had also further matured.

During the intermediary period, from about 1959 to 1964, with the peak occurring about 1963 (Belz 1972, 74), a popular revival of so-called "folk music" appeared to materialize, perhaps attractive particularly among the adolescent part of the former rock-and-roll audience who had gone on to attend college. Despite any effort to portray it otherwise, however, the kind of folk music that was produced and gained popularity during this period remained, most likely unbeknownst to many of the members of its audience, mostly a well-crafted, commercial product, ostensibly beginning with the success of the Kingston Trio and Peter, Paul and Mary.

Emerging primarily within urban centers and performed often by persons raised in like environments, the seemingly sudden resurgence of interest in folk music during the early 1960s[1] has been variously described as an "urban folk revival," although the tradition of urban origins for the sort of folk music that was produced during this period actually began in the 1930s (Malone 1968, 334), as I roughly addressed above. It is also worth mentioning that not only did the revival consist of "re-productions" of traditional ballads, but also involved the advent of "pseudo" folk tunes, as they have sometimes been characterized, such as "Hanging Tree" (Malone 1968, 302), "Ten Thousand Drums," and a variety of other "pseudo-cowboy" songs, such as "El Paso," which happened to be a relatively successful commercial release by Marty Robbins in 1959 (Malone 1968, 302; cf. 342). Accordingly, as Malone described the situation, the folk music revival actually consisted of a range of folk-like music performers, stretching from "ethnic" performers, whose interest seemed to be to "recreate the sounds of the authentic folk," for example, Bob Dylan or the New Lost City Ramblers, through individuals and bands who would "interpret the folksong as an art form," for example, John Jacob Niles or Richard Dyer-Bennett, and onward to "popularizers" like the Kingston Trio or Peter, Paul and Mary. In contrast to the two former groups, more or less, these latter "popularizers" seemed less interested in the scholarship of folk song itself according to Malone. Instead, their approach appeared to be to model what they are doing on the work of other "urban folk singers . . . who had come before them" such as "the Weavers, Woody Guthrie, Pete Seeger, et al." (Malone 1968, 337–38).[2]

It is these "popularizers," I take it, that Nat Hentoff had in mind, at least for the most part, when he used the expression "folkum," a term he credits with being originally coined by the *Little Sandy Review* (Hentoff 1961, 91), in contrast to a presumed "authentic" though "popular" folk music. As a matter of fact, this "folkum," if not even the whole genre of the so-called "folk" music that comprised the folk revival of the 1960s, would seem to be dogged by the sorts of issues of authenticity, of being some kind of "real thing," that were also faced by a structurally similar development which occurred in German folklore studies, and that Regina Bendix has insightfully noted, namely *Folklorismus*, "second-hand folklore," or "fakelore" (cf. Bendix 1997, 13).

Be that as it may, Malone is certainly correct to imply that the urban folk "revival" of the early 1960s did not just appear on the popular music scene, "out of the blue" so to speak, but is clearly linked, in particular, to the precedent musical work of the Weavers, Woody Guthrie, Pete Seeger, and other company, and the associations and musical projects, such as the Almanac Singers, hootenannies, and *People's Songs*, to which they contributed, if not made wholly popular. Beginning around 1940, future Weavers, Pete Seeger, and Lee Hayes had first formulated what eventually evolved into a quasi-cohabitational collective of musicians called the Almanac Singers, later to be joined by the likes of such left-leaning musicians as Woody Guthrie and *Broadside* cofounders Sis Cunningham and Gordon Friesen (cf. Jarnow 2018,

22). Alan Lomax, collector of folk songs, some may add "extraordinaire," and former supervisor to Pete Seeger when Pete previously worked at the Library of Congress, was also in the wings. Their residence, or at least gathering place, eventually became, correspondingly, the Almanac House. A loose collective, in that various contributors came and went, the Almanac Singers frequently hosted hootenannies, a kind of group sing along party, often conducted in the basement of the Almanac House, and the term for which Pete and Woody Guthrie first introduced to the group having imported the idea from Seattle (Jarnow 2018, 21).

In the early months of their original configuration, the first major performance of the Almanac Singers occurred in 1941 at the Turner Arena in Washington, DC. for the American Youth Congress. It was there, according to some interpretations, that the Almanac Singers and their seemingly "out of the mainstream," or dare I say "communist" attitudes first became conspicuous to wartime surveillance activities, hosted by such agencies as the Federal Bureau of Investigation, when they received a booming response to their singing of an impromptu lyric in the course of delivering the "Ballad of October 16th," namely "I hate war and so does Eleanor, but we won't be safe 'til everybody's dead." This line, incidentally, was contributed by the Almanac Singers' newest member at the time, namely Millard Lampell, who, according to Jesse Jarnow, was merely imitating the socially resistant tone of Woody Guthrie (Jarnow 2018, 13–14) while aligning the music with the "pro-peace" political stance of the "Popular Front," a wing of American and Soviet Communist initiatives that had materialized around 1935, and a theme likely precipitated, at least to some degree, by the nonaggression pact struck between Adolf Hitler and Joseph Stalin. Soon thereafter, in May of 1941, the association between the Almanac Singers and the use of music as a means of furthering political ends, particularly those of a leftist nature, was reinforced through their performance at Madison Square Garden in front of twenty thousand members of the Transport Workers Union (Jarnow 2018, 18).

Pete Seeger, a soon-to-be fixture or central touchstone of the folk revival to come, had certainly been attracted to organized communist enterprises from an early age, with his own personal subscription to *New Masses*, a "Marxist literary Journal" by the age of fourteen (Jarnow 2018, 16), and his membership in the Young Communist League at the age of eighteen. This attraction continued into his early adult years with his official membership in the Communist Party at the age of twenty-two (Jarnow 2018, 20). It was also likely influenced by his father, Charles Seeger, an "avant-garde composer," and "[a] Communist in the utopian early days of American communism, even before the Russian Revolution," who "almost single-handedly invented musicology" (Jarnow 2018, 16). In any event, the Almanac Singers, such as Woody Guthrie, were firmly wedded to the conviction that music could somehow change the world, that "[s]ongs could be weapons" (Jarnow 2018, 16), a belief no less exemplified by the notorious message "THIS MACHINE *KILLS* FASCISTS" pasted and sometimes painted on Guthrie's guitar.

In those days, other friends who congregated during their rent parties, and who pretty much "constituted the whole of the New York folk scene as it existed" included "Huddie Ledbetter, known as Lead Belly," "Burl Ives, Josh White, and Aunt Molly Jackson" (Jarnow 2018, 15), half-sister of Sarah Ogan Gunning "from Kentucky coal country" (Jarnow 2018, 13). As a matter of fact, by the Spring of 1941, a small folk music community had started to gather around New York City, centering, to some degree, at the record store the Music Room on West Forty-Fourth Street. In addition to offering its customers access to various rare 78s such as Woody Guthrie's *Dust Bowl Ballads*, and recordings of the Carter Family and Dave Macon that Victor had recently re-released, "sensing an emerging new market" (Jarnow 2018, 17), its owner and former treasurer of the Communist rag *New Masses*, Eric Bernay, also agreed to release the Almanac Singers' "triple 78 debut" *Songs for John Doe*, which quickly made its way from coast to coast, according to Pete Seeger, "in this narrow circle of leftwingers, and peaceniks of one sort or another" (Jarnow 2018, 17). The release also likely helped to further solidify the connection in the public imagination of the Almanac Singers in particular, and other folkish music generally, to leftist politics and various seditious activities. As Jarnow reports "[e]ven the *Daily Worker* had touted the collection as 'pretty seditious stuff,' though it did so almost admiringly. An article in the *Atlantic* titled 'Poison in Our System' called the album 'strictly subversive and illegal.' It was 'a matter for the Attorney General,' the magazine wrote" (Jarnow 2018, 20). Moreover, although the Almanac Singers were fortunate for a time to enjoy a more inviting reception by some mainstream media outlets, including a photographic spread in *LIFE* magazine and exposure to thirty million listeners as part of a "thirteen-week series broadcast coast-to-coast over all four major networks" which was entitled *This is War*, soon their *John Doe* recording and its "Ballad of October 16th" reemerged in such headlines as "Singers on New Morale Show also Warbled for Communists," which appeared in the *New York World-Telegram* (Jarnow 2018, 23). In fact, according to Jarnow, "[w]hen the record made it to the White House, even folk-enjoying Franklin D. Roosevelt couldn't see the humor, wondering briefly if he could arrest the Almanacs somehow. Eric Bernay destroyed his remaining stock" (Jarnow 2018, 18).

All of that said, "by 1943 the Almanac Singers were defunct, diffused, defused" (Jarnow 2018, 11), perhaps assisted, to some degree, by the negative press from the right-wing, the drafting of Pete Seeger in the summer of 1942, and the somewhat widespread "all hands on deck" contra-union-issues sentiment spurred on by the entrance of the United States into the war. For example, as FBI files were being opened on Pete Seeger and Woody Guthrie early in 1942, Sis Cunningham, Woody, and Pete were fortunate to land a gig at the Waldorf Astoria, which turned out to be a bit prickly. As Jarnow reports:

> "Bring on the girls!" someone in the very rich and extremely sauced crowd shouted a few songs into their set, and Pete Seeger flipped.
>
> "What are you, human beings or bunch of pigs?" Pete snarled into the microphone. "Don't you care that American boys are dying tonight to save your country for you, and many more thousands will die before this is over? Great God Almighty, haven't you got any shame?"
>
> From one of the tables, someone shouted for "She'll Be Comin' Around the Mountain."
>
> And they played it, and when Woody took a verse, he took it loud, clear, and direct into the microphone: *"She'll be wearin' a union button when she comes. She'll be wearin' a union button when she comes . . ."* When they finished there was a hush in the room. The Almanac Singers showed themselves out. (Jarnow 2018, 24)

By 1943, however, the then chief of the FBI, J. Edgar Hoover, had given up his quest to track the Almanac Singers down. The agency's own copies of the Almanac Singers' 78s, "collectors' items" as they had become in the interim, had been originally broken in transit, which Hoover apparently memorialized in the marginal note of a report: "[s]ee to it that records are more carefully packed, in order that incidents of this type will not reoccur" (Jarnow 2018, 11). That said, by that time the FBI had filed their music "under 'Gramophone Records of a Seditious Nature'" (Jarnow 2018, 11).

As Pete and Woody returned from their respective wartime duties, they quickly launched the enterprise People's Songs near the end of 1945, the purpose of which was, like the previous iteration of the Almanac Singers, to "facilitate a singing labor movement and change the country through song," beginning with a "semi-reunion of the Almanac Singers to rally 8,000 striking electrical workers in Pittsburgh" (Jarnow 2018, 34) in March of 1946, at which they sang "Solidarity Forever." Although one of the local newspapers labeled it a "Communist song," unions and labor movements were back in for some audiences. Woody wrote "Oh. Well. . . . Any song that fights for the cause of the workhand is a communist song to the rich folks" (Jarnow 2018, 35).

Pete had numerous ideas for their new initiative, People's Songs. These included, naturally, a newsletter, collections of songs that could be retooled for any morally worthy political occasion, the development of a "national network of song sharers and performers," hootenannies of course, and the organization of "workers' choruses for every union" (Jarnow 2018, 34). People's Songs even undertook a two-year struggle to secure a license to broadcast on the nascent FM band under the auspices of The People's Radio Foundation (Jarnow 2018, 42–43).

The Weavers evolved, more or less, directly out of People's Songs activities and performances, coincidental with the latter's last gasps as a formal organization, which were primarily due to a lack of sustainable funds (Jarnow 2018, 59). Having dedicated much of their recent effort to supporting and performing for the Progressive Party's 1948 candidate for the U.S. presidency, namely Henry Wallace, former Vice President to Franklin Delano Roosevelt, some other source of revenue needed to be identified to keep People's Songs afloat once Wallace predictably lost the election. Meanwhile, Pete Seeger and Lee Hayes had both been itching, for some time, to develop a chorus drawing from the collection of "People's Songsters" that came and went, but "something like a less sloppy iteration of the Almanac Singers" (Jarnow 2018, 5). And so, having secured the Irving Plaza, "the frequently hooted 1,000-capacity ballroom just east of Union Square" for a Thanksgiving hootenanny in the wake of Wallace's defeat, People's Songs advertised "the new singing group of Lee Hayes, Fred Hellerman, Jackie Gibson and Ronnie Gilbert" (Jarnow 2018, 54). In retrospect, according to some reports, this would become the first performance of the Weavers. Its highlight was, given the political climate of the times, an arguably subversive arrangement orchestrated by Pete and Fred which they originally labeled "Around the World," what would, decades later, be reworked by Disney artists for an amusement park ride, and eventually renamed "It's a Small World, After All" (Jarnow 2018, 56). In addition to other numbers that had been collected over the years through the work of the Almanac Singers and People's Songs initiatives, the repertoire of this group also adopted some numbers from Woody Guthrie and Lead Belly (Jarnow 2018, 56, 58).

Given the success of the Thanksgiving hoot, another one followed at Christmas that year, also at Irving Plaza, for which seven hundred people were turned away, and Lee Hayes also managed to get the group scheduled to perform on "WNYC's *Folk Song Festival*" as the "No-Name Quartet." The *Daily Worker* merely referred to the group as "People's Songs' new vocal quartet" (Jarnow 2018, 58). The next big gig was to play for the Peekskill benefit for the Civil Rights Congress which, notoriously, did not go well and led to rock throwing, verbal assault with racist, antisemitic and political slurs, hospitalization for some, and all things "fascist" that the Weavers, philosophically, were on a mission to confront through music. As a matter of fact, while they were under attack in their vehicle during the melee that ensued, Woody led its passengers in Lee and Pete's new "Hammer Song," "I'll sing out danger, I'll sing out warning" (cf. Jarnow 2018, 63–68).

Somewhere during this time, they named themselves The Weavers. When asked once on a radio broadcast what the name meant, Lee said "It's just one of those ridiculous *brand names*." Despite being somewhat of an exaggeration, Fred Hellerman further confirmed this account years later when he said "[w]e wanted a name that didn't mean anything" (Jarnow 2018, 58). That said, beyond more metaphorical connotations that seem appropriate, there also appeared to be some affinity between the sort of historical material the group chose to adopt, such as union songs from bygone days, and the name of the band.

Not long after the Peekskill disaster, the Weavers played for a Madison Square Garden rally, kept up their leftist associations by agreeing to sing "for Benjamin Davis Jr., the black congressman from Harlem, the sole elected Communist in the House of representatives, and certainly the only candidate running a reelection from jail" (Jarnow 2018, 70), and conducted weekly hootenannies at the Photo League, a popular front–inspired "visual equivalent of People's Songs" (Jarnow 2018, 72). However, in search of additional revenue, given the insolvency of People's Songs, Pete finally approached Max Gordon, owner of the Village Vanguard, a local nightclub, and agreed on behalf of the group to play a regular gig for $200 a week. Pleased with how things were going, Gordon extended the opportunity into 1950. As a result, the Weavers eventually attracted the attention of Gordon Jenkins, "bandleader, producer, arranger, and star performer" who, in 1948, also became a musical director for Decca (Jarnow 2018, 82). Jenkins, who saw the Weavers perform at the Vanguard on many occasions, and who was otherwise pretty oblivious about political realities (Fred Hellerman once remarked "I don't think he knew who the President was") (Jarnow 2018, 82), simply loved what the Weavers were doing, and soon set up an audition with the executives at Decca. The audition, however, did not go very well. After a handful of songs, the president of Decca prepared to leave while remarking that they were uncommercial, and another executive said, "You're good. . .but you have to decide if you want to be good or commercial," to which Lee responded, "We hoped we could be good and commercial" (Jarnow 2018, 83). After the meeting, Jenkins reassured the group that he would work them into some production of his in any case. Meanwhile, the Weavers enlisted Harold Leventhal as their manager, who, in turn, enlisted his childhood friend, Pete Kameron. Both had show business experience in one sense or another, Leventhal in Tin Pan Alley promoting Irving Berlin, and Kameron as a road manager in the South (Jarnow 2018, 84). Employing an old duplicitous business strategy, Kameron quickly approached Columbia Records to inform them that Decca was going to sign the Weavers. Columbia, in turn, responded with an offer. When the band told Jenkins of the Columbia offer, Jenkins asked them to hold off signing while he told Decca, and reassured Decca that he would even be willing to pay for the Weaver's sessions himself and release the product under his own name "if it made them feel any better" (Jarnow 2018, 85). Adopting a bifurcated strategy of a single of the Weaver's "global folk," and another on the flip-side with Gordon Jenkins and his symphonic accompaniment, Decca agreed to the project (Jarnow 2018, 86).

The choice for the "global folk" turned out to be "Tzena, Tzena, Tzena," and the Gordon Jenkins accompaniment was "Goodnight Irene," with an editing of some offending lyrics (cf. Jarnow 2018, 87). Both helped to catapult the Weavers into the spotlight of popular music. "Tzena, Tzena, Tzena," "an English-language arrangement of an Israeli folk dance" (Jarnow 2018, 2), approached the Top 10 by the summer of 1950, and "Goodnight Irene," a song they had learned from their friend and colleague, Lead Belly, "a former convict and underground folk-music hero" (Jarnow 2018, 2), surpassed it on the charts by the fall. "Goodnight Irene" was something Lead Belly originally learned from his uncles and had played for years, eventually becoming one of his "signature" tunes. But its history may extend, as a matter of fact, to a nineteenth century product of Tin Pan Alley originally composed by Gussie Davis (Jarnow 2018, 75). In any event, covers of "Goodnight Irene" proliferated, leading to over one million records sold. According to Jarnow, these covers included versions by

> Eddie Grand, Gene Autry (two versions), Cliff Steward, Jack Shook and Dottie Dillard, the Harmony Bells Orchestra, Gunter Lee Carr, Lenny Dee, Ted Maksymowicz and His Polka Orchestra (translating it into Polish, "Zegnaj Irene"), Mad Man Maxwell, Moon Mullican (rewriting the verses), the Alexander Brothers, Dennis Day, and the Paul Gayten Orchestra, along with a straight knockoff of both sides credited to Ray Jenkins and Choristers (cheeky, cheeky). (Jarnow 2018, 93)

Nonetheless, the Weaver releases were immediately met with complications. First, problems of copyright emerged in connection with "Tzena, Tzena, Tzena" when the original authors surfaced, contractual arrangements in hand with another publisher (Jarnow 2018, 90). Secondly, as it was implied by Decca executive Milt Gabler's comment "Oh, yeah . . . I know you, Pete. Always liked you" during the Weaver's initial audition, the Weaver's "communist"-laced associations with the earlier iterations of the Almanac Singers and People's Songs continued to dog them. Milt Gabler was likely sympathetic, though, having been principally responsible for the release of Billie Holiday's "Strange Fruit." In any case, just about the time they were slated for a TV show sponsored by Van Camp Beans, and an appearance on NBC's *Broadway Open House* in May of 1950, a supplementary newsletter entitled *Counterattack*, asserted that the Weavers were "well known in Communist circles" and that "the folk songs they sang for *Broadway Open*

House are not the 'folk songs' they sing for the subversive groups they frequently entertain" such as the "fighting songs of the Lincoln Brigade (which fought for Stalin in the Spanish Civil war) and other Communist song favorites" (Jarnow 2018, 88). Be that as it may, this did not bode well for their Van Camp Bean arrangements, which were soon withdrawn, as were the beans Van Camp had been graciously gifting to the band. To smooth things over, however, Pete Kameron approached the staff of *Counterattack*, who asked for $5,000 to back off. Not having that kind of money, Kameron instead promised not to book the Weavers with any group with Communist affiliations, and to discourage them as individuals from engaging in any "pro-Communist activity" (Jarnow 2018, 89). The attacks of *Counterattack* momentarily subsided. Meanwhile, the Weavers began playing regular gigs at the upscale Blue Angel, and the Strand Theatre.

Gordon Jenkins soon after chose Woody Guthrie's "So Long, It's Been Good to Know Yuh" to follow the productions of "Goodnight Irene" and "Tzena, Tzena, Tzena." Given its lyrical associations with Dust Bowl plight, a decisively unsexy topic for a post-Depression, post-war audience, Woody had to change the lyrics to make it commercially viable. This Woody eagerly agreed to do, having previously refitted the song for another commercial purpose, namely an advertising effort for a tobacco company, as well as for Henry Wallace's campaign (Jarnow 2018, 95). Moreover, insofar as the House Unamerican Activities Committee was busy at the time firing up its inquiries into communist affiliations of various public figures, and the Weavers remained under the lens of organizations and readership of such publications as *Counterattack*, Pete Kameron encouraged band members to distance themselves as much as possible from political involvement to further bolster the commercial brand. Motivated, perhaps, by a desire to "get the music as far as possible," and in particular "onto television," Pete reluctantly agreed, asserting "I'll go along with it . . . but I will feel like a prisoner" (Jarnow 2018, 97).

"On Top of Old Smoky," although previously recorded by other artists, as well as being a regular staple of the Weaver's repertoire from the Vanguard days, soon followed the success of "Goodnight Irene" as the Weaver's second "biggest single" (Jarnow 2018, 102). "Kisses Sweeter Than Wine" was also reworked from something Pete heard Lead Belly play, namely "If It Wasn't for Dicky," which Lead Belly, in turn, had picked up at a house party from the Irish artist, Sam Kennedy, under the title "Drimmen Dow," "about a recalcitrant cow" (Jarnow 2018, 105). Meanwhile, the fallout of *Counterattack*'s publications continued to unwind, leading to the cancellation of a performance scheduled at the Ohio State Fair. Having learned of the scheduled gig through an ad, one of *Counterattack*'s subscribers, a certain

Roger E. Sherwood, contacted the governor of Ohio, who contacted J. Edgar Hoover, who provided the governor, off the record, "a bundle of clippings from the FBI's private files" (Jarnow 2018, 110). Nonetheless, with contract to perform in hand, and being, as they were, members of the American Federation of Musicians, the Weavers showed up nonetheless and were paid (Jarnow 2018, 110). That being said, other organizations soon piled on with their outing of the Weavers, including the American Legion and the Catholic War Veterans of America (Jarnow 2018, 111). For example,

> [i]n Syracuse, members of the American Legion had been visiting local television and radio stations, jukebox distributors, and record stores, brandishing *Counterattack* and a copy of the "Banks of Marble"/"The Hammer Song" 78. . . . The A-side with its lyrics about how "the vaults are stuffed with silver that the farmer sweated for," was bound to set anti-Commie radars bleeping. (Jarnow 2018, 111)

Nevertheless, by 1952, the Weavers, ostensibly some kind of "folk" group with eclectic and international tastes gone-popular-music, had become, by all accounts, wildly successful. "Tzena Tzena Tzena," "Goodnight Irene," and "On Top of Old Smoky" were soon followed with the success of "Wimoweh," what was "a shifting chant capped by a soaring and mysterious falsetto melody, not an English word within it" (Jarnow 2018, 3) which would eventually become an even greater hit retitled as "The Lion Sings Tonight," in addition to "the Bahamian sailor song 'The Wreck of the John B.'" (Jarnow 2018, 3). "Wimoweh," incidentally, had an equally interesting, albeit commercial, history beginning with the performance of "Mbub" by Solomon Linda and His Original Evening Birds (Gallotone GB-829) with which Pete Seeger had become enthralled once while listening to records from South Africa that Alan Lomax had shared with him (Jarnow 2018, 78). Similarly, like "Dig My Grave," the adoption of "The Wreck of the John B" by the Weavers, a song originally collected in Carl Sandburg's 1927 *American Songbag*, was the result of reviewing Alan Lomax's 1935 recordings from the Bahamas, which included a version performed by the Cleveland Simmons Group (Jarnow 2018, 79).

Contemporaneously, the "activities" of the House Unamerican Activities Committee raged on, dragging in various presumed communists for testimony. Although former employee of People's Songs, Harvey Matusow, had previously testified before the committee in February of 1952 (Jarnow 2018, 115), Burl Ives, former Almanac Singer, "became the first significant folkie to name names" (Jarnow 2018, 119). Irwin Silber, "[a] hardline sectarian Communist" (Jarnow 2018, 103) and editor of *Sing Out!*, a folk music publication often surprisingly unsympathetic to the Weavers, given that it was cofounded by Pete Seeger, wrote "[t]he future of Burl Ives should be interesting. . . . We've never seen anyone sing while crawling on his belly before" (Jarnow 2018, 120). In any event, the names of the Weavers soon littered the records of the committee. Eventually each member of the group would receive a subpoena to testify, and as the unfavorable associations to leftist enterprises continued to leak out from the committee and were reiterated and leveraged by like-minded organizations, the commercial opportunities to practice their craft significantly dried up and, as the years unfolded, their commercial success would further ebb and flow, with their first "reunion" in 1956, and the change in personnel precipitated by the departure of Pete Seeger from the group in 1958.

Albeit mostly unrelated to the Weavers' work, it is worth acknowledging that what would become for some a touchstone of one aspect of the subsequent folk-revival of the late 1950s was also released in 1952 by Folkways Records, a shoestring operation owned by an electrical engineer named Moe Asch and located in a one-room "studio"-slash-office on West Forty-Sixth Street in Manhattan. What passed as the studio was, in fact, recording equipment that was built "right into his desk" (Jarnow 2020, 122). The release was entitled the *American Anthology of American Folk Music* and was composed by an eclectic thinker named Harry Smith, who carefully selected, organized, and packaged eighty-four songs recorded between 1926 and 1934 that he had previously collected. Soon thereafter, as Jarnow describes, "[t]he *Anthology* . . . became a beacon . . . [and] began a new branch of the folk scene, those committed to tending to the music itself in its purest form" (Jarnow 2018, 124). Among the members of this other branch would be Robert Zimmerman, a.k.a. "Bob Dylan."

Despite this seemingly continuous tradition of "urban" and "popular" folk music that preceded the 1960s "folk revival," shepherded, as it was, principally by the previous, quasi-activist work of the Weavers and company, it has been commonplace to mark the formal onset of that "revival" with the Kingston Trio's national debut as a folk group in 1958 when they released their recording of "Tom Dooley" (Malone 1968, 335; Denisoff 1983, 194), which happened to be a rearrangement of the "North Carolina Ballad, 'Tom Dula'" (Lund and Denisoff 1971, 397). As Jarnow articulates it, although "the expression 'folk revival' had circulated for at least a decade . . . no one had conceived it on this scale, maybe not event Pete Seeger. Just as with 'Goodnight Irene,' in popular American folk music, there was before 'Tom Dooley' and after 'Tom Dooley'" (Jarnow 2018, 187). That being the case, to characterize this event as their national debut as a folk group may seem worth pausing to consider as we gage what kind of music comprised the urban folk revival, because the Kingston Trio did not appear to begin their musical career in folk music, at least as some might imagine such music to be. Instead, despite their triggering of what was to become a very widespread and lucrative interest in some version of folk music, the Trio had previously branded themselves, at least according to some accounts, as a "pop-calypso group organized to cash in on the brief calypso fad generated by Harry Belafonte in 1957" (Lund and Denisoff 1971, 396). Indeed, the genre of "calypso" itself had become a brief fad moving into the late 1950s, principally because of, it is sometimes asserted, Belafonte's success with "Day-O" (cf. Belz 1972, 74).

On two scores, however, this characterization of the situation might be somewhat misleading considering, first, that Belafonte had maintained indirect ties to the Weavers' work, such as through Fred Hellerman, who at times worked directly for Belafonte (cf. Jarnow 2018, 157), and, second, because "Dave Guard, the trio's banjo player, was inspired to pick up the instrument after catching the Weavers in San Francisco on their reunion tour in 1957" (Jarnow 2018, 187). As Guard further remarked "[w]e were sort of trying to sound like the Weavers. . . . It was really Weavers energy" (Jarnow 2018, 187). Be that as it may, it should also not go entirely unmentioned that, on the eve of the Kingston's folk revival breakout, there were simultaneous commercial efforts underway to resuscitate rock and roll through the production of the so-called "Philadelphia Schlock," which, despite being released by independents, had been spurred on by Dick Clark's American Dance Band (Chapple and Garofalo 1977, 5–51), and that at least targeted, if not also appealed to, the precollegiate white middle class.

Regardless of these commercial attempts to fill the industry vacuum created by the demise of rock and roll, the popular folk music of the Kingston Trio, Peter, Paul and Mary, and eventually Joan Baez and Bob Dylan, were likely perceived by the general public as a move away from rock and roll, from the rebellious, juvenile music of teenagers, toward a "serious" music of adults. Evidence for this may be further gleaned by reflecting on the fact that both the musicians and audience were somewhat associated with colleges and universities, as can be seen reflected in the dress. The bad boy leather jacket and jeans were replaced, as in the case of the Kingston Trio, with an "Ivy League" appearance of white slacks, and striped shirts, or armless sweaters, and eventually with the seemingly plain dress of Joan Baez, with little to no apparent make-up. In addition, the general perception of pop folk as adult music was, according to some, additionally reinforced by the fact that it was released mostly on LP 33s rather than 45s (Belz 1972, 80–81).

Thus, for some contemporaries, the folk revival may have seemed, at first, to align more with mainstream, that is, "wholesome," values than had the music of rock and roll. That said, the seemingly "plain" or "normal" appearance, relatively speaking, sported by the folk musicians and members of their audience, together with the reliance, dare I say "insistence," on unamplified music or the use of so-called "natural" instruments and sounds that harkened back to some putatively "historical" or "traditional" music, may have actually represented, at least for other persons, a push away from where the so-conceived mainstream culture was perceived to be heading, a place, perhaps, most aptly represented by the commercial and formulaic *kitsch* pop that continued to gush from Tin Pan Alley and that persisted in popularity with the *Sinatra* crooner crowd, who appeared to relish overproduction in all its forms. For the music of the folk revival, at least at first, may have been experienced as somehow tapping into a growing dissatisfaction of the up and coming adult generation with the commodification of all of the reality that their future lives would seem to likely soon suffer, as well as a desire for some kind of authenticity, truth, or genuine contact with reality that could be accessed, at least in part, through a musical experience. In other words, the music of the folk revival was, perhaps, attractive to some swath of the maturing society because it was perceived as "authentic" music attended with authentic emotions, as opposed to a "commercialized" and, therefore, "simulated" music and its "simulated" emotional delivery. In this respect, one might say, that music complemented the emerging and other seemingly countercultural attitudes that began to be prevalent by the late 1950s and into early 1960s.

Still, because its origins were, in fact, commercially orchestrated, and its very essence commodified, the result was, paradoxically, a commercialized "noncommercial product." The Kingston Trio was certainly packaged to appear authentic in their personhood and music, and that package managed to convey, at least for a brief period, the intended appearance. However, that appearance soon faded and the music of such groups as the Kingston Trio began to appear commercialized, particularly when it was juxtaposed to that of Peter, Paul and Mary, in conjunction with the latter's crafted images, who, similarly, came to appear like spurious "Folkniks" when considered alongside of the likes of Joan Baez (cf. Belz 1972, 81–82).

That it was precisely some widespread thirst for authenticity in general, and particularly such as might be embodied in a musical experience, which served to fuel the so-called "folk music revival" of the early 1960s is perhaps best exemplified by the notorious audience push-back to Bob Dylan's performance at the 1965 Newport Folk Festival. As Belz described the event:

[a]t the Newport Folk Festival in that year, Dylan completed the first half of his performance with the acoustic guitar, the harmonica, and the song style to which his listeners had become accustomed. But when he returned for the second half of his concert, accompanied by a set of electric guitars, he was jeered and driven from the stage. He returned, in tears, sang one his greatest songs, "Mr. Tambourine Man," and temporarily regained the support of his audience. (Belz 1972, 162)

As a matter of record, the song Dylan apparently played when he "plugged in" was "Maggie's Farm," which Sean Wilentz characterized as an amplified twist on "Down on Penny's Farm," a tune originally recorded in 1929 by the Bentley Boys. Moreover, while Dylan was plugging in and the crowd "jeered," it is reported that renowned ethnomusicologist/folk scholar Alan Lomax, in cahoots with the then folk giant Pete Seeger, was going to town backstage in an effort to hack the power cords to Dylan's amplifiers with an ax (Wilentz 1998, 100, 104).

Now the reason often proffered for this audience reaction to Dylan's "plugging in," an event which subsequently signaled for some rock historians the apparent birth of the "folk-rock" genre, was that Dylan had somehow "sold out" to commercial forces, that is, "the man," by choosing to play electric, rather than using the "authentic" or "real," which is to say "noncommercial" sound of acoustic instruments, that had been the trade-mark and distinguishing characteristic of the folk revival, in contradistinction to the manufactured and so-called "pop" music of the commercial music industry—that Dylan was attempting to transform himself into a rock, or what was soon to become, a "folk-rock" artist in order to capitalize on the blitz-like popularity that had just issued from the advent of the Beatles and the accompanying "British Invasion." However, I venture to propose, as others have done before, that this perception by audience members was quite mythological. For commensurate with what the foregoing hopefully has shown so far, there had existed for some time, and certainly well in advance of the occurrence of the folk revival, highly entrenched and commercial forces and structures, quite beyond the control of the creative talents and will of any given musical artist, let alone any single human person, that had consistently served to shape the trajectory of all mass-music dissemination in the United States. Moreover, Dylan's career itself, as illustrious as it is, did not start off with him being some pure, free-wheeling, mendicant poet, some quasi-wandering minstrel, dare I say "hillbilly," spinning off charming, authentic, topical songs in an isolated vacuum, perhaps a cabin in the woods, untouched by any of the evil forces and corruption of the corporate, commercialized, simulated, urban and suburban, but ultimately robotic, world and the money it stood for. Indeed, such an image itself was entirely choreographed, manufactured, and commercial in its origin. For example, it certainly does not take a lot of digging to determine that Bob Dylan's first single release happened to be "Mixed-Up Confusion" in 1962, which was recorded with an electric band, and that Columbia Records swiftly took it off the market at the height of the folk revival in 1963 (Lewis 1970, 308). To make matters even more confusing, what presumably was subsequently popularized as Dylan's folk rock, "led by the Top-40 deejay Murray the K," Dylan, himself, actually characterized as "historical traditional" music (Wilentz 1998, 105). Perhaps he meant historically and traditionally commercial music, as I intend to further suggest below.

In any event, interest in popular folk music, at least of the non-amplified variety, began to wane after 1963. One reason that has often been cited for its decline in popularity, as intimated above, was that the advent of the Beatles in 1964 (Belz 1972, 87) blew the non-electric folk genre, in its myriad forms, off the charts. Having said that, and lest it, therefore, be imagined that the product of the Beatles represented something wholly new, it should be noted that their art also emerged out of an amalgamation of folk-laced musical genres, including Skiffle,[3] as exemplified, in part by John Lennon's association with the Quarry Men (Belz 1972, 72). Moreover, the impact of the Beatles on the popular music scene should not be exaggerated, as there were other commercially successful, though distinct, musical genres pursued by the record business that paralleled the Beatles to some degree in popularity as well as the resurgence in rock and roll and folk-rock. Herb Albert and the Tijuana Brass, for example, is often cited as "out-grossing" the Beatles in 1966 by selling almost eleven million albums (Denisoff 1983, 195).

NOTES

1. Archie Green appears to date the folk music revival as occurring a little earlier in the 1950s (Green 1959, 7).

2. Perhaps it should be noted that among the individuals ostensibly not listed by Malone in this excerpt, but "like" those in the "ethnic" class in terms of her "loyalty to song sources" is Joan Baez, although, according to Malone, she does not attempt to "duplicate styles (except in her guitar work)" (Malone 1968, 344).

3. According to Jesse Jarnow, skiffle actually emerged out of the success of an English pop star, namely Lonnie Donegan, who made his mark in 1956 from a cover of the Lead Belly tune "Rock Island Line" that "reached a rockabilly-like intensity similar to what Elvis was channeling concurrently in Memphis" (Jarnow 2018, 162). However, despite its contributions to the fusing of folk and pop, and the impact of its "locomotive rhythm" on future Beatles, skiffle did not gain the sort of traction in the United States that it enjoyed in England. As Jarnow further articulates: "[a] brief but powerful explosion in British pop culture, skiffle was in its own way—without exaggeration—as significant as the discovery of atomic energy" (Jarnow 2018, 163). All of that said, it should not be overlooked that, "paired . . . with a Memphis rhythm section," Donegan ended up touring with Chuck Berry (Jarnow 2018, 163).

Chapter 6

Rock and Roll as Social Protest

Against the foregoing backdrop of some factors that arguably helped shape the evolution of the American music industry, let us now turn to consider to what degree rock and roll might be construed as social protest music. To begin this evaluation, I think it is heuristically productive to enlist a distinction prominent in Plato's dialogues and particularly highlighted in the *Republic*.

In the *Republic* and other dialogues, one finds Plato often addressing or implying the existence of a difference between the "appearance of things" and the "being of things" (or "appearance" in contrast to "being"). Now, for Plato, the appearances of things are considered representations. As such, they must possess the quality of being referential in that they must refer to the things they represent, or the things of which they are the appearances, in order to be, in fact, representations or appearances of them. Because of this, appearances as representations may also be said to possess the quality of being "about" the things of which they are the representations or appearances.

In contrast, the "being of things" is suggested to apply to the things of which the appearances are appearances or representations, that is, to the things to which the appearances or representations refer, or the things of which the appearances or representations are "about." So considered, the "being of things" itself, does not possess any representational or referential quality; it does not possess the quality of being "about" something else, since it does not refer (or "re-present") anything outside itself, any more than one might say an undetected rock on Mars may be said to be representational, or possess any referential quality. Being, like that rock, simply "is." Being is reality, pure and simple.

It is important to mention, however, that the appearances of things can certainly cease to be appearances and become the being of things to the extent that they lose the quality of being referential and representational, that is, to the extent that they lose the quality of being "about" something else. Conversely, the being of things can cease to be being to the extent that it begins to function representationally, referentially, or to the extent to which it acquires the quality of being "about" something. When this happens, being ceases to be being to that extent and begins to function as an appearance or representation of "being."

In the *Republic* and elsewhere, Plato frequently underscores this difference between being and appearance and often aligns it with a difference that he implies between words and deeds, where words operate like the appearances of things, and deeds operate like the being to which words refer. Indeed, unlike the being of things, but like the appearance of things, words function as words by referring to something, and, as such, they possess the quality of being "about" something, and so are like appearances or representations. Furthermore, to say that words "refer" is, I suggest, to say that they have a "discursive" quality. "Being," on the other hand, lacks this quality of being referential, of being "about" something else, of being representational, and so is "nondiscursive" in its nature.

This ontological distinction or "gap" between appearance and being is particularly significant for Plato because, on the one hand, if appearance and being were the same, then no conflation or confusion between them would be possible; there would be no chance that appearance could be mistaken for being, since they would, in fact, be identical. And if it was not possible to mistake or confuse appearance with being, then all deception, as well as ignorance of one's ignorance (that is, thinking one knows when one does not), would not be possible. So, the ontological divide or "gap" between appearance and being is necessary to maintain the possibility of all deception and ignorance of one's ignorance. This is, I suggest, part of the lesson to be gleaned from Plato's so-called "Allegory of the Cave."[1]

In fact, this ontological divide or gap between appearance and being (reality) presents a fundamental philosophical puzzle, or *aporia*, about the nature of the human condition that is, perhaps unfortunately, iterative, whether it applies to words or the appearances in our heads, or any attempt to address, discursively, the very distinction itself. For, certainly, what is "said" (or more accurately "written") in the *Republic* and other dialogues about the gap between appearance and being must also, if true, apply to these very texts themselves, and so also to the discursive accounts offered therein about the nature of the gap. After all, the *Republic*, according to the *Republic*, is in part a discursive account about appearance and being, and the gap between the two, and so must itself be a mere appearance or representation of being, and not being itself. So, if what the *Republic* says about the gap is true, that is, if it is an accurate representation of the gap, then there must be a gap between what the *Republic* says about being, appearance, and the gap, and the actual reality of being, appearance, and the gap. And so, as an appearance, or representation about being and appearance, what the *Republic* "says" is not the "real thing," and should not be confused as such, lest one be ignorant of one's ignorance, and come away from reading the *Republic* with the impression that one knows when one does not.

To complicate matters further perhaps, because, according to the *Republic*, there is a difference between appearance and being, it is possible that what is "said" about being in the dialogues, including the *Republic* of course, might in one place serve to confirm, amplify, or clarify what being is, while at another juncture what is "said" might serve to contradict, or misrepresent what being is. The so-called "truth" of what being is and how it differs from appearance may then only be grasped by assessing the nature and various connections among these confirmations, amplifications, contradictions and misrepresentations.

It is perhaps important to also mention at this point that all of this should not be interpreted to deny that being or reality, unto itself, can have meaning. I certainly think a rock can mean something, just as the murder of John F. Kennedy or that of Martin Luther King Jr. can mean something. Hopefully, it is plausible to say that we can learn about things from a rock, or the murder of John F. Kennedy or Martin Luther King Jr., or, for that matter, the cluster of historical events themselves which one might collectively refer to by the expression "The Vietnam War." Hopefully, that is, we can learn what they "mean," even if they are not themselves appearances, representations, or words.

Similarly, when we consider music only in terms of its instrumental or auditory and, therefore, nondiscursive quality, or as Judith McCulloh appears to mean it when she defines music as "sound *per* se" (McCulloh 1970, 180), it would seem to be a kind of being that functions nonrepresentationally, unlike a word. Music, considered merely in its "sonic" respects, does not seem to have any representational and referential quality to it. Music simply is. But that does not entail, I hope, that it cannot mean anything, any less than do the events themselves to which the expression "The Vietnam War" may refer. Likewise, perhaps, as "the late saxophone genius, John Coltrane, was quoted as saying, 'when I hear a man play, when I know a man's "sound" . . . that's *him*'" (Pratt 1986, 60).

As a matter of fact, I provide this simplistic account of Plato's distinction between appearance and being, between what might be otherwise be called "discursive" and "nondiscursive" reality, to offer what I believe to be a useful lens through which one may better assess the extent to which rock and roll could have entailed elements of social protest, both at the advent of its original emergence as popular music during the mid-1950's, as well as its subsequent evolution through the 1960s, and beyond. For by appeal to this lens, I suggest in what follows that rock and roll, from its inception, was a form of protest in terms of its being, that is, its nondiscursive aspects, broadly construed, far more than it ever was considered purely from the standpoint of its discursive aspects: its words or lyrics. Although these latter discursive aspects certainly sometimes served to underscore, complement, further articulate, or even at times contradict, particular protest messages conveyed through lyrics, I suggest that it is more revealing to *assess* whether rock-and-roll music counted as social protest, not merely on the basis of the presence or absence of controversial, and seemingly political lyrics contained in the music, but rather by focusing on its nondiscursive dimensions, such as the "being" or sound per se of the music itself.[2]

Now this approach appears to stand in stark contrast to what John Platoff has described as "a long tradition of thinking about popular songs more or less exclusively in terms of their words" (Platoff 2005, 250).[3] Likewise, the tendency to construe music as social protest, only if the discursive meaning of its lyrics implied some kind of "message" of protest, appears quite widespread over the years. Serge Denisoff, for example, often seemed to employ this strategy of assessing the political or protest quality of a song by mere appeal to its lyrics. As Denisoff implies it: "[t]he exceeding small number of songs [during the 1950s] commenting on topics outside of the romantic love situation suggests that the Top Forty was not a vehicle of social protest" (Denisoff 1983, 32). Indeed, Denisoff strongly appeals to the discursivity in music when he concludes, from a review of the discursive content of 1950s hits, that a predominant theme was "social resignation," with Doris Day's *"Que Sera Sera"* being highlighted as emblematic of this attitude (Denisoff 1983, 30).

To consider another example of appealing purely to the discursive dimension of music to identify its social protest quality, it would seem the motivation for Richard Cole's analysis of the lyrics of the Top 10 songs, during each year of the 1960s, was guided by the thought that, above all else, it is lyrics that make the difference as to whether a song is one of social protest. According to his coding, "Love-sex" themes accounted for 71 percent of the songs, and "social protest" accounted for 10 percent during the second half of the decade, all appearing during the years of 1968–1969, and none in the first half (Cole 1971, 392, 396). Furthermore, according to Cole, not one Top 10 song treated drugs as a "predominant" or "secondary" theme, and "no lyric made a clear-cut reference to drugs or to common slang terms for them" although "Let the Sun Shine In" recorded by the Fifth Dimension did mention Timothy Leary (Cole 1971, 396).[4]

Part of the problem with assessing the degree to which rock and roll was a form of protest by mere appeal to the lyrics of songs is that it can, mistakenly I suggest, lead to the view that the genre does not appear to be subversive, deviant, or a form of protest at all. Consider Michael Allen's conclusions, for example:

Rock and Roll [*sic*] was not political music. Rock and rollers were much more interested in girls (and cars) than politics. Yet rock and roll was born because, despite overt racism and segregation, black and white musical forms had already integrated. Rock and roll was a product of that cultural integration, and it served as a huge symbol of the change that was moving across America. Rock and roll music showed that turbulent change could also be joyous, and that folks could dance to it. (M. Allen 2015, 115)

Meanwhile, however, there certainly appears to be plenty of evidence, quite apart from any clear appeal to its lyrics, to suggest that rock and roll was identified with deviance and juvenile misconduct, with deviation from "outward symbols of respectability and the basic normative order" (Denisoff and Levine 1970, 40), and in this respect at least, it somehow seemed to embody a certain social protest quality for some people. For despite the lyrics of rock and roll being predominantly about cars and "girls," there was something else about rock and roll that, ostensibly, appeared to trouble mainstream adult society. Indeed, even assuming the lyrics were at times experienced as vulgar or objectionable to certain segments of mainstream society, it is hard to imagine how that, by itself, could explain the extent of the visceral public distaste and objection often openly expressed about the genre and its proponents. Consider, for example, that Peter Potter "master of ceremonies on the Hollywood Juke Box Jury [said] 'All Rhythm and Blues records are dirty and as bad for kids as dope'" (Orman 1984, 3), or that an *Encyclopedia Britannica* yearbook once described rock music as "insistent savagery" (Orman 1984, 4). Perhaps one of the most memorable and public condemnations of the genre, however, was what Frank Sinatra enunciated, while complaining about the motion picture and recording industries during an appearance before Congress in 1958, namely that the "bulk" of rock and roll was:

the most brutal, ugly, degenerate, vicious form of expression it has been my misfortune to hear . . . [i]t fosters almost totally and destructive reactions in young people. It smells phony and false. It is sung, played and written for the most part by cretinous goons and, by means of its almost imbecilic reiterations and sly—lewd—in plain fact dirty lyrics, and . . . manages to be the martial music of every side-burned delinquent on the face of the earth. (Grendysa 1978, 22; cf. Chappell and Garofalo 1977, 46)

One reason for thinking that reactions such as these cannot plausibly be attributed to the lyrics of rock and roll alone, is that there had been numerous instances of lyrics contained in otherwise widely disseminated and commercially produced popular music that were far more socially problematic, one would think, prior to the advent of rock and roll. That such socially problematic lyrics existed and were perceived by some persons to be such at the time of their incorporation in commercially produced music is, for example, suggested in one letter drafted by the daughter of Reverend Andrew Jenkins, namely Irene Spain, who had been enlisted by Polk Brockman to transcribe the words and music to Fiddlin' John Carson's recordings for future sheet music publication.[5] In this letter, she writes:

> Daddy (Jenkins) and my husband were both ministers and we were quite ashamed to be playing such records in our house for some of them were truly vulgar. But we would close the windows and doors and sit by the hours and sweat them out until we got them. Daddy, being blind, had a more sensitive ear that I [*sic*], and he could understand words that I could not. So we worked together. (McCulloh 1967, 228)

In fact, according to Richard Peterson, at times it was even a struggle to get the Jenkins Family and John Carson to perform in proximity to one another on Atlanta's radio station, WSB. Whereas the Jenkins Family "sang sacred numbers," some family members disliked John Carson because he demanded "to get drunk and be chewing tobacco to perform" (Peterson 1997, 29).

This "vulgarity" was certainly not unique to John Carson, however. For in addition to some pretty explicit sexual lyrics in so-called "race records," there had been quite a long history, according to D. K. Wilgus, of "bum and jail songs" (Wilgus 1970, 159), "protest" songs (Wilgus 1970, 166) and "sin-sex-booze patterns" in so-called "Country-Western" music, leading back to its roots (Wilgus 1970, 178), which also entailed "a white copy of the Negro 'party blues' (such as 'She's Sellin' What She Used to Give Away')" (Wilgus 1970, 169).[6] As Wilgus further elaborates:

> Sex, drink and illicit love . . . [were] outstanding characteristics in a good percentage of country-western songs. The subjects were far from absent in early hillbilly music and in the folk music that preceded it. Folk and hillbilly music borrowed Paul Dresser's song of a repentant whore, "Tell Them That You Saw Me"; and hillbilly music produced the song about the fate of the wayward girl in "Unloved and Unclaimed." (Wilgus 1970, 176)

As a matter of fact, this history of recording sexually explicit and socially undermining "folk" or "hillbilly" songs certainly stretches as far back as the 1920s and 1930s when it was commercialized specifically for white "folk" or "common" consumers (cf. Hoeptner 1959, 17). Consider also, for example, Fiddlin' John Carson's "The Old Hen Cackled and the Rooster's Going to Crow" released by Okeh in 1923, or the Allen brothers' "Shake It, Ida, Shake It" and "Misbehavin' Mama," or "No Low Down Hanging Around" that happened to include the lyric "Come here mama, just look at Kate / She's doing her living in a Cadillac Eight" (Wolfe 1993, 39).

Another concern that generates doubt about the strategy of assessing rock and roll as social protest music merely by appeal to its lyrics is that those lyrics, especially later in rock and roll's development, were often widely misunderstood, sometimes through no fault of the audience because some recordings appear to have been mixed in order to make the lyrics quite inaudible or at least ambiguous, as John Platoff implies with the Rolling Stones' "Street Fighting Man."[7] Certainly, if the intention of the music was to be one of social protest only through the content of its lyrics, it would not seem that deliberately making its lyrics unintelligible or at least potentially misinterpreted, would help much to facilitate that goal. And yet, according to studies of audience reactions to rock-and-roll lyrics that were conducted by Paul Hirsch, there appeared to be a noteworthy trend of apparent misinterpretation. As Hirsch reports

[W]e saw . . . that the vast majority of teenagers sampled in two Michigan cities, including those attracted by the social protest song style, were unable to interpret the messages these records allegedly contained in the same terms as research scholars and social critics . . . [M]ost teenagers made no reference to drugs, sex, or politics when asked to interpret the meanings of songs which we believe said a great deal about each of these subjects. (Hirsch 1971, 380)

Moreover, citing a study by Denisoff and Levine (1972b), Platoff has also confirmed this trend of misinterpretation: "[i]n 1965, during the height of popularity of Barry McGuire's 'Eve of Destruction,' . . . nearly half of San Francisco State College students who had heard the song and were supplied the lyrics could not interpret the meaning of the song correctly" (Platoff 2005, 251; Denisoff and Levine 1972a, 217).

Even so, and despite the audience's difficulties interpreting the lyrics of rock and roll, critics such as Carl Belz have continued to maintain that "rock was from the start a protest art . . . that is what rock meant, even in its early history: a protest against the music of the past and of an older generation, and against the values of that generation" (Belz 1972, 31). Likewise, Paul Linden concurs, rock and roll, characterized as "essentially an up-tempo black pop music," served as "the vehicle for a new youthful defiance" by giving the white youth "a voice to an entire set of topics held to be taboo by the older generation: those that revolved around human sexuality, overt emotionalism, and even self-determination" and to "identify themselves against the Victorian values by which they would have otherwise been restricted" (Linden 2012, 52–53).

Yet why, if the social protest quality of rock and roll could not be plausibly anchored simply in the lyrics, was the genre so typically construed or perceived to be deviant or somehow subversive by so-called "mainstream" society? Appealing to publications from some media outlets, such as *Time Magazine* and the *New Times*, Shane Maddock, for one, attributes much of this disdain of rock and roll to inherently racist sentiments toward the genre (Maddock 1996, 189–93), sentiments, which I will suggest, were actually triggered by the nondiscursive, rather than the discursive features, or lyrics, of rock and roll.

Of course, by encouraging this attention on the nondiscursive dimension of rock and roll to assess its social protest quality, I do not wish to understate or wholly ignore the significance of its discursive dimension.[8] I do not wish to deny that rock and roll, at times, contained discursive content that was explicitly of a social protest nature. For one thing, as Serge Denisoff and Mark Levine have underscored, the first "universally considered" rock protest song was Eddie Cochran's "Summertime Blues," which was released in August of 1958 and which, in particular, emphasized "the hardships of part-time jobs, getting the car, and adolescence" (Denisoff 1970, 43; Denisoff 1983, 32). Moreover, there were certainly other songs with overtones of protest that even preceded "Summertime Blues," such as Chuck Berry's "Too Much Monkey Business," which was released in 1956 and which Joe Ferrandino associates with Bob Dylan's "Subterranean Homesick Blues" (cf. Ferrandino 1969, 270). Relatedly, as the 1960s unfolded it certainly seemed as if rock and roll became progressively nonconformist in terms of the "messages" of its lyrics, which began by then to, perhaps more explicitly, question basic values and institutions of the society (Denisoff and Levine 1970, 40–41).

In addition, it is probably also a mistake to overlook the fact that there were likely a variety of extra-musical reasons that transcended rock and roll's discursive and nondiscursive elements that may have contributed to the association of rock and roll with rebellion and deviance in the public consciousness. It probably did not help, for example, that the roots of its very namesake may have conjured up notions of sexual intercourse (Denisoff and Levine 1970, 40; cf. Denisoff 1969, 225) at a time when such references could have been deemed objectionable for more conservative audiences descendant from the Reverend Jenkins variety. Rock and roll had also been associated with the film *Blackboard Jungle*, and the film *Rock Around the Clock* had been ostensibly connected to a riot that broke out at Princeton in 1955 (Belz 1972, 36). Furthermore, the sort of attention rock and roll often received from "establishment" sources may have reinforced associations of it with subversion. In 1955, for example, a "congressional subcommittee held hearings on the perceived relationship between juvenile delinquency and rock 'n' roll. Disc Jockeys broke rock 'n' roll records during air time to show their disgust with the musical form" and "[t]he Juvenile Delinquency and Crime Commission of Houston, Texas, banned more than fifty songs in one week" (Orman 1984,

3). Roman Catholic leaders in Boston also called for a ban on rock and roll in 1956 (Orman 1984, 4).

That said, it seems reasonable to suppose that these extra-musical associations were, at least for the most part, more likely the effect rather than the cause of the public disapprobation expressed toward rock and roll. Accordingly, I propose that one of the understated reasons that motivated the identification of rock and roll with so-called "social" protest, be it juvenile or otherwise, stemmed from its nondiscursive "being," including, no less, "the presentation of the material, such as the dress, styles and stage presence of performers" (Denisoff and Levine 1970, 40). Carl Belz, for one, vaguely intimates the relevance of such factors when he proposed that Mick Jagger not only discursively "described his frustration and alienation" and "spoke to youth's similar feelings about the world" in the song "Satisfaction" by the Rolling Stones, but that Jagger's discursive description also helped to inform "why the Stones looked and acted the way they did" (Belz 1972, 155).

Like Richard Peterson, when he suggests that "[m]eaning is communicated in the rhythm, orchestration, color, accent, etc., as well as in the words" (Peterson 1971, 592; cf. Fox and Williams 1974, 357; Rosenstone 1969, 142: Lewis 1970, 307–8, Rodnitzky 1971, 44), or "as veteran white saxophonist Bud Freeman put it . . . [t]he jazz man is expressing freedom in every note he plays" (Pratt 1986, 57), I think one can only adequately assess the extent to which rock and roll was a form of social protest by interpreting its discursive content, its lyrics, within the wider context of the being, or nondiscursive dimension, of the music, including in some cases, additional nondiscursive factors that may attend its presentation or delivery. In fact, I venture to say that some music can even qualify as a form of protest when it is entirely unaccompanied by a discursive element, such was arguably the case during Jimi Hendrix's performance of the Star-Spangled Banner at Woodstock.

To reflect in greater detail on how both discursive and nondiscursive elements, together with their interplay, can be relevant to the overall meaning of a particular piece of music, it may help to consider, for example, George Lewis's treatment of punk rock, where the nondiscursive apparently conflicts with the discursive:

> Punk rockers are not expected to play together, nor play well. The idea is to create a din of amateur, uncoordinated sounds, to make a statement about the structure of contemporary music—and of the society that produces it. And yet, their very energy precludes one from hearing their often stinging lyrics concerning society. *Punks create a potent message on one level, yet destroy it in its musical translation.* Along with this tremendous focus on social criticism and concern, punk rockers usually adopt the stance that they don't care about anything, including whether anyone hears their music, gets their social message, or not.

Contradictory and irreconcilable—yet seemingly not for those who make and listen to this music, perhaps the most powerful musical art form to emerge from the late 1970s and early 1980s." [*sic*] (Lewis 1983, 139; my italics for emphasis)

Furthermore, to demonstrate how the constituents of the meaning of the music can even extend beyond the proximate discursive and nondiscursive fabric of a piece of music to include the relevance of a wider social, political, and cultural context in which its appearance may be intentionally orchestrated, Lewis asks us to consider "[w]hat is the meaning of disco for West Africans? The music of Bob Marley for non-Jamaicans? Elvis Presley for the Japanese?" (Lewis 1983, 139).

Now it may be quite apparent to some persons that this approach to assessing the social protest quality of rock and roll by examining its nondiscursive dimensions is by no means original nor recent. Certainly, *Rolling Stone* columnist and author, Greil Marcus, appeared to allude to something similar when he asserted:

[s]inging protest songs on a sit-in or on a demonstration can be different; sometimes you have to applaud yourself just to keep going. Even then, I think, the words are irrelevant. They are an excuse to start singing, to have "something to sing," because people still think that words are "something" and that music is what you hang that something on. But it is the experience of letting the rhythms of the music capture you, together, that affirms the group, strengthening the will to fight and keep the struggle going. It is the act of singing, not the message mouthed as the words are sung. That's why when Phil Ochs gets up to sing protest songs to people getting ready for a demonstration, to tell them that they are right and that their opponents are wrong, he always sounds flat and empty compared to the singing that begins when the cops move in. That's why no one ever argues about what song to sing when the time for singing comes." (Marcus 1969b, 92)

Moreover, according to a study they conducted on lyrics in 1969, William Fox and James Williams concluded, perhaps surprisingly, that it was musical styles, and not lyrics, that appeared to be directly linked to "ideological orientations" (Fox and Williams 1969, 371). Likewise, Serge Denisoff appears to have something like this approach in mind when he wonders "whether the music itself is viewed as protest or is it the lyrical content which is viewed as protest" (Denisoff 1983, 28), when he proposes that "Presley's deviance, then, stemmed more from his choice of musical idioms and his stage appearance rather than his lyrical statements" and when he states that "[t]he deviant aspect of Rock 'n' Roll, it appears, was tied to the emergent genre of 'rock-a-billy' rather than lyrical content" (Denisoff 1983, 30). Furthermore, in contradistinction to a reference in an article by Robert L Root entitled "A

Listener's Guide to the Rhetoric of Popular Music" that, John Platoff claims, "discusses lyrics almost exclusively, with no more than brief mentions of musical features of songs," Platoff adds,

"[a]s with any vocal music, however, an understanding of the meaning of a rock song must go beyond the words (or even the juxtaposition of the words and the music, treated as separate entities) to a more comprehensive view, in which the meaning stems not from the words alone but from the way they are expressed in the music." (Platoff 2005, 250)

As a matter of fact, perhaps credit for applying this approach should be specifically paid to John Platoff for the excellent effort he made describing the significance of the sonic elements of rock and roll to its meaning and articulating the dangers of simply relying on its lyrics. By focusing on the Beatles' two versions of "Revolution," [9] but certainly just as much applying to their song "Back in the U.S.S.R.," Platoff plausibly demonstrates how songs can generate multiple perceptions of meaning when the wider public merely focuses on their lyrics.[10] In the case of "Revolution" and "Back in the U.S.S.R.," some persons perceived these songs as clear cases of advocacy of communistic ideology or even revolution, while, perhaps more realistically, others, particularly in the case of "Revolution," appeared to conclude that the Beatles had actually "sold out." On the one hand, for example, Gary Allen concluded: "[t]he song ["Revolution"] makes it perfectly clear that The Beatles are on the side of, and working for, 'Revolution'—and that their war is going to be successful (*it's gonna be alright*) . . . No wonder the Communists have had some very good things to say about The Beatles" (G. Allen 1969, 163). And in regard to "Back in the U.S.S.R.," Allen wrote: "[t]urn on your radio, tune in a rock station, and listen to The Beatles' new hit about how great it is to be out of America and 'Back in the U.S.S.R.' Pretty crimson propaganda to be coming from Capitol Records, isn't it" (G. Allen 1969, 152). Meanwhile, on the other end of the political spectrum, one finds Susan Lydon writing, in an article entitled "Would You Want Your Sister to Marry a Beatle?" that appeared in the publication, *Ramparts*: "'Revolution' is a narcissistic little song . . . that, in these troubled times, preaches counter-revolution . . . The chorus of the song is, 'And [*sic*] you know it's gonna be all right.' Well, it isn't. You *know* it's *not* gonna be all right; the song, in fact, is one of the few Beatles songs that, even artistically, lacks conviction" (Platoff 2005, 248). And a vein similar to Susan Lydon, Ellen Willis summed up her reaction to "Revolution" in the *New Yorker* by saying "'Revolution' . . . reminds me of the man who refuses a panhandler and then can't resist lecturing him on the error of his ways. It takes a lot of chutzpah for a multimillionaire to assure the rest of us, 'You know it's gonna be all right'" (Platoff 2005, 248). Indeed,

Greil Marcus noted that because of the release of "Revolution," "[a] lot of the people were mad at the Beatles because their 'politics' didn't agree with ours. We felt tricked because we had expected the Beatles to be *our* spokesmen (whoever 'we' were)" (Marcus 1969a, 95; cf. Marcus 1972, 130). However, Marcus also seemed to imply that "Revolution" may be more complicated than a mere review of its lyrics would suggest:

> [t]he radio executives ought to be more careful, those men that smugly program *Revolution* every hour in the hope that it will keep the kids off the streets. Those men like the "message," but there is a "message" in that music which is ultimately more powerful than anyone's words. The music doesn't say "cool it" or "don't fight the cops." Rock 'n' roll music at its best, and it's at its best in *Revolution*, doesn't follow orders—it makes people aware of their bodies and aware of themselves. (Marcus 1969a, 97; cf. Marcus 1972, 132)

One thing that complicates matters about the meaning of "Revolution" was the fact that there were, as implied above, two versions released that differed in slight lyrical respects and significant nondiscursive ways. First, the two versions are lyrically distinguishable, as Platoff points out, in that the first composed and recorded version (what is identified as "Revolution 1") contains the line "But when you talk about destruction, Don't you know that you can *count me out—in*" [my italics], while the second version (typically identified as "Revolution") deletes the "-in" of the first version, so that the line reads "count me out." In addition, the first version involves Paul McCartney and George Harrison providing an additional background chorus of "bow-oom, shoo-bee-doo-wah," while the second version omits this background chorus (which, for simplicity sake, I would treat as a discursive difference). Although it may end up muddying the waters even further, it seems also noteworthy that the original demo of "Revolution," recorded more or less in advance of the recording of "Revolution 1," contained "count me out" (but not "-in"), whereas the promotional video that was produced after "Revolution" included "-in" in conjunction with "count me out," as well as the "bow-oom, shoo-bee-doo-wah" chorus, which was absent from "Revolution."

Added to these lyrical differences, the nondiscursive and sonic differences between "Revolution 1" and "Revolution" included the use of acoustic instrumentation, such as guitar, trumpet and trombone, together with occasional electric guitar chords in the background ("Revolution 1") in contrast to distorted electric guitars and an electric piano ("Revolution").[11] Furthermore, what Platoff describes as "sexual panting" is heard in "Revolution 1," while "Revolution" begins with "a wild high scream" by John Lennon and is punctuated with an emphatic "alright" at the end. In "Revolution," Platoff also notes the presence of "(an awkward overdub of the third syllable of the word 'evolution,' at 0:22). The effect is of an unreliable radio transmission from the middle of a riot or a war zone" (Platoff 2005, 252).

Now, for Platoff, these differences help, on the one hand, to convey an impression of some kind of contemplative, at times "playful" if not light-hearted, reflection away from some aggressive commotion ongoing in the distance ("Revolution 1"), as if, perhaps, the narrator is thinking to himself while lying in a field and observing clouds go by on a summer afternoon. And, as a matter of fact, Platoff reports that Lennon recorded at least part of "Revolution 1" while "singing lying on his back on the studio floor" (Platoff 2005, 251). In contrast, on the other hand, the sonic elements of "Revolution" may seem to convey an impression of being "in the thick of it," up-close to the action of some sort of ongoing riot or battle.

What might help to make even more sense of the differences between these versions of "Revolution" is to understand them within the wider social context that arguably was in play during the period in which they were released. Unlike one commonplace view that there existed a single, unified and particularly revolutionary countercultural movement underway during this period, other persons, such as Fred Turner, have suggested that there were actually at least two quite distinct "countercultural" movements taking place more or less simultaneously,[12] but that they have often been conflated, perhaps because one of those movements may have had something further to gain, political speaking, from such conflation. On the one hand, there was what I would call the countercultural "hippies proper," namely of the San Francisco Diggers variety, and which Fred Turner has labeled the "New Communalists." It should be noted, however, that the term "hippy" was a label mostly used by persons outside of this group to refer to people inside it and I only use it here for the sake of clarity to designate to whom I am refer-ring because it is more familiar to a general audience; as far as the members of this group themselves, they typically referred to themselves as "freaks." That said, this group appears to be what Platoff has in mind when, drawing a page from Richard Neville, he refers to the "psychedelic Left . . . the hip-pies, the social drop-outs and commune-organizers. They were the people who felt that the appropriate response to social and political oppression was a personal transcendence, a search for a purer and less compromised way of living" (Platoff 2005, 264). On the other hand, there was the very political "New Left"[13] activist element. That movement was comprised of the sorts of folks who might have shown up at the Democratic Convention in 1968, and which is typically associated with the activities of such groups of individuals as those, for example, who organized Vietnam War protests, the Students for a Democratic Society (SDS), the Student Nonviolent Coordinating Committee (SNCC), and the Free Speech Movement. At least in the case of the Bay Area of San Francisco, it might even be said that these two factions were more ostensibly separate, and the differences between them more clearly noticeable, since their geographical hubs of origin tended to be located on one of two sides of that body of water that exists between the City and Peninsula of San Francisco and the cities of Berkeley and Oakland, California.

Be that as it may, according to this account of what some people have located under the umbrella of "the 1960s Counterculture," the differences between the two groups had to do with the fact that whereas the hippies proper really had little interest, and more likely even shunned, working within the extant social structures to foster any kind of social change, those that formed the activist New Left were attempting to do just that. The hippies proper, on the one hand, believed that the royal road to the salvation of their human "being" required a kind of internal or personal revolution that may have, at times, been further facilitated by experimentation with psychedelic drugs. Anarchists as many appeared to be, their goals were advocated by the likes of such signature personalities as Timothy Leary, who some may recall notoriously proposed at the 1967 Human Be-In in Golden Gate Park that people "Turn on, tune in, and drop out . . . drop out of high school, drop out of college, drop out of graduate school, drop out of junior executive, drop out of senior executive . . . turn on, tune in, drop out!" Accordingly, as the 1960s counterculture continued to ripen, drop out they did, as these folks went off to establish alternative communities and ways of living, often in rural areas of the United States, although sometimes beginning in urban centers. The other group, typically subsumed under the banner of the "New Left" and likely populated primarily by more college-leaning young adults, sought salvation through some kind of Marxist-flavored ideology that called for an "external," "material" and somewhat "muscled" social change, including the eventual installment of "communist" or "socialist"-laced governance structures to be ultimately realized through activist pressure brought to bear on the "Establishment." Moreover, as this latter group veered toward the end of the 1960s, some of its constituents became increasingly disillusioned with the more passivistic strategies that had been undertaken to achieve social change and that had been formerly advocated by the likes of Martin Luther King Jr., or grounded in the political philosophy of Mahatma Gandhi, and so they began to talk of, and take measures to realize, revolution in a more garden-variety sense.

It is within and by appeal to this wider social context that perhaps both the lyrical and sonic differences between "Revolution 1" and "Revolution" may make more sense. Lyrically speaking, for example, it may help to explain the ambiguity posed by the presence of "out-in" in "Revolution 1," and the presence of a definitive "out" in "Revolution." If, that is, one associates the electric, aggressive, crashing of "Revolution" with the kind of revolution we normally think about, namely the sort of revolution that involves physical force and that occurs outside of oneself, that may have been the sort of revolution that John Lennon was suggesting "you can count me out" of. If, however, one associates the slower, folkie, playful and somewhat dreamy "Revolution 1" with a contemplative mental revolution far away from any loud commotion, and that must come to pass inside of oneself, perhaps John Lennon was suggesting: "That is the sort of revolution I'm game for"; "you can count me 'in' [to that revolution]." Indeed, the continual juxtaposition of lyrics that address external states of affairs and activism, such as "You say you'll change the constitution" and "You tell me it's the institution," to calling for change presumably to occur within one's mind, such as "We all want to change your head" and "You better free your mind instead" would seem to support the view that both versions of the song advocated for the internal revolution of the hippies proper and against the sort of external revolution of the New Left.

Returning to our Platonic distinction between the discursive and nondiscursive, it might be surprising to learn that appeals to something like it, along with specific references by Plato to music, appear quite prevalent within the fears and virtues expressed early on about rock and roll. As a matter of fact, a review of analyses and criticisms crafted by popular authors and scholars at the time of rock and roll's inception, curiously reveals a relatively consistent pattern of evoking Plato's *Republic* to articulate some subversive quality or danger of rock and roll in relation to the wider society as such (cf. G. Allen 1969, 53). The appeal to Plato, no less, was so widespread in discussions of protest music, generally, that Serge Denisoff once declared "[i]n discussing this phenomenon [the protest song] it is quite easy to fall into Platonic clichés about the power of music to corrupt the young and unaware" (Denisoff 1983, vii; cf. also Denisoff 1983, 19, 190; Fox and Williams 1974, 352; Lewis 1983, 133). To offer one such noteworthy example, John Orman began *The Politics of Rock* by referencing Socrates's and Adeimantus's frequently quoted remarks from Book IV of *Republic* about the subversive power of music to change the nature of the state (Orman 1984, 1–2).

Part of the reason for this common appeal to Plato to express concerns about rock and roll, I suggest, had in fact to do with an underlying worry about its nondiscursive dimensions, although I think it is reasonable to suppose that what Plato considers about discursive "form" and "content" in relation to healthy or unhealthy trajectories of human communities may have, at times, also been relevant for certain critics. When various conservative Christian leaders, for example, objected to rock and roll, and often invoked Plato to do so, it was primarily its nondiscursive nature, rather than any discursive accompaniment, that they seemed most concerned about. As Anna Nekola has characterized this attitude:

David A. Noebel, Bob Larson, and Frank Garlock preached on the threat of rock music, arguing that not only was the culture of this music morally threatening, but the sounds themselves were inherently dangerous and fundamentally evil, and thus could harm the bodies and minds—and souls—of listeners. These Protestant conservatives essentialized the sonic components of rock music as physically, psychologically and spiritually hazardous for individuals and their salvation. (Nekola 2013, 408)

According to Nekola, these conservative thinkers "critiqued the actual *sounds* of rock music, not just its lyrics and cultural connotations" (Nekola 2013, 409). Rock and roll was "inherently *dangerous* music" for Noebel and his Christian colleagues because

it was sonically bad and innately immoral. Good music, they [the predominant Christian critics] claimed, was harmonic, coherent, organized; it appealed to the intellect and uplifted the spirit. Bad music, by contrast, was primarily rhythmic, unbalanced towards tension and dissonance. Through its appeal to the base and physical elements it could cause long-lasting harm to both the body and the mind. (Nekola 2013, 411)

In particular, Noebel "argued that the syncopated beat of rock 'n' roll music hypnotized American youth and brainwashed them into godless communism" (Nekola 2013, 411), and Bob Larson asserted:

[t]his subordination of the melody line in rock music to a pulsated rhythm has further psychological consequences . . . Any monotonous, lengthy, rhythmic sound induces various stages of trance. It is quite obvious to any qualified, objective observer that teenagers dancing to rock often enter hypnotic trances. When control of the mind is weakened or lost, evil influences can often take possession . . . (Larson, 1970, pp. 69–70). (Nekola 2013, 413)

Although he also addressed other properties of rock and roll, Larson was particularly focused on its "back-beat" ("rock's off-beat accent on beats two and four"), which he believed specifically encouraged a "sensuous response from the body" (Nekola 2013, 413). Meanwhile, other conservatives, like Frank Garlock, went so far as to insist that rock and roll's sonic elements were dangerous to living things, "citing as proof . . . a series of now (in)famous experiments in which plants that were exposed to rock music died while those shielded from rock flourished" (Nekola 2013, 413). Sometimes these Christian critics even offered graphs to further demonstrate the psychologically harmful effects of rock and roll's sonic qualities.

For Anna Nekola, and I believe rightly so, this conservative Christian targeting of the sonic dimension of rock and roll as a threat was not merely convenient, but had to do with an otherwise deeply engrained, and pervasive, belief that has, at least according to my understanding, permeated much of Western thinking since the time of Plato, and which is probably due partly to Plato's own doing, however unintentional that may have been in the first place. This belief consists of the assumption that there exists an ontological schism of sorts between the mental and the physical, the mind and body and, alas, the immaterial and the corporeal. Not only has this widespread belief been plausibly linked to Plato's writing, but I think there is a case to be made that it was further promulgated and, thereby, tightly woven into the fabric of Western civilization, through its ongoing and deliberate incorporation into the framework of Christian Theology over the course of many centuries. As Nekola further articulates the schism and its related implications:

> all three conservative Christian critics' claims about rock's beat [Noebel, Garlock, and Larson] were grounded in the concept of a duality between the mind and body. . . . white men were most associated with reason, "the spirit" and the mind, while women, children, and so-called "primitive" or non-Western peoples existed outside of rationality and were thus associated with the physical, "the flesh" and the body. (Nekola 2013, 414)

In other words, not only had this Platonically-laced intellectual distinction between mind and body fully permeated the mechanics of Christian Theology up to the time of these critics (and for good theological reasons, I might add, since it certainly helped to make sense of the possibility of immortality), but with that, it had also been frequently pressed into service to cultivate a widespread and invidious cultural perception that mind was somehow morally superior to the body, and so to whatever was physical or material. Consequently, over many years, through the toil of many thinkers, and embedded in the trappings of many cultural artifacts and institutions, "reason" or "mind" came to be associated with "civilization" and all that was good, while the materiality of the body came to be associated with what was "primitive," "savage," and "bad." Furthermore, within the context of religion and perhaps occurring in tandem, those aspects of "man" which were construed as ungodly came to be associated with what was physical, while the mental, the immaterial or "reason," was treated as the aspect of man which was morally worthy. After all, the physical, according to such Western monotheistic religions as Christianity, was the source of "man's" depravity, and that from which "man" should yearn in some sense to escape.[14] The mind, the mental or "reason," in contrast, was the respect in which "man" was good because it was the respect that man exemplified the immateriality of God and, accordingly, "God's image": a non-spatial, non-corruptible, and therefore, eternal and immortal being—a being that, by definition, did not possess any material properties.[15] Naturally, then, any human persons, non-human animals, and any inanimate objects, including those of cultures, who or that may have been deemed to exemplify qualities of the body more than those of the mind had historically been treated as inferior, and morally debased, to that degree. The persistence of such a widespread invidious attitude has certainly been apparent in sexist, racist, ethnocentric, and anthropocentric attitudes down to the present day. As a matter of fact, the association of the material with moral depravity became so entrenched within the fabric of Western culture, that, arguably, some members of the culture became, and to some degree remain, inculcated with an emotive reaction of moral repugnance toward whatever may be associated with the body.

Be that as it may, it was not simply conservative Christian critics who latched on to the nondiscursive sounds and rhythms of rock and roll as the root of its threat to society. There were others not so clearly affiliated, such as Republican congressman James Tustin of California, who Ralph Gleason credited with saying "the Beatles and the other rock musicians 'use Pavlovian techniques to provoke neurosis in their listeners'" (Gleason 1969,138). Even academics, such as A. M. Merrio, associate professor of psychiatry at Columbia University, warned of a threat from the nondiscursive dimensions of rock and roll when he said "[i]f we cannot stem the tide of rock and roll with its waves of rhythmic narcosis and of future waves of vicarious craze, we are preparing our downfall in the midst of pandemic funeral dances" (Orman 1984, 4). Most notably, perhaps, there was Professor Joseph Crow, who Gary Allen characterized at the time as "[p]ossibly the country's number one expert on music subversion," and who, according to Allen, also thought rhythm could be used for hypnosis. According to Crow:

> [b]y changing the rhythm within a musical piece you can have a strong impact on the listener and the subliminal effect is to push the "message" much more strongly. Some people actually have a physiological response when, for instance, a beat is switched from three-four time to five-four time. Pop music now does this type of poly-rhythms all the time, because it accentuates the message. We were taught never to do this in music school, but we were not trying to use music for mind conditioning. (G. Allen 1969, 162)

Indeed, the supposition that the source of the real problem with rock and roll, socially speaking, was to be located in the nature of the very music itself, if not also in combination with the lyrics, was frequently underscored by folks such as Gary Allen, who often built his criticisms out of the conservative writings of thinkers such as Professor Crow. As Allen further remarks:

[t]he changes in rhythm and other musical techniques used to sell attitudes and concepts are not unrelated to brainwashing. As Dr. Crow informs us: "Many of Pavlov's experiments were conducted with a metronome to research the effects of rhythms as a conditioning agent. His famous experiment done with lights, controlling the salivating of a dog, was repeated with metronomes. A dog was conditioned only to eat his food when the metronome was playing at 50 beats per minute, and not to eat his food when the metronome was set for 120 beats per minute. By switching back and forth, or playing both rhythms simultaneously, an artificial neurosis was created." (G. Allen 1969, 161)

But it was not just the conservative critics who pointed to the efficacy of the nondiscursive qualities of rock and roll. After mentioning Plato, again on forms and rhythms in music and their relationship to political change, seemingly sympathetic Ralph Gleason also gave a nod to the significance of the nondiscursive dimension of rock and roll:

[t]he content of rock lyrics has had the most obvious effect on our "customs and manners" . . . But the movement in pop from foxtrot rhythms to black variants of 6/8 time or triplets over a 4/4 beat has brought blues, always an underground communication against the oppressor, overground. There's been a parallel development in dancing, from the rigidity of Arthur-Murray-type box-stepping to a sensuous, individual expression. Dylan's message is in his lines, the Grateful Dead's is in the form of their music, its relation to drug and sexual experiences, its improvising freedom—and in the way that's shown though their collective movements and creation on stage. (Gleason 1969,138–39)

In any event, whether the meaning of the music was grounded in its nondiscursive quality, or its discursive dimension as manifested in the lyrics, or both, did the conservative adversaries of rock and roll not have a point when they characterized rock and roll as a threat, as somehow subversive in relation to the "mainstream," that is, the particularly white, middle-class American culture as they understood it, or were they simply expressing, perhaps again, some misplaced paranoia, some "hallucination" about the wider changing culture? Ralph Gleason, for one, seemed to think so:

American Opinion and other organs of the radical right, as well as fundamentalist religious publications, are vehement in their protest against the music of electric guitars. When radical rightists talk about telstars and satellite H-bombs hung in the sky by Russia, when they discuss George C Marshall as a Communist, they are hallucinating. When they talk of the Beatles as communists, they are not hallucinating—they are merely mislabeling the contents. They correctly define the Beatles as their enemy. (Gleason 1969, 138)

Finally, all the foregoing emphasis on the materiality of rock and roll, on its "sound *per se*" as primarily embodying its protest quality is, by no means, intended to overshadow the important effect that its lyrics, in certain circumstances, could have. Even so, I maintain that it was the being of the music more so than the lyrics that was the primary issue. When Gary Allen claimed, for example, that "Jefferson Airplane takes you on a 'trip,' i.e., it simulates a drug experience" (G. Allen 1969, 152), I, for one, doubt very much that what Allen meant was that Grace Slick's mouthing of the words of "White Rabbit" took people on a trip, although it may have contributed a little window dressing to the experience.[16]

NOTES

1. At least according to my reading of Plato, in fact, the relationship between the distinction of appearance from being (or "reality") and the possibility of deception is essential, not only to understanding the whole of Plato's political philosophy, but to understanding Plato's general account of the human condition, as well as the narrative presented in Plato's *Apology* as to why the Delphic Oracle deemed Socrates the wisest of all.

2. Of course, it is important to note that just as appearances may be said to sometimes lose their referential and "aboutness" quality, at which point they are said to become being, so too the lyrics of songs themselves may sometimes be treated as part of the nondiscursive, auditory, and instrumental body of the music itself, namely at those junctures where they begin to function in a nondiscursive respect, which is to say, when their purely auditory qualities, nondiscursively experienced, become part of the melody and rhythm, for example.

3. In reference to this long tradition of construing songs in terms of words divorced from the accompanying music, Platoff adds: "The reasons for this are not hard to find: Words are concrete, they refer to specific things, and we have an established vocabulary for talking about them" (Platoff 2005, 250).

4. Be that as it may, Cole's study was specifically restricted to singles and to the Top 10, and what Cole does conclude, perhaps in part correctly, is that "deviant messages in lyrics and popularity did not correlate" (Cole 1971, 398).

5. Incidentally, Brockman had previously become associated with Reverend Jenkins in 1923 when the Jenkins's family recorded a few tunes for Brockman. Having learned from that experience that Jenkins had some talent for song writing, Brockman shared some newspaper clippings with Jenkins about the Floyd Collins's dilemma, while attempts to rescue Floyd were underway, and suggested that Jenkins write a song about it for a field-recording session in Atlanta, which eventually occurred on April 15, 1925. However, by that time Floyd Collins had died. Nevertheless, Brockman purchased the song from Jenkins for $25 and gave it to Fiddlin' John Carson to record. However, since, according to Richard Peterson, Carson was unable to read music, he made a "stiff" recording of what thereafter

became Carson's release of "The Death of Floyd Collins" that did not sell well, and so Brockman "licensed the performance rights of the song to Frank Walker of Columbia Records who then placed the song with Vernon Dalhart" (Peterson 1997, 24). Dalhart then made a recording that became a "national hit" (Peterson 1997, 36). Reference to the Floyd Collins incident, perhaps further assisted in notoriety by the popularity of the song, is also made by Kirk Douglas in the 1951 film *Ace in the Hole*.

6. Cf. footnote 15, "She's Sellin' What She Used to Give Away," Buddy Jones, Decca 5613 (1938).

7. With regard to "Street Fighting Man," Platoff remarks: "[b]ut listening to the song also reminds us that the words are virtually incomprehensible. Mick Jagger was quoted once as saying that in rock and roll, the lyrics shouldn't be too easy to hear, and his maxim certainly applies to this song. (In fact, generations of listeners have insisted that line 2 reads 'fighting in the streets,' though with headphones one can hear that he sings 'rising')" (Platoff 2005, 256).

8. "Boston's Very Reverend John P. Carroll declared that 'the suggestive lyrics on rock 'n' roll records are a matter for law enforcement agencies'" (Chapple and Garofalo 1977, 46).

9. In what may have been an unfortunate confluence of events regarding the song "Revolution," its first release as a single coincided with the first day of the Democratic National Convention on August 26, 1968, just as violent protests outside the convention hall were getting underway.

10. That said, it should not be overlooked that Paul McCartney apparently expressed concern that the song may have been too much of "an overt political statement" (Platoff 2005, 246).

11. In a footnote, John Platoff notes that "[t]he guitar distortion was, in producer George Martin's words, 'done deliberately because John wanted a very dirty sound on guitar and he couldn't get it through his amps.' It was created by putting the guitars through the recording console, thus over-loading the pre-amp on the mixing board. The Martin quotation is in Nicholas Schaffner, *The Beatles Forever* (Harrisburg, Pa.: Cameron House, 1977)" (Platoff 2005, 252–53, footnote 36).

12 Fred Turner, for example, theorized this bifurcation of movements in his book From Counterculture to Cyberculture: Stewart Brand, The Whole Earth Network, and the Rise of Digital Utopianism.

13. The use of the term "New Left" extends back to the 1960s itself and refers to a new flavor of Marxist-informed activism spawned by a generation younger than the sorts of Marxists who had previously dominated the Union movements in the United States and elsewhere. See, for example, Theodore Roszak's reference to "daddy's politics" (Roszak 1969, 4).

14. Perhaps this is not due solely to the adoption of Platonic philosophy by Christianity but may also be related to Plato's works themselves. Consider, for example, the last words that Socrates is represented as expressing in Plato's dialogue the *Phaedo*. At least according to an interpretation which is often credited to Nietzsche, for some persons they may suggest that Socrates perceived his death as a healing from an illness because he was finally liberated from the body which hitherto had been his prison in life.

15. In *De Libero Arbitrio*, for example, St. Augustine argues that it is because (1) the mind must be akin to the objects that it knows (so that it can mingle with and thereby know them), and (2) the objects that it knows, such as numbers, are non-corruptible, timeless entities, that (3) the mind (or "soul") must be non-corruptible, timeless, and hence immortal.

16. In contrast, it is arguably true that the music of the Grateful Dead was designed to take people on a "trip." Not only were many of the songs designed and delivered in that way, but the whole unfolding of the sets served to constitute an extended "trip" of sorts, which explains, in part perhaps, why the Grateful Dead was notorious for long shows. As the Grateful Dead matured over the years, this design became more explicit for decades of Deadheads, with the first sets setting the stage for the more fluid and psychedelic later sets. For a paradigmatic example of this along the path of their overall evolution as a band, consider the Grateful Dead's performance at the closing of Winterland on New Year's Eve, 12/31/1978.

Chapter 7

Authenticity and Social Protest

Commensurate with the sort of outrage expressed by the 1965 Newport Folk Festival audience toward Bob Dylan's so-called "plugging in," concerns about "authenticity" in relation to rock and roll, and particularly in terms of the extent to which it might possess some social protest quality, were certainly not unique to it. For the issue of authenticity has repeatedly dogged, if not cut to the heart of, what could possibly count as "real" or "genuine" folk music in North America from the time of its widespread public exposure. At first, it may have been supposed that true, or "authentic," folk music was to be captured in its pristine form, and from its "native" habitat so to speak, through various field recordings that were produced in the backwoods of Appalachia, as well as other remote, and sometimes hard to get to rural corners of the United States of the day. As Bill Malone notes, some of these field recordings were sponsored through the Works Progress Administration (WPA) Federal Writers' Project as well as the Library of Congress, which began its own "field recording of Southern folk material" in 1933 under the direction of John and Alan Lomax (Malone, 1968, 105). Alan Lomax also produced what was referred to as a "Check-List" that was eventually issued in 1942 and which indexed "nearly 10,000 field recordings" of "American singers in the English language" that were made between 1933–1940 (Green 1959, 9). Prior to that endeavor, however, the folklorist Robert Winslow Gordon conducted field recordings in 1927 "from the Southern Appalachians to the Canadian side of the Great Lakes" under the sponsorship of Harvard University. From that expedition Gordon is said to have made a thousand cylinder recordings that became "the original nucleus of the Archive of American Folk Song" (Malone 1968, 104–5). Even so, prior to Gordon's effort in 1927, namely in June of 1923 in Atlanta, one finds what may be the first field recordings to identify regionally renowned performers, such as Fiddlin' John Carson, being undertaken by Polk Brockman for commercial purposes, with the aid of equipment designed by the engineers at Okeh Records (Peterson 1997, 19). Moreover, the business of conducting field recordings to capture some sort of "authentic" folk music was not limited to these efforts, nor to the United States for that matter. For during the first decade of the twentieth century, thousands of "field recordings" had been made in India by the Gramophone Company (Peterson 1997, 241, note 14).

At the time and periodically since then, many of these recordings were often presumed to count as genuine or authentic examples of the original forms of folk music. One problem with this perception, however, is that both before and while these field recordings were being conducted, which occurred over a number of years, the rural artists who were recorded did not remain wholly immune from outside influences of commercial musical works. Rather, those commercial products, originating as they did in the more urban centers of commercial production such as Tin Pan Alley and vaudeville, often found their way to the rural locales of these artists by passing through surrounding areas by means of traveling shows, which occasionally even ended up employing some of the local musicians looking to gain professional experience (Malone 1968, 19). Meanwhile, barn dances and radio broadcasts also contributed to the shaping of what would subsequently count as the "authentic" form of folk music.

Not only were the rural and urban landscapes peppered by such entertainment venues, the venues themselves were also quite lucrative and extensive undertakings in some cases. For example, Malone reports that the Chicago WLS road shows launched six thousand performances starting in 1932 which grossed $500,000 between 1939 and 1942. The Hoosier Hot Shots, what Malone described as "a small instrumental combination featuring home-made instruments," took in $3,000 to $5,000 during any given performance day. Lulu Belle and Scotty, who also performed on WLS in Chicago and WLW in Cincinnati, earned roughly $500 a day, plus transportation of course, and the *Renfro Valley* show generated roughly $5,000 a week, with its greatest single day revenue of $9,500 being due to two shows, one that was delivered in Indianapolis and another that took place in Dayton, Ohio (Malone 1968, 194).

Now, in addition to these live performances, the influence of commercial "folk" music on the genres being recorded in the rural world also transpired by way of previously released commercial recordings. Despite specialists and field recorders of folk music acknowledging any awareness of such circular influence, there is plenty of evidence to suggest that what was often deemed to be "genuine" folk music was, by the time of its recording, already under the influence of commercial recordings of the genre (cf. Malone 1968, 350). Indeed, the list of professional musicians seemingly implicated in this circular influence is significant, including such signature artists as Uncle Dave Macon and Charlie Poole, who had also performed in vaudeville and medicine shows (Malone 1968, 45), the Carter Family (Malone 1968, 350), Carson Robinson (Malone 1968, 59), Roy Acuff, [1] Vernon Dalhart, and

Jimmie Rodgers. Jimmie Rodgers, who Malone characterized as a "hillbilly star," appears to have had a particularly monumental role in shaping the so-called "folk" genre of his day. For, according to Malone, the people who could plausibly be identified as "folk," if anyone could reasonably qualify, bought his records, learned how to play his songs, performed them for traveling folklorist recorders, and their recordings, in turn, were eventually logged in the Library of Congress checklists and became listed in various folklorist publications (Malone 1968, 94). However, only Vance Randolph ever noted Rodgers's name according to Malone. And at least as of the publication of his book *Country Music U.S.A.* in 1968, Malone claimed, no one had yet undertaking a comprehensive investigation to determine just how many of Rodgers's songs had become adopted by the "folk" or been incorporated into any of their oral traditions (Malone 1968, 92).

In much the same sense, the trajectory of Dalhart's career further underscores how commercially produced music came to influence so-called "original" or "authentic" folk music. Although Dalhart was born in Jefferson, Texas, within a family of modest income, his professional career actually began in New York, as a popular and "light opera" singer who worked with the Century Opera Company, and who also appeared in a Gilbert and Sullivan production through 1913–1914 (Malone 1968, 56). Confronted with various professional and financial difficulties that impeded his efforts to break through as a popular singer, however, and despite numerous recordings across the stylistic spectrum, together with his use of a collection of pseudonyms presumably adopted to further enhance his brand, Dalhart eventually approached Victor to record "hillbilly" numbers, and subsequently became one of the most successful recording artists of the 1920s, boosting Victor's deflated sales, due to the advent of radio, with such tunes as "The Wreck of the Old 97," as well as "The Prisoner's Song" (Malone 1968, 56). In fact, Malone reports that the "The Prisoner's Song," with almost six million sales, was Victor's greatest hit prior to transitioning to electric recordings (Malone 1968, 58). Coupled with this, it might not be too far a stretch to propose that a bit of Hawaiian influence could have found its way into the portfolio of so-called "authentic" American rural folk music in this fashion. For, apparently, Dalhart was accompanied on his first Edison "hillbilly" recording by no other than Hawaiian guitar player Frank Ferera, the Hawaiian native of Portuguese lineage mentioned above, who presumably also claimed for himself the honor of having originally introduced Hawaiian guitar to Americans (Malone 1968, 58).

The point is that because these commercially produced musical styles and songs had been attractive to and accepted by the rural "folk," for whatever reason, and later became incorporated, in varying respects and to varying degrees, into their own noncommercial musical efforts and repertoire, what was eventually recorded in the field and deemed to be "authentic" folk music had previously been substantially shaped by commercial music produced in "professional" hubs such as Tin Pan Alley (Malone 1968, 25). Accordingly, it should be no surprise to learn that even prior to the advent of the Library of Congress's field recording program in 1933, as Archie Green asserts, "[m]any—perhaps thousands—of authentic folksongs traditionally sung" had already been "released on American labels" (Green 1959, 9).

Now it seems worth noting that the artificiality of the commercial music that inevitably influenced whatever "folk" music was subsequently "discovered" in the field did not remain limited to the music itself, strictly speaking. Instead, that artificiality eventually extended to elements of the commercial music's presentation, contrived as that became through the adoption of various attendant mannerisms, garb, and promotional materials, all deliberately designed to foster an impression of some kind of "natural," even though ultimately counterfeit, habitat of sorts: a kind of accompanying visual fantasy fabricated entirely for the purpose of further stimulating the purchase and consumption of the music it attended. This fantasy consisted of a sort of pure or pristine universe existing free from and in contrast to the sorts of fetters that were often perceived to attend the modern, urban world, a universe that, incidentally, may have never existed in the first place, or if it did, certainly no longer remained in quite the manner that the fantasy intended to depict it.

To be more specific, this sort of fabricated fantasy can be seen in the kinds of materials that were designed to promote the "original" Hillbillies, the group that Brockman and Peer had recorded in Atlanta. One might consider, for example, how members of the group are photographed with crumpled (but, no doubt, clean) hats, neck scarves, and bib-overalls. Or one might examine the second publicity photo of The Fruit Jar Drinkers, who are dressed in "hillbilly" overalls, in contrast to the standard dress of Sunday suits and ties that such performers originally wore when performing, and as pictured in their appearance at the Grand Ole Opry during its early years (Peterson 1997, G2.3-G.2–4). Furthermore, quite a bit of effort, it would seem, was undertaken to represent early "hillbilly" or country performers competing in popular "Old-time fiddling contests" as primarily anti-modern, rustic, old men, bordering on 'a dying breed,' and that harkened from some fantastically depicted backwoods. John Carson, arguably one of the poster children of these early contests, was certainly "rural born," but he had actually lived most of his life in Atlanta and had been employed primarily in the city's largest and most technologically advanced cotton mill. Despite that being the case, however, when twenty-two year old Marcus Lowe Stokes beat out the rustically characterized John Carson at the annual Atlanta Old Time Fiddler's Convention and Contest of 1924, with Carson's own favorite contest song no less, namely "Hell's Broke Loose in Georgia" (a song, incidentally, that "was not an ancient Smokey Mountain Song"), the *Atlanta Journal* carried no story at all of Stokes' accomplishment. Instead, a story appeared in the *New York Times* (reprinted in the *Literary Digest*), that falsely characterized Stokes as a "mere novice" who had "come down from the Blue Ridge foothills primed with all the Southern tunes that he had learned from his grand-dad (*Literary Digest* 1924: 70)," an account that happened to be further embellished in the narrative poem "The Mountain Whipporwill" by Stephen Vincent Benet (Peterson 1997, 58).[2] Meanwhile, according to Peterson, "none of this was true. The young Stokes at the time lived in Atlanta and was a member of the modernizing faction of fiddlers that gathered around Clayton McMichen" (Peterson 1997, 58).

Such strategies of fabrication, moreover, were seemingly applied in contexts of the existing culture beyond the strictly commercial, such as, for example, when John Lomax is reported to have marketed the blues artist Lead Belly to academics, as Aaron Oforlea has suggested:

Lomax presented Lead Belly as having a lawless background, which was a significant draw to intellectuals and general audiences because this gave him credibility as an authentic Southern African American folk singer. . . . At the Modern Language Association meeting in Pennsylvania Lomax arranged for Lead Belly to sit on a banquet table while performing serval work and folksongs for researchers and academics. Included in Lomax's biography is a picture titled "Negro Folksongs as Songs by Lead Belly" that played up his lawless past . . . This picture looks natural but it is staged and represents the sentimentality of folk revivals. The photo depicts Lead Belly, barefoot, sitting on sacks of grain playing a guitar. (Oforlea 2012, 27)

Despite whatever rural origins they may have originally possessed, artists such as Lead Belly, John Carson, the Fruit Jar Drinkers or the Hillbillies were arguably a far cry from being untainted by urban commercialism by the time they recorded. They had already become showbusiness.

Of course, one should not overstate the ignorance of folklorists about the influence of commercial music on the field recordings produced, nor of their ability to decipher residual traces of some degree of noncommerciality therein. Citing D. K. Wilgus, for example, Malone and others acknowledge that Robert Winslow Gordon was one of the first scholars to identify the influence of contemporary artists on the folk performers he recorded (Malone 1968, 104–5). Meanwhile still, according to Archie Green,

[c]ommercial recording does not necessarily mean departure from folk style or traditional sources. Kelly Harrell is as true a folksinger as any Library of Congress field informant. Many hillbilly and race records preserve stark, authentic versions of folksong, but the evaluation must be made record by

record with the same meticulous care that a student gives to texts in published collections. (Green 1959, 11)

That said, Green cautioned:

⌊w⌋e must remember that careful attention to phonograph records by American folklorists is rare and recent [as Green writes in 1959]. In general, academicians viewed hillbilly and race records of the 1920's with jaundiced eyes as instruments of corruption. An honorable exception was Howard Odum who bought race records as they appeared and wrote in 1925, "One thing is certain, however, and that is that the student of Negro song tomorrow will have to know what was on the phonograph records of today before he may dare speak of origins." (Green 1959, 11–12)

To make matters perhaps even more confusing when it comes to questions of authenticity, of what is the "original" or the "real deal," it is also possible that some folklorists may have deemed some hillbilly songs inauthentic because they "did not conform to the scholars' esthetic standards or to the "esthetic standards that the folk were 'supposed' to have" (Malone 1968, 350).

In any case, whatever was recorded during the field recordings and taken to be a record of a "genuine" article was already likely influenced by commercially produced live performances and commercial recordings. At the very least then, it seems unclear, epistemologically speaking, as to how one might proceed to determine when songs are "authentically" rural, or "folk" in origin. And so, to handle this issue, Malone proposes something vaguely similar to what other students of music have suggested, namely that one should not appeal to a song's origin to determine whether it is "folk" or "country." Instead, he suggests, it should depend on whether "rural people accept it as one of their own and perform it in their native manner" (Malone 1968, 23). Accordingly, although a given song might have been composed by a professional composer and tailored to the tastes of an urban audience, "[i]f the folk accept a song" and it becomes part of their oral tradition, "then it is a folksong regardless of its origin or quality" (Malone 1968, 23, note 46). One such example of a song that, while urban in origin, eventually became indistinguishably absorbed into the so-called "traditional," and hence, presumably, "authentic" folk song category was "Floyd Collins" (Malone 1968, 361).

Compatible to some degree with this account, John Greenway offered a somewhat more nuanced characterization of folk song, specifically in order to assist his effort to adequately characterize so-called "folksongs" of social protest. To do so, he began, like Carl Belz, by first proposing a distinction between folk music, on the one hand, and "conscious art" (Greenway 1953, 5) on the other, where the "lowest level" of the latter may be said to entail "popular" music (Greenway 1953, 8). Whereas "conscious art," for Greenway, issued out of an intentional, self-conscious reflection on the aesthetic style, genre, or literary quality of the work, a folk song was not "a consciously composed piece," or at least it had to lose that identity by the time it could qualify as a folk song (Greenway 1953, 5). Furthermore, Greenway rejected many of the requirements that had traditionally been proposed for "authentic" folk songs, such as that they be transmitted by oral tradition and not from any print materials (Gordon 1938, 3), that their oral transmission occur over "a reasonable period of time," that "all sense of their authorship and origin has been lost" (Pound 1922, xiii; cf. Greenway 1953, 5), that the songs had adopted some verbal changes during their oral transmission, or that they had been sung for some time (Greenway 1953, 5). For, according to Greenway, adhering to requirements such as these would seem to exclude many songs from qualifying as folk songs, and particularly those of social protest with which Greenway was primarily concerned. As Greenway explained:

> [s]ongs of protest are by their very nature ephemeral; most are occasional songs that lose their meaning when the events for which they were composed are forgotten, or displaced by greater crises. Since many are parodies of well-known popular songs or adaptations of familiar folk melodies, they forfeited another attribute of traditional songs—at least one widely known identifying tune. Except for the very simple ones ("We Shall Not Be Moved") and the very best ones ("Union Maid") they are likely to become forgotten quickly because it is easier to set to the basic tune new words more relevant to immediate issues and circumstances than it is to remember the old. And the songs cannot lose their sense of authorship, because they rarely outlive their composers. (Greenway 1953, 6)

So while Greenway required that an "authentic" folk song lack a self-conscious quality, he dispensed with the requirement that genuine folk songs must possess some degree of longevity since, as he put it, this criterion was "a gauge of popularity, not of authenticity" and "[i]t excludes from folksong nearly all Negro secular songs, which are so slight that they have no more chance than a scrap of conversation to become traditional" (Greenway 1953, 7). As Greenway perhaps correctly noted "'The Kentucky Miners' Dreadful Fight' became a folksong the moment Aunt Molly Jackson scribbed it on a piece of paper; 'Barbara Allen' was not a folksong until the folk had worn off its music-hall veneer" (Greenway 1953, 7). Meanwhile, by appealing to Aunt Molly Jackson's remark that "[t]his is what a folk song realy is the folks composes there own songs about there own lifes an there home folks that live around them" [*sic*], Greenway added the requirement that in a folk song the singer must not speak "for himself but for the folk community as a whole, and in the folk idiom; he must not introduce ideas or concepts that are uncommon, nor may he indelibly impress his own individuality upon the song . . . It is impersonality of authorship, not anonymity of authorship, that is requisite of genuine folksong" (Greenway 1953, 8). Accordingly, Greenway further clarified that folk songs must be "in the possession of the folk, communally owned, so that any member of the folk may feel that they are his to change if he wishes" and that the "folksong should be concerned with the interests of the folk, whatever they may be" (Greenway 1953, 8). Of course, Greenway realized that these last definitional elements naturally called for some further explanation as to who the "folk" were before it could be operationally useful. And so, Greenway suggested that:

> "[f]olk" in our culture is an economic term; when the milkmaid put down her pail and went down the river to the cotton mill, she did not necessarily cease to be a member of the folk . . . The modern folk is most often the unskilled worker, less often the skilled worker in industrial occupations. He is the CIO worker, not the AFL worker, who is labor's aristocrat . . . The mine community as a whole is still folk; the textile community similarly; part of the farm community is still folk; the seaman has almost left the folk culture . . . Individuals in these communities may have acquired sufficient acculturation to take them out of the folk, but their enlightenment has so far not leavened the entire group. If we do not accept people like Aunt Molly Jackson, Ella May Wiggins, and Woody Guthrie as the folk, then we have no folk, and we have no living folksong. (Greenway 1953, 9–10)

It certainly seems Greenway has a point with his examples of folk, obscure as this effort to define the folk may otherwise be. Even so, what would appear indisputable is that many of the songs and styles performed by rural artists as they were captured in field recordings, and sometimes later further disseminated and identified as "Old Tyme" tunes, had often been previously primped, performed, and recorded by professional artists, and then packaged and promoted to rural audiences by various commercial interests, and strictly for commercial purposes.

At this juncture, it is important to note that the process of mistaking a fabricated version of rural folk or "hillbilly" music for the so-called "real" thing, together with the accompanying contrived representation of the rural folk artist, all deliberately undertaken and engendered to enhance the commercial success of the musical product, certainly occurred in relation to other musical genres, and often to various crafted representations of their artists, although sometimes a particular case of mistaking was cultivated putatively for less commercial reasons, as implied above by John Lomax's primping of Lead Belly's appearance for academics. Ingrid Monson, for example, explores how something like this mistaking of the fabricated for the real may have been prevalent in various aspects of the kind of image promulgated for, and to some extent by, bebob and jazz artists, and perhaps further fostered by such efforts as Norman Mailer's "The White Negro: Superficial Reflections on the Hipster" and Ross Russell's *Bird Lives: The High Life and Hard Times of Charlie Parker*. Even though, according to Monson, representations of these artists were often tailored to emphasize or even exaggerate qualities which were taken to be socially subversive by swathes of mainstream society and culture, including, for example, an heightened emphasis of drug use, sexual virility, and a general "badness" that bebob and jazz musicians were presumed to possess, such qualities were frequently emphasized and exaggerated in the representations of these artists precisely because doing so seemed to attract the interests of certain segments of white audiences, and, therefore, led to further commercial profitability. In some cases, in fact, the fabricated representations were further exaggerated by deliberately omitting other respects in which the artists and their lives may have more closely resembled qualities typically associated with mainstream if not elite society. One natural consequence, of course, was that these false or "inauthentic" representations came to be mistaken (or treated) for the real thing. As Ingrid Monson describes the process:

> African American performers have frequently been caught in a bind with respect to self-presentation, for the image of "unabashed badness" and sexual transgression has sold extremely well in the twentieth century, thanks in part to white fascination with it. Male jazz musicians have not infrequently enjoyed their reputations for virility and have constructed accounts of themselves that play into the market for this image and its transgressive aspects. There is indeed a stream of African American cultural criticism that find some performers complicit in the reinforcement of negative images . . . While African Americans evaluate the image of "badness" knowing that it violates more mainstream African American values, non-African Americans have tended to presume that "badness" is the "real thing" or even the "only thing." (Monson 1995, 419–420)

On the one hand, for example, Monson points to Charles Mingus's detailed "accounts of his sexual and musical exploits" in *Beneath the Underdog*, and how Miles Davis "advertises his ill-treatment of women" in his autobiography (Monson 1995, 420). On the other hand, and despite Charles Keil's claims to the contrary in *Urban Blues*, Monson reports a recurring emphasis on "discipline and responsibility" by the jazz musicians she interviewed (cf. Monson 1995, 420).[3] Moreover, she recites bassist Phil Bowler's comments about Roy Eldridge "as a family man" and that Eldridge said "when he died that one of his wishes would be to let the public know that we jazz musicians have families that we love very much, too. We have a house, we want our kids to go to good schools. We're family men too. We care about our money for the kids" (Monson 1995, 418). Furthermore, Monson mentions Charlie Parker's interest in reading, talking politics and philosophy, and his disdain for thinking that drugs somehow contributes to creativity: "Some of these smart kids who think you have to be completely knocked out to be a good hornman are just plain crazy. It isn't true. I know, believe me" (Monson 1995, 414). In addition, she notes Dizzy Gillespie's remarks about the publicity that bebob was getting around 1946:

> I felt happy for the publicity, but I found it disturbing to have modern jazz musicians and their followers characterized in a way that was often sinister and downright vicious. This image wasn't altogether the fault of the press because many followers, trying to be "in," were actually doing some of the things the press accused beboppers of—and worse. (Monson 1995, 414)

In short, it seems, part of the reason for emphasizing traits of some kind of anti-assimilationist "badness," sexual aggressiveness, virility or promiscuity, and drug use inherent in artists of this genre is that these qualities appeared to be attractive, in some respects, to a particular subsection of white Americans yearning for bohemian idols, and so they served to boost the market for the musical product. Their deemphasis, in contrast, could have been met with disillusionment, which would have presumably affected profitability, at least to some degree (cf. Monson 1995, 418). More strangely still, perhaps, but nevertheless aligning with what often happens in other cases of contrived inauthenticity in American society, an unintended consequence of the promulgation of a false image for the African American jazz artist is that it may eventually come to serve, at least in part, as part of the "true" criteria for what it took to be a "real" African American, such that, if a particular African American jazz artist somehow failed to fulfill that image, that artist might not so qualify, if only in the popular, "white" American imagination. As Monson suggests, "[t]he most damaging legacy of the mythical view of the rebellious, virile jazz musician may be perhaps that when African American musicians emphasize responsibility, dignity, gentleness, or courtship, some hip white Americans presume that the artist in question may not be a 'real' African American" (Monson 1995, 415–16).

Returning now to the genre of rock and roll, it is perhaps obvious that from its very inception it was quite saturated with an imitative quality because of the impact of the commercial forces and motivations that fostered its "mass-mediafication," as ostensibly indicated particularly through the repeated practice of manufacturing "covers." For it has been repeatedly implied, both above and elsewhere, that many qualities of the rock-and-roll genre certainly predated its widespread manifestation on the popular music scene. It seems apparent, to reiterate, that rock and roll incorporated many elements of the so-called "folk" music that preceded it, including, for example, "folk" roots music which, in many cases, was composed and performed by black artists, having been, in the words of a number of scholars, "co-opted," "appropriated," and "sanitized" (Monson 1995, 418) or, as some have further characterized it, "bleached" (Linden 2012, 43, 49) in the course of the commercialization and eventual packaging of rock-and-roll products. In fact, many of these sorts of "borrowings" began as early as the assimilation of ragtime into popular music, and no less amid the American Federation of Musician's own condemnation of ragtime in 1901. Ryan, for one, emphasizes that there is "considerable evidence that the music industry worked to 'sanitize' the contributions of black musicians and composers," most notably through the "control" of the "lyric content of the 'race' music" (Ryan 1985, 67). For example, "[i]n 1921, under the pressure from music distributors to 'clean up' jazz lyrics, the Music Publishers' Protective Association began censoring popular songs" (Ryan 1985, 67).

And yet, as the characterization of such "borrowings" implies, there has been a tendency to conceive this form of mimicry by adoption of musical trope as an attempt to abscond or confiscate the original creativity, or unique cultural attributes, of individuals as well as whole classes of people, or, perhaps sometimes conversely, in order to assimilate the qualities of a dominant social group,[4] but in either case typically for the purpose of maximizing profit. Most notably perhaps, it has been frequently suggested that the music of Elvis Presley, understood as encompassing all the nondiscursive elements of his performances, was, in large part, seemingly comprised of "disinfected" (Linden 2012, 54) strains of so-called "folk" or "poor" people's audio and visual "tropes." As an aside, one might even venture to speculate that part of the threat of Elvis Presley's music to some corners of mainstream white culture was not merely that his music came to symbolize, through imitation, black and "hillbilly" musical style and rhythm, but that, in so doing, it served to depict some version of "racial mixing" itself (cf. Linden 2012, 46). And yet, clearly Elvis was not the first instance of this sort of mixing of otherwise racially associated musical genres that appeared to enjoy phenomenal success, although the other instances did not seem to trigger quite the same intensity of disapprobation. After all, Jimmie Rodgers, a.k.a "America's Blues Yodeler" (on the one hand) and "The Singing Brakeman" (on the other) also mixed "the sounds and sentiments of blues, jazz, and traditional country music" to produce "a new kind of music that in its musical informality and earthy sentiments stood in stark contrast to the Tin Pan Alley-based urban popular music of the time" (Peterson 1997, 50). In fact, according to Peterson, it was precisely this mix that, only a couple of generations after Rodger's death, would reemerge "under the rubric of 'rock 'n' roll'" (Peterson, 247, note 34).

Be that as it may, it would appear to be problematic to loosely characterize such forms of mimicry or imitation as bluntly mere co-optation, assimilation, subsumption, or even "blanching" (Linden 2012, 54)[5] of otherwise "racially"

or "ethnically" specific genres, despite the prevalence of "covers" by predominantly white bands of previously produced music by black artists. For
to assume that the covered music was "co-opted" or "appropriated" in these
cases would seem to require that, at least to some degree, one also assume
the preexistence of some primordial and authentic originality that had been
"absconded" by whatever might count as the musical "knock-offs." And
yet, what appears to be the case in rock and roll was that the commercially
produced "cover" was just another copy, or "parody," of certain musical
products that were themselves comprised of "borrowings" from previously
commercialized packages of rhythm and blues and country-western music,
and hence, mimicries that resulted from previous instances of putative co-
optation of various forms.

To make matters even more convoluted when it comes to the question of
what may justifiably count as an original musical form and what may count
as an imitation, and accordingly to whom the so-called "original" should
ultimately be credited, it is probably worth acknowledging that the tendency
to engage in imitation of musical tropes in general, either in recordings or
performances, can sometimes even extend to the artists to whom those tropes
are originally credited. Consider, for example, the case of one-time hit artists who, once successful, may have inadvertently derailed their later artistic
efforts by doing their best to somehow re-create or mimic in new work elements they believed were responsible for their initial commercial success.
As Belz has explained, by becoming "self-conscious with regard to the art in
hand, namely the first recording," such artists "try to duplicate those magical
ingredients with only minor or barely perceptible variations, thereby hoping
to achieve a second success," while, in the end, "they produce only a superficial imitation of the original work" (Belz 1967, 138). That is, these artists end
up mimicking their own previous work in their effort to produce an additional
successful recording. And I think it can also be reasonably demonstrated that
many musical artists with long successful careers have often succumbed to
this inclination to imitate their own previous successes, both in their recordings and in their performances, so much that their later output might border
on becoming a parody of their early work.

In any event, concerns about authenticity, as I have suggested, have consistently surfaced in the study of music, perhaps originating in folk music,
but appearing as well in examinations of rock and roll or pop music, jazz and
blues time and again,[6] and arguably extending to punk (K. Fox 1987), hip-hop
(McLeod 1999), and rap. Yet these concerns have not been limited merely to
music studies. A modest degree of reflection will likely confirm that some
concept of, and concern with, authenticity appears to be deeply rooted in
most, if not all, fields dedicated to the study of culture, underlying or serv-
ing to legitimate (cf. Bendix 1997, 4) many of the projects of anthropology,

ethnology, and folklore studies[7] themselves, insofar as these disciplines appear to be primarily dedicated to the business of "uncovering," understanding, and preserving something "genuine" (cf. Bendix 1997, 4). Indeed, it may even be supposed that these disciplines require the existence of some authenticity for the object of their study, and therefore, for their very raison d'etre.

Meanwhile, still, the question of authenticity has apparently permeated a myriad of other facets and cultural phenomena of industrial society. For example, concerns expressed about music might equally be seen expressed about the proliferation of abstract expressionist-style tableaus that have, for decades now, mimicked the likes of such artists as De Kooning and Pollock, and that certainly appear to continue up to the present day. But perhaps more to the point, concerns about authenticity appear to have peppered numerous aspects of Western civilization from the time of the "pre-Enlightenment" down to the present day. There have been concerns expressed about the authenticity of texts, of scriptures, of relics and their power during the early Christian world (cf. Bendix 1997, 14; Peterson 2005, 1083). People have also been concerned, for obvious reasons, with the authenticity of money since its inception, most ostensibly beginning with weights, and extending to the authenticity of coinage, if we are to put any stock in Adam Smith's reflections about the origins of money in *Wealth of Nations*. In addition, Peterson describes a variety of other deliberate efforts undertaken to promote or "fabricate" a sense of authenticity in his article "In Search of Authenticity." These include such things as forging associations, beginning in the late Renaissance, with wines and the seemingly regal establishments of chateaus in Bordeaux, France, to generate impressions that the wine product possessed a greater, more authentic value through a connection to bygone days (Peterson 2005, 1084). There has also been the increasingly pervasive trend to fabricate travel destinations of all sorts, such as "authentic Ireland." There is the custom of showcasing the founding date of establishments of business to foster some sense of greater authenticity. There is "the invention of traditional Scottish clan tartans by a Quaker Yorkshire coal mine owner" during the nineteenth century. There has been the effort to fabricate history, such as the storming of the Bastille as the characteristic event that earmarks the French Revolution. In like fashion, there are the fabrications of reputations of U.S. presidents and CEO's of corporations, and various ideas of how democracy comes to pass that "were accepted by 19th and 20th century non-Western nation-builders as the model for creating democracy" (Peterson 2005, 1085). There has been the fabrication of narratives about the origins of pop bands specifically tailored to mystify and entice fascination and excitement in order to achieve, or augment, commercial success.[8] Finally, although not explicitly discussed by Peterson, there are the innumerable commercial efforts that have been undertaken to conflate, as much as possible, various commodities with something genuine, as in authentic New England chowder, or genuine Chicago pizza and New York subs.

Philosophical concern with authenticity also seems to have gained notewor-thy traction beginning in the so-called age of Enlightenment, through works such as Jean Jacques Rousseau's *Discourse on the Origin of Inequality*. It may have even attended the arguably related impetus to the burgeoning quest for individuality and freedom that eventually may have facilitated the democ-ratization of certain Western nations, assuming the best about philosophy's efficacy to permeate popular culture. For some thinkers, such as Marshall Berman, for example, "the concern with authenticity [was] the product of the rise of radical individualism" (Peterson 2005, 1094). And there have been multiple treatments of the nature, conceptualization, and concern over authenticity that idiosyncratically relate it to the so-called "modern period" in one sense or another, if not also on occasion to whatever may be deemed to qualify as "modernity," equivocally speaking.[9] For example, "in his famous 1936 essay, [Walter] Benjamin (1969) argued that works of art lost something of their sacred aura in the present industrial era because they can be so eas-ily reproduced. Thus only with the mass reproduction of symbols does the authenticity of an art work emerge as a quality to be prized" (Peterson 2005, 1094).[10] Similarly, Regina Bendrix mentions Lionel Trilling's assertion that "[a]t a certain point in its history, the moral life of Europe added to itself a new element, the state or quality of the self which we call sincerity (1974: 2)." According to Bendix, Trilling held that

> [t]he imperative of sincerity began to "vex men's minds" in the sixteenth century. . .and the most poignant sources are, not surprisingly to be found in theater—the domain that is constructed out of pretense and artifice, and hence "insincerity." Actors' ability to move one to tears or anger rousted suspicions in the audience. Drawing on Goffman, Trilling observes how the fascination with theater led to an awareness of role play in life and to the realization that role play compromises sincerity. (Bendix 1997, 16)

Now it is true that there appears to be plenty of evidence to suggest that concern with authenticity seemed to flourish around the sixteenth and seven-teenth centuries, which is to say, on the eve of the industrial period in Europe. However, with all due respect to Trilling, it does not seem obvious that one of the reasons for this had to do with fascination with theater, rather than, say, treating that fascination as an outgrowth of a greater concern for authentic-ity. Instead, concern with authenticity in general may have grown in tandem with an emerging supposition that there existed a duality between a kind of ontologically posited (if only fabricated) core self, on the one hand, and, on the other hand, a plethora of manners or ways of "appearing" in public life that people increasingly felt pressured to adopt in order to fend for themselves and, as it were, for survival's sake, as the "modern" industrial environment unfolded. Although Jean Jacques Rousseau does not explicitly connect such a duality with "modern" life specifically, however that term is to be understood, and perhaps for obvious reasons he certainly seems to imply in the *Discourse on the Origin of Inequality* that this duality emerges in concert with the emergence of "civilized man," as Berman further notes in connection to Rousseau in *The Politics of Authenticity*. That said, this human downside to modernity certainly seems to be what Rousseau vaguely had in mind when he placed the advent of deception at the cusp of "civilization," broadly construed, while situating its putative antithesis, namely authentic existence, in so-called "savage man." But equally commensurate with Rousseau's coupling of "civilization as such," in contrast to "modernity" proper, with the materialization of human "two-facedness," I think it is plausible to suggest that worries about authenticity, in at least one philosophical sense, may be traceable to certain ethical concerns about morally right ways of being and acting that significantly predated the modern period or "modernity," however that term is likely to be defined. For it seems that moral prescriptions to circumvent tendencies to engage in duplicity, which is to say the business of deliberately intending to appear other than the way one is, either in deed or word, and particularly for personal advancement, political or otherwise, were certainly discussed by, and were arguably a recurring theme for, the likes of philosophers as far back as Plato.[11]

Be that as it may, philosophical treatment of authenticity, whether correctly or not, has frequently identified interest in, and concern for it with some sort of specifically "modern" problem for human existence. Regina Bendix, for example, asserts that:

> [t]he quest for authenticity appears to be a peculiar longing, at once modern and antimodern. It is oriented toward the recovering of an essence whose loss has been realized *only* through modernity, and whose recovery is feasible *only* through methods and sentiments created in modernity ... The continued craving for experiences of unmediated genuineness seeks to cut through what Rousseau called "the wound of reflection," a reaction to modernization's demythologization, detraditionalization, and disenchantment. (Bendix 1997, 8; my italics.)

In fact, Bendix continues, "[f]olklore has long served as a vehicle in the search for the authentic, satisfying a longing for an escape from modernity. The ideal folk community, envisioned as pure and free from civilization's evils, was a metaphor for everything that was not modern" (Bendix 1997, 7), a view that would certainly seem to align with a gloss Peterson offers of the press release, as well as the attending narrative poem by Stephen Benet, about the young Stokes defeating Fiddlin' John Carson. For according to his gloss, "[t]he best music was seen to be carried by a pure youth newly come from a more remote mountain region . . . Clearly the idea of a place uncontaminated by urban-industrial society and peopled by unchanging descendants of Daniel Boone-like old-time folk was lodged firmly in the American imagination" (Peterson 1997, 58). In fact, the view that links concern with authenticity to "modernity" is found frequently echoed in literature on authenticity. One finds it, to offer another instance, in Allan Moore's comment that "the social alienation produced under modernity, which appears to me the ideological root of such striving for the authentic, and of which we have been aware for decades, grows daily more apparent" (Moore 2002, 210), as well as in his attribution to Georgina Boyes that "authenticity" is juxtaposed to "modernity" (Moore 2002, 212). Likewise, Weisethaunet and Lindberg, based on Richard Middleton's "post-structuralist reading of Charles Taylor's *The Ethics of Authenticity*," attribute to Taylor the coupling of key concepts like "expression, authorship, and truth" to "the Enlightenment and the Romantic era" (Weisethaunet and Lindberg 2010, 466–67).

Now regardless of whether this linking of concern for authenticity to "modernity" may be ultimately wrong-headed, traces of a desired flight from "modernity" toward some form of authenticity may be found to persist in and underlie, however uncritically, more recent concerns with authenticity. For traces of that general inclination, along with its attending assumption that some core authenticity actually exists and may be eventually captured or somehow regained, certainly seemed to be present in consideration of what originally qualified as folk songs in the mid- to late-1920s and 1930s, in the quality of the folk revivals starting in the 1950s and into the early 1960s and, perhaps more notably, in the attitude that presumably precipitated the apparent audience outrage with Bob Dylan's so-called "going electric" at the Newport Folk Festival in 1965. Moreover, residual traces of it may also be found embedded in concerns over appropriation of musical styles of various blues performers such as Robert Johnson by the likes of Eric Clapton and other British performers, as I have suggested above. Finally, such traces may even play a role in fostering an ongoing desire for some kind of "unmediated expression"[12] between an imagined "pure" or "original" musical intent and a performer's attempt to express it unfettered by other considerations, such as what might sell or what might align with what an audience believes, so that its "originator (composer, performer) succeeds in conveying the impression that his/her utterance is one of integrity, that it represents an attempt to communicate in an unmediated form with an audience" (Moore 2002, 214).

Be that as it may, perhaps the longing for authenticity is more fundamental to human existence, and not merely specific to a particular culturally and momentarily informed sort of consciousness, such as one that uniquely emerged during a "modern" period, or only within the context of the Western intellectual trajectory. Rather, in line with the methodological spirit of David Hume, perhaps humans, in general, gravitate toward the authentic and shun or avoid inauthenticity, the hypocritical, or the duplicitous. Perhaps, that is, concern over authenticity persists because, as Weisenhaunet and Lindberg suggest (albeit loosely and, untechnically employing the term "existential"), the concept of authenticity "seems to respond to existential needs" (Weisenhaunet and Lindberg 2010, 481). For whether or not they are evolutionarily hardwired to do so, it would seem that humans frequently experience strong emotive responses to inauthenticity, hypocrisy, insincerity, and the like.[13] When conditions are right, they often smile when they are presented with what they believe to be authentic and they tend to grimace when they are confronted with what they belief to be inauthentic or insincere. Taking a page from the corpus of *Plato*, one may even be so bold as to propose that these emotive responses issue from the fact that humans frequently experience a life permeated with the duplicitous actions of others, afforded in part because human thought itself, being symbolic in nature, entails an ontological gap between sign and signified, or appearance and reality, that can be exploited in ways, for example, deception and lying, that often adversely affect their well-being. Indeed, one might suggest that humans, though perhaps neither exclusively nor exhaustively,[14] have struggled against an inevitable current of duplicitous existence from time immemorial and are duplicitous beings for the most part.On the one hand, humans sometimes appear to do things sincerely. On the other hand, they often appear to foster an impression of sincerity for personal gain when they do not actually mean it. And because much disenchantment, disappointment, and grief are often linked to insincerity, along with the kindred discovery that what was believed to be authentic is only mere simulacra, they end up enhancing their yearning for the sorts of things they believe to be authentic or "real," and shunning the things they take to be imitations, counterfeits, or "knock-offs."

Along these lines, one might further propose that the yearning for the real and the disappointment precipitated through confrontation with inauthenticity and deception are connected to something quite fundamental to human existence as such, which Jean Jacques Rousseau implies in his *Discourse on the Origin of Inequality*, namely dependency. When one human becomes dependent on another, according to Rousseau, a split materializes between what that human is and how they attempt to represent themselves to others, a split which is motivated by their need to manipulate the interests of others so that those interests align with their own. In somewhat less sterile and more deprecating terms, Rousseau hints at such a human condition on the cusp of civilization:

[i]t was necessary, for his advantage, to show himself to be something other than what he in fact was. Being something and appearing to be something became two completely different things; and from this distinction there arose grandiose ostentation, deceptive cunning, and all the vices that follow in their wake. On the other hand, although man had previously been free and independent, we find him, so to speak, subject, by virtue of a multitude of fresh needs, to all of nature and particularly to his fellow men, whose slave in a sense he becomes even in becoming their master; rich, he needs their services; poor, he needs their help; and being midway between wealth and poverty does not put him in a position to get along without them. It is therefore necessary for him to seek incessantly to interest them in his fate and to make them find their own profit, in fact or in appearance, in working for his. This makes him two-faced and crooked with some, imperious and harsh with others, and puts him in the position of having to abuse everyone he needs when he cannot make them fear him and does not find it in his interests to be of useful service to them. (Rousseau 1754 [2011], 77)

As a matter of fact, such a two-faced manifesting "split" as this may arguably align, at least to some degree, with various Marxian and Neo-Marxian[15] worries about the sort of alienated or "estranged" existence that Karl Marx appeared to causally attribute to the structure of capitalism as such, if not also to other stages of human social development. Likewise, it may align with what Karl Marx had in mind when he described the sort of reunification with oneself which "pure" communism promised, as articulated in his *1844 Economic and Philosophic Manuscripts*. After all, rhetorically speaking, was not the core idea of Marx's "alienation," as described in the *Manuscripts*, the thought that, under capitalism, one remains somehow "split," detached, or separated from what is, in fact, that which constitutes one's true self or nature, which is to say, one's essence? For Marx it would seem, at least at that juncture of his work, but possibly stemming from Rousseau, capitalism and perhaps most, if not all social organizations that predate it, create a split in the human person, a sort of schizophrenia loosely speaking, between what the human person "is" and what the human person must become under capitalism. It is a split between their essence, nature or being, on the one hand, and what the economic conditions within which they find themselves necessitate them to manifest, on the other hand: a servant to others, and hence, one who, out of necessity, is driven to fabricate an inauthentic or inhuman self that would be of interest and use to others. The business, then, of pure communism, in contrast, is to afford human persons the means to heal or remove this rift between the essence of the self and the way of being that the self has undertaken to be of service to others. It is the condition by which human persons may become "one" once again.[16]

Finally, it seems worthwhile to acknowledge that this theme of recovering some kind of primordial being of the human person, of a return from an artificial state of being to a real or authentic one, was certainly prevalent in various existentially-flavored accounts of the "human condition" that followed. For example, one finds it in Heidegger and Sartre, as expressed in *Being and Time* and *Being and Nothingness* respectively, in addition to subsequent critical works, such as Theodor Adorno's *Jargon of Authenticity* (Bendix 1997, 19; cf. Weisethaunet and Lindberg 2010, 466), all of which certainly helped to further shape elements of the dominant philosophical threads of twentieth century intellectual history as I will further touch on below.

Returning now to music studies specifically, what one means by claiming that music possesses authenticity has by no means been made clear despite much popular or academic discourse dedicated to the subject. Contrasting accounts about authenticity in music over the years have certainly littered academic literature and popular media and have been applied to music in varying contexts with differing connotations by academics and popular music critics alike. To make better sense of these accounts as a whole, at least to some extent, it might be fruitful to begin first by saying that they tend to coalesce into two general categories that mostly align with whether authenticity is approached from an emic (that is, ordinary or "life-world" to borrow an expression from Edmund Husserl) or an etic (that is, reflexive) perspective.

First, congruent with the more emic perspective, an account may be an "objective" or "essentialist" treatment that characterizes authenticity as some kind of property inherent in the music itself and, accordingly, something to be sought, found, and verified within it (cf. Taylor 1997, 21; Moore 2002, 209; Weisethaunet and Lindberg 2010, 466). Here, authenticity is some sort of objective property of authentic entities which, perhaps, depends for its existence on a specified relation those entities bear to their origins. In this camp belong Mol and Wijnberg, who appear to adopt an objectivist approach when they suggest that "[t]he most straightforward definition of 'authentic' is that something is genuinely what it seems to be or the producer has truly made what is ascribed to him/her; the most abstract is that the product and producer are as close to possible to the essence of the particular category to which they belong" (Mol and Wijnberg 2007, 704). Likewise, Allan Moore references the objectivist approach when he asserts, albeit opaquely:

[i]n rock discourse, the term [authentic] has frequently been used to define a *style* of writing or performing, particularly anything associated with the practices of the singer/songwriter, where attributes of intimacy (just Joni Mitchell and her zither) . . . and immediacy (in the sense of unmediated forms of sound production) tend to connote authenticity. It is used in a socio-economic sense, to refer to the social standing of the musician. It is used to determine the supposed reasons she has for working, whether her primary felt responsibility is to herself, her art, her public, or her bank balance. It is used to bestow integrity,

or its lack, on a performer, such that an "authentic" performer exhibits realism,
lack of pretence, or the like. (Moore 2002, 211)

Perhaps less opaquely, the notion of an "inauthentic authenticity" or "fabricated authenticity," insofar as it posits a dichotomy between the true and the
fake or artificial, likewise appears to operate within a presupposed objective,
or essentialist, framework (cf. Weisethaunet and Lindberg 2010, 473). In
fact, I think it is fair to say that such an objectivist conception of authenticity frequently co-implicates the instantiation of "the fake, spurious, and even
illegitimate" (Bendix 1997, 9), where the attribution of "authenticity" to
things thereby "elevates" them "into the category of the noteworthy" (Bendix
1997, 7), while discursively denigrating the latter, often the mere "copy," as
ordinary discourse implies.

   Now it seems reasonable to me to also suppose that it is precisely this
sort of "objective" construal of authenticity that precipitated the formation
of various cultural studies fields in the first place, insofar as they appeared
to presuppose the objective existence or some original to be recovered. For
those fields, at least in terms of their inception, appeared to be on a quest to
find some kind of "authentic" original as I suggested above. In addition, it
would seem to be this sense of authenticity that continues to underlie concerns about authenticity, as well as the longing for it. When people appear to
long for the original or authentic, they seem to be longing for something they
believe to be an objective property of things. Likewise, theories that malign
the effects of mass media on musical production as yielding "knock-offs," as
opposed to delivering the "real" thing, appear to presuppose this objectivist
treatment of authenticity. Furthermore, old school charges against performers for "selling out," for not being, or keeping it "real," seem to assume such
a theoretical framework, as do accounts that imply a distinction between a
real artist, or rock-and-roll star, as opposed to a "poser" (cf. Weisethaunet
and Lindberg 2010, 471, 475).[17] Similarly does this appear to be the case
with regard to concerns over the "truthfulness" of a performance or a performer, or, as Weisethaunet and Lindberg refer to it, "authenticity as self-
expression" wherein "truth is conceived in terms of the degree to which a
representation is taken to offer access to the inner world of an exceptional
subject" (Weisethaunet and Lindberg 2010, 471). Moreover, it seems reasonable to subsume into the objectivist category of authenticity the numerous
analyses and charges that suggest that something is inauthentic because it is
the result of ethnic appropriation, blanching, and the like, or those analyti-
cal approaches that serve to "essentialize" "categories like 'black music' or
'white music'" (Weisethaunet and Lindberg 2010, 480), or for that matter
"folk." Accordingly, theories that strive to attribute authenticity to a particular musical style, musical composition or performance appear to make such

objectivist assumptions about the conditions of that authenticity's existence. Finally, theories that ascribe authenticity to a work of art on the grounds that it possesses "originality" or "creativity" appear to assume that objective existence pertains to that originality and authenticity.

In contrast to and more recent than the foregoing emic and "objectivist" group, instances of the etic or reflexive group construe authenticity subjectively as something that is not inherent in but rather ascribed to things, typically through various subjective acts of consciousness.[18] To offer an example of such an approach, consider Moore, who asserts:

> I start . . . from an assumption that authenticity does not inhere in any combination of musical sounds. "Authenticity" is a matter of interpretation which is made and fought for within a cultural and, thus, historicized position. It is ascribed, not inscribed. As Sarah Rubidge has it: "authenticity" is . . . not a property *of*, but something we ascribe *to* a performance" (Rubidge, 1996, p. 219). Whether a performance is authentic, then, depends on who "we" are. (Moore 2002, 210)

Indeed, according to Moore, authenticity is "a construction made on the act of listening" (Moore 2002, 210). Likewise, Richard Peterson's account may also be identified as a member of this etic group insofar as he conceives authenticity as a "social construction." For Peterson "[a]uthenticity, like 'creativity' . . . and 'entrepreneurship' . . . does not inhere in the object, person, or performance said to be authentic . . . Rather, authenticity is a claim that is made by or for someone, thing, or performance and either accepted or rejected by relevant others" (Peterson 2005, 1086), which is to say, variously empowered authenticators (Peterson 2005). Reminiscent of Hirsch's earlier research of the popular music industry during the 1960s (Hirsch 1963), Peterson elaborates how this conception of authenticity plays out in the production of country music:

> no one person or group authenticates country music. Rather there is a cycle of authentication involving everyone active in the field . . . performers and songwriters offer their best efforts at producing what they think country music to be. A few performers and songs are selected by the record companies with an eye to authenticity . . . Any given song has to run a twisting gauntlet of a decision chain . . . Decisions are made ostensibly to fan tastes, but in practice they are made largely to satisfy the expectations of the next gatekeeper in the decision chain. (Peterson 2005, 1091)

In other words, for Peterson, authenticity as it pertains to music is ultimately a social construction that emerges in the context of marketing musical products, where things come to be deemed authentic by way of the experiences and mutual affirmations of producers, consumers, and critics.

Further down this subjective path of construing authenticity as a product of individual or collective consciousness, there has not even been consensus about whether concerns about authenticity are even warranted, let alone intellectually justifiable. Some persons have believed, as Moore quotes Born and Hesmondhalgh, that the very concept of authenticity "has been consigned to the intellectual dust-heap" (Moore 2002, 210), while others have questioned whether it has any epistemological usefulness in gaining insight into the nature or value of specific forms of music. Regina Bendix, for one, even hoped that her work, *In Search of Authenticity: The Formation of Folklore Studies*, might succeed in "removing authenticity—in particular, its deceptive promises of transcendence from the vocabulary of the emerging global script" (Bendix 1997, 7, 9; cf. Titon 2012, 229). More ominous, it would seem, Bendix has highlighted how the very idea of authenticity, in the sense of the original or the "pure," has sometimes been historically employed to provide disturbing traction for nationalistic movements.[19]

It is probably worth acknowledging that the emergence of all of this subjective treatment of authenticity, this "subjective turn" in the various strategies adopted for the ontological appraisal of authenticity, likely occurred in tandem with a flourishing rejection of the supposed existence of an ontological unified "subject" that occurred during the latter half of the twentieth century, thanks principally to the post-structural efforts of thinkers such as Michel Foucault and Jacques Derrida.[20] Whether such a suggestion is completely accurate, it would seem nonetheless plausible to argue that these subjectivist accounts tend to be more recent and more academically produced, appear to be commensurate with the general trend that occurred during the latter half of the last century in the fields of humanities and related intellectual circles of reducing much to subjectivism, constructivism, and the relativity of reality, and are typically lumped together with various contemporaneous post-structuralist flavored reasonings inspired by Foucault and Derrida.[21]

Be that as it may, whether or not some version of a "subjectivist" account of authenticity is correct, it seems pretty clear that the sort of subjectivity these accounts ascribed to authenticity only presents itself through a reflexive analysis. It is not, in other words, the sort of reality that authenticity is typically perceived to possess from a pre-reflective, or "life-world" perspective. For by being construed to pop into existence through some kind of social construction, or some patchwork of individual-specific acts of consciousness, authenticity is thereby conceived to be, in actuality, merely imaginary or illusory, and not in fact part of the objective furniture of the world. But a personally or socially constructed, subjective and illusory authenticity, which is revealed only through a reflexive analysis, is certainly not the sort that appears to be what one desires or seeks when one desires or seeks the so-called "authentic"; that is not the sort of authenticity that is taken to be the object which people appear to yearn or long for when they yearn or long for the authentic or real. Rather, they long for an authenticity that they perceive, imagine, or assume is objective.[22] In other words, whether or not authenticity is merely *ascribed* to things or to people and does not actually inhere in so-called "authentic" things, people still long for "the real deal." Likewise, they seek the artist who is "being real," or actually "being themselves," not a "being themselves" that they project onto the artist. They do not long for a thing that they might understand to be a product of their own consciousness, their own culture, and the like. And so, despite the plethora and plausibility of the subjective treatments that have emerged, and regardless of the intellectual popularity they have enjoyed within certain circles, it is not surprising that these theories have not, to date, managed to gain traction in altering the ordinary discourse that people use, or the popular criticism that continues to be drafted, when talk of the original, the real, or the authentic is undertaken, nor have these theories done much to ostensibly curb, diminish, or substantially alter any longing for the real in ordinary life. For certainly much evidence of it continues to persist down to the present day.

In any event, how might all this talk about authenticity matter to social protest music? Authenticity, it would seem, stands in a somewhat unique position in relation to social protest music, unlike most other musical genres, with the exception, perhaps, of cases like folk music. For authenticity is important to social protest music because it is essential to it being social protest music; authenticity, that is, must be possessed by music in order that it function as protest. The reason for this, I maintain, is because social protest itself, in whatever form it takes, cannot survive the loss of all authenticity. Social protest cannot be inauthentic through and through and still be social protest; it cannot survive being imitated, counterfeited, feigned, or faked. And if this is the case for social protest, then it would seem to be true that social protest music cannot survive the loss of authenticity. It cannot survive mimicry.

Perhaps this is, in the end, what troubled Pete Seeger like others, when the Weavers went fully Pop (cf. Jarnow 2018, 178–79), and which may have ultimately contributed to his departure from the group. Meanwhile, as far as it concerns the roots of rock and roll, rock and roll itself, and whatever else followed in terms of the folk revival and folk rock, it seems reasonable to claim there were instances when these genres imitated a social protest quality because it was attractive to a commercially consuming audience to do so and thus had the prospect of generating profit. At other times, it seems plausible to insist that were instances when the music served as an authentic dissent toward the norms and status quo of society, or specific governmental policies and projects, such as the Vietnam War. The question one might ask, accordingly, is how are we to distinguish the instances that were merely imitative from those instances that were "genuine"?

At first glance, the difference between something that is an imitation and something that is genuine or original would seem to be a relatively straight-forward conceptual matter, especially when one briefly reflects on the difference typically supposed to exist between a genuine pair of *Nike* shoes or *Ray-Bans*, and some "knockoff" typically available in various corners of the world. However, the distinction can quickly become quite murky, conceptually speaking, through the slightest degree of reflection. Consider, as one case, this difference in relation to the sort of practice sometimes engaged in by certain visual artists, who on occasion, have imitated the "style" of other visual artists by quoting it in their own works, in contrast, say, to quoting the "content" of a particular work, as when Edouard Manet appeared to have quoted some of the content of Titian's *Venus de Urbino* in *Olympia* (Clark 1985). Let us imagine, for example, that Henri Matisse created a variety of artworks over the course of his earlier years from which, collectively, a general "style" of that work may be identified. Furthermore, let us suppose that once that style was established, more or less, other artists may have attempted to "quoted" it in their own works on occasion, although the actual content they may have presented in that style could have varied from any actual work of Matisse, assuming a reasonable distinction can be maintained between style and content. One might suppose, for example, that Pablo Picasso may have quoted Matisse in some of his works, and, by extension, Matisse may have quoted Picasso on occasion. Similarly, one might suppose this could have been true in relation to Marcel Duchamp and Picasso, say, or Paul Gauguin and Vincent Van Gogh to some degree, and so on.

Now even though quotes of this sort might be correctly identified as cases of imitation of one form or another, it seems reasonable to assume that they are not, at least ostensibly, clear cases of forgery or counterfeit, in the sense, perhaps, that was charged in the infamous case of the forgeries created by Henricus Antonius ("Han") van Meegeren of various works by Johannes Vermeer during the 1920s and 1930s. That said, they seem to be clear forms of imitation nonetheless, at least to the extent that they are not the original thing itself, but rather some kind of "copy" of the real thing and intended as such.

However, to further muddy the conceptual waters, let us consider whether it is ever possible for an artist to imitate their own style and, if so, to what extent those imitations might be able to qualify as cases of forgery or counterfeit.[23] First, it seems reasonable to speculate that it was possible for Matisse to have imitated a Matisse painting in one of his paintings, even if, in fact, the imitated painting was never something the original of which Matisse ever painted. That is, it seems possible to imagine that Matisse, himself, could have "quoted" his own style, in much the same respect as Picasso might do. Meanwhile, it also seems possible, I propose, that Matisse could have imitated or mimicked his own style on occasion simply to produce additional revenue, given the outstanding public interest in his work and the commercial success it enjoyed. In these cases, however, I would suggest that Matisse would not be quoting Matisse in quite the same sense that either Picasso or Matisse might be said to quote Matisse as I described above. Instead, I suggest that Matisse would be engaged in a project similar to "forging" a Matisse. Imagine, for example, that Matisse produced some simple lithographs involving a line or two depicting a partial representation of a person's head. One line might serve as the contour of a forehead, cheek, and jawbone. Another line might be quickly added to represent the point where a neck intersects with the contour of the face. Still another few lines might serve to indicate the presence of lips, an eye, and an eyebrow. In two minutes or less, say, voila—one would have an image in the style of Matisse. Once signed, these lithograph copies, depending on the market, might then sell for thousands of dollars each. Similarly, it does not seem much of a stretch to suppose that Picasso could have engaged in like efforts, say on certain pieces of pottery produced at his studio in Vallauris, France, given a mere splash of colored glaze here, and another splash there, on the interior of a bowl perhaps. Indeed, the practice is equally imaginable in relation to any number of quick sketches by Salvador Dali, Marc Chagall, or other notable visual artists.

Of course, I do not wish to imply that Matisse, Picasso, Dali, or Chagall would ever engage in such mimicry or forgery of their own work merely for profit. However, despite whether such speculation about Matisse, Picasso, et al., is merely some kind of dull philosophical fancy, still it seems plausible to me to suppose that an artist, such as Matisse, could imitate or mimic her or his own style on occasion, and that this mimicry could rise to the level of being wholly inauthentic in the sense of counting as a sort of forgery. Granting that possibility, the question one might then entertain is what the difference could be between such mimicry *cum* forgery and any "original."

To answer this question, it may be helpful to take a page from Robert Elliot's work on "faking nature" (Elliot 1987) and suggest that the relevant difference is to be found, not within the very substance or materiality of the respective works, the constitutive elements of their "visuality" as it were, but rather beyond that materiality, namely in their etiological differences. To elaborate, the difference between an original "Matisse" and an imitation of a "Matisse" by Matisse, one which rises to the level of a sort of forgery, may be locatable in the nature of the intention that prompted the creation of the artworks in the two cases. In the one case, that purpose, superficially stated to be sure, may have been to create the artwork for its own sake, let us say, because there was some core, artistic urge of some sort to create the artwork, such as was presumably the case of various draft sketches Matisse made in advance of his stain glass windows in the *Chapelle du Rosaire de Vence* in Vence, France. In the case of mimicry, in contrast, other considerations may have yielded the "Matisse." Imagine, for example, Matisse producing a quick sketch of a child's face on a napkin as a gift to a restaurant owner, say of *La Colombe d'Or* in St. Paul de Vence in return for a good meal. In this latter case, one can plausibly imagine, what could have prompted the artwork may have had little to do with producing any artwork for its own sake; instead, one can imagine that the so-called "artwork" was motivated by some other reason, such as casually repaying the gift of a good meal with something of greater value on the open market, and from which the owner might someday be able to financially benefit.

Assuming there is some conceptual plausibility to drawing a distinction between the authentic and the inauthentic, an original and an imitation in the sense of a counterfeit, in this way, how it might it be applied to how, when, and to what degree rock and roll, folk-rock, or folk could qualify as social protest music? With regard to a given recording or live performance, one might suggest that there could be respects in which it qualified as an authentic form of social protest music, and there could be respects in which it qualified as a case of mere mimicry or fakery of social protest music, a forgery or counterfeit of such, where whether these respects were genuine or counterfeit depended on the intentions that attended their manifestation. In fact, one of the advantages of this view is that it accounts not only for how whole performances could qualify as either original or fake instances of social protest, but also for the possibility that a given musical work might contain a mixture of both genuine and fake elements. For given that the nature of music requires that its coming to be in any form occurs over time, and that the intentions of persons, and in this case musical artists, can fluctuate from moment to moment as various actions are elicited, it is possible to think of a particular musical work, in its entirety, as actually being composed of a battery of elements, each aligned with a specific intention. Accordingly, rather than following from a singular, unified intention, the work as a whole may be understood as following from a bundle of intentions, some of which may be responsible for genuine dimensions of the work, and some for features of the work that are merely imitative. During a given live or recorded performance, for example, it is not too difficult to imagine that, at one moment, the mouthing of specific lyrics and the corresponding plucking of strings are motivated by a desire for commercial profit, and a minute or even a second later, if not during another performance entirely, the mouthing of the same words and the plucking of the same strings may be motivated by some feeling or intention that one might reasonably associate with being authentic in relation to the kind of music being produced.[24] At least, based on testimony, it certainly seems plausible that witnesses of performances experience such a difference on occasion. Likewise, the same could be true in the process of producing studio numbers for commercial release. Some elements present in the final product are the result of one kind of intention. Some are due to another kind of intention.

As a matter of fact, it may be realistic to extend this distinction to many human behaviors that materialize during the course of everyday human life, be it in the home, at the office, or, say during a eulogy delivered by a pastor or a funeral director. It is not too difficult to believe, for example, that pastors and funeral directors, on occasion, deliver eulogies without knowing much of anything about the persons for whom they deliver the eulogies. In such cases, perhaps, a pastor or funeral director might speak sincerely about the loved one. At other moments, the eulogizer might mouth prepared words while thinking about the time needed to prepare the venue for the next customer. In cases such as these, the words mouthed in real time might not be anything "meant" at all; in fact, the speaker might not even be cognizant of mouthing them. Here, they are merely imitating or faking sincerity.

In any event, within the advanced industrial society of the contemporary world, the apparent tendency of human beings to yearn for something real, genuine, original or authentic, has certainly not been overlooked by commercial endeavors. In fact, these enterprises have actively sought to tap into that yearning at every opportunity that is likely to excrete some profit, like everything else. It may even be said that the entire commercial environment has been so perforated with instances where products are touted as "the real thing" that *Coke* was once motivated to implement a promotional campaign centered on the mere use of a variant of that expression.

Meanwhile, the yearning for the "real" has also often been leveraged to consolidate power of one form or another. It has, of course, been a staple strategy of strictly political undertakings, such as fostering support from various constituencies, as well as commercial dealings and the various confluences of the two. After all, was it not a charge of the absence of "being real" or "authentic," of somehow being deceitful, that unnerved the public when it came to the 1960 congressional payola proceedings? For it appeared, at least to some degree, that segments of the public became disappointed with disc jockeys when they learned that some had presumably elected to play songs, not because they believed the music was great, but, instead, because they were paid to do so. These segments, it seems, were disappointed with news that the disc jockeys may have not been "real" with their audiences, that they had been "inauthentic" or deceitful, that they had "duped" the public about their actual beliefs and intentions. In many cases, in fact, although certainly not exhaustively speaking, the whole reason for engaging in imitation in the first place is in order to substitute something that is not "real," "original," or "authentic" for something that is and to have people conflate or confuse the former with the latter because people are fundamentally attracted to the latter rather than the former, and something can be gained by fostering that conflation or confusion. Put in simpler words, one primary reason for imitation, at least in most cases, is to gain something through deception.

It is also true that the human longing for the real, genuine, or authentic, and the leveraging of it for gain, have been particularly salient characteristics of the way of life for many Americans. Throughout their history, Americans have yearned for authenticity, and yet they are, time and again, seduced by the duplicitous use of that yearning. The largely inescapable business and commercial world into which they mature, and within which they must find a way to manage their lives, continually practices a business plan that involves a bait and switch. The bait is a promise of something authentic, something sincere. When the switch is made, it involves the delivery of something less than the real thing because making such a substitution is profitable under the circumstances.

Certainly, this major characteristic of advanced industrial American culture has significantly influenced the trajectory of rock and roll, and its status as protest music, just as it has for a myriad of other commercial products down to the present day, with little to no exception, and with no obvious end in sight. For, certainly, rock and roll was no less exempt from the pressures of this prevailing cultural environment than any number of other artifacts. Even though, in fact, part of the essence of the counterculture of the 1960s, together with its soundtrack, may have involved an effort to push-back against such a duplicitous manner of being, in the hopes, perhaps, of regaining some assumed bedrock quality of what the human being actually was or should be, like many elements of the cultures that proceeded it or followed in its wake, it also quickly succumbed precisely to the thing it was protesting or resisting, as the San Francisco Diggers tried to exemplify through their "Death of the Hippie" gig. In much the same sense, as Michael Lydon asserted in "Rock for Sale," "[r]ock, rather than being an example of how freedom can be achieved within the capitalist structure, is an example of how capitalism can, almost without a conscious effort, deceive those whom it oppresses" (Conroy 1986, 128). Likewise, as Doors manager, Bill Siddons once expressed, "[i]t's funny, the group out there on stage preaching a revolutionary message, but to get the message to the people, you got to do it the establishment way" (M. Lydon 1969, 318), or as Stephen Conroy further inferred, "groups or stars become part of the big commercial show business and lose whatever commitment to rebellion they once hand" (Conroy 1986, 128).

As a matter of fact, Stephen Conroy describes the pattern to which the fascination with rock and roll and the previous fascination with hotrods both appeared to conform. As Conroy characterizes it:

a new rebellious movement, a fierce opposition to it by the establishment, an overwhelming of the opposition by the growing popularity of the movement [*sic*], a seizing of the movement by the commercial interests, and the inevitable loss of the rebellion's content as the movement is institutionalized and made part of the dominant culture (Conroy 1986, 128).

Here, what was once authentic and real is inevitably replaced with something which is mere simulacrum, precisely because the former possessed an attractive authenticity and its confusion with the latter is far more profitable. That being the case, as Conroy adds, "[a] Dodge Charger is [still] not a 'chopper,' and the Monkees are not the Rolling Stones" (Conroy 1986, 132; my emphasis in brackets).

NOTES

1. In reference to Roy Acuff, Bill Malone also specifically notes that listening to "hillbilly" records was one of Acuff's influences (Malone 1968, 201).

2. Peterson further notes that a common motif of the time of a fiddling contest occurring between a brash youth and the devil, which was also appealed to in the Benet poem, may "be heard in the Charlie Daniels Band's 'Devil Went Down to Georgia'" (Peterson 1997, 247, note 4).

3. As Monson notes this tendency, "[i]n 1966, when *Urban Blues* was written, Keil might have attributed such a response to sanitization: 'Almost any Negro in the presence of a white or black bourgeois interviewer or social worker can recite a stream of conventional American values and beliefs without a hit, halt, or second thought. Yet it is also true that these are rarely the cultural guidelines by which the person reciting them lives' [footnote 80: Kiel, *Urban Blues*, 12]. Family-oriented values expressed by jazz musicians historically have been dismissed as being a protective cover hiding the 'true,' 'unassimilated' African American male" (Monson 1995, 418).

4. Ingrid Monson, for example, claims that "Amiri Baraka devoted an entire chapter of *Blues People* to criticizing the black middle class for what he claimed was its desire to erase blackness through the emulation of mainstream white culture" (Monson 1995, 416).

5. Incidentally, Linden appeals to Max Horkheimer's distinction between authentic and mass or commercial culture, where authentic from subordinate classes is assimilated, repackaged, and marketed by dominant culture (Linden 2012, 49), although Linden prefers the terminology of "subsumption" to "blanching" and "assimilation" (Linden 2012, 60).

6. For example, Peterson suggests, "[b]efore the Second World War, liberal critics and intellectuals asserted that only blacks could play jazz properly . . . and by the 1960s those in the black pride/black power movement said that only blacks had the right to play jazz. . . . However as Grazian (2003) shows in the case of blues music, questions of the right and ability are still hotly contested, and tourists at the turn of

the millennium generally believe that blues must be played by African Americans to be authentic" (Peterson 2005, 1094).

7. Regina Bendix asserts that "the idea of authenticity pervades the central terms and the canon of the field [of folklore]. It has contributed a vocabulary that . . . has been of amazing durability despite changing theoretical paradigms. The authenticating claim through its subject matter was also a means through which folklorists have staked institutional claims" (Bendix 1997, 8).

8. In particular, Peterson points to the narrative provided on the website of N'SYNC, a band that, he asserts, actually resulted from "a casting call by a professional manager associated with the Walt Disney Company." According to the website narrative, in contrast, "[i]n 1996, five guys got together, formed a band made an album, and changed the world all in one shot. That's the basic story behind the quintet known as 'N SYNC. Five talented young men from across the country, joined together in Orlando and created one of the most successful groups in music history" (Peterson 2005, 1085).

9. For the sake of avoiding confusion, it probably should be mentioned that the term "modernity" is often used in equivocal senses by various academics presumably due to their diverse disciplinary backgrounds. For some, it may refer to the rise of individualism and so-called "Enlightenment" science, say beginning around the late 1500s CE to about 1850 CE. For others, it might refer more proximately to industrialization and the establishment of mass media, and even to something that applies exclusively to the twentieth century. In a number of cases, unless it is otherwise specifically defined, it is unclear to what the term actually refers. Because of this ambiguity, the referent of the term "post-modern," and sometimes "post-structuralist," are also sometimes implicated.

10. By "authenticity," which he suggests might be subsumed under "aura," Benjamin means "the essence of all that is transmissible from its [the art work's] beginning, ranging from its substantive duration to its testimony to the history which it has experienced" (Benjamin 1936 [2019], 228), which is to say, perhaps more concretely, "the domain of tradition," or more precisely "its presence in time and space, its unique existence at the place where it happens to be," which determines "the history to which it was subject throughout the time of its existence. This includes the changes which it may have suffered in physical condition over the years as well as the various changes in its ownership" (Benjamin 1936 [2019], 227). As Benjamin further explains, "[o]ne might generalize by saying: the technique of reproduction detaches the reproduced object from the domain of tradition. By making many reproductions it substitutes a plurality of copies for a unique existence. And in permitting the reproduction to meet the beholder or listener in his own particular situation, it reactivates the object reproduced. These two processes lead to a tremendous shattering of tradition" (Benjamin 1936 [2019], 228).

11. In like manner, and in reference to Bendix's paraphrase of Tilling's position above, it certainly seems plausible to suppose that the concern over authenticity that Tilling specifically links to sixteenth-century theater productions could equally extend to ancient Greek audiences enjoying *Oedipus Rex* at Epidaurus. Was there, after all, not a lot of two-facedness going on therein, I wonder.

12. Building on Timothy Dean Taylor's "authenticity as primality" argument, presented in *Global Pop: World Musics, World Markets* "wherein an expression is perceived to be authentic if it can be traced to an initiatory instance," Allan Moore characterizes the "unmediated expression" as one "perceived to be authentic because it is unmediated—because the distance between its (mental) origin and its (physical) manifestation is willfully compressed to nil by those with a motive for so perceiving it" (Moore 2002, 213).

13. And so, as Bendix asserts, "[t]he search for authenticity is fundamentally an emotional and moral question" (Bendix 1997, 7).

14. That is, duplicity may not be a uniquely human trait or a trait that must be possessed by all humans. Instead, it may be argued by some, depending on the epistemological assumptions they might hold, that members of other species sometimes attempt to lie or deceive, and there may be rare cases where a given human is never duplicitous.

15. What I have in mind in this context are those worries of Marxists or Neo-Marxists that are specifically traceable to the thought of Karl Marx, and not necessarily to thinkers who might have vaguely or indirectly followed in his footsteps broadly construed.

16. According to Marx in the *1844 Manuscripts*, it is only through the transcendence of private property, which is to say "capital" or "profit," a transcendence which entails "pure" communism, that this "split" can be overcome. As Marx expresses it: "Communism as the *positive* transcendence of *private property* as *human self-estrangement*, and therefore as the real *appropriation* of the *human* essence by and for man; communism therefore as the complete return of man to himself as a *social* (i.e., human) being—a return accomplished consciously and embracing the entire wealth of previous development [*sic*]. This communism, as fully developed naturalism, equals humanism, and as fully developed humanism equals naturalism; it is the *genuine* resolution of the conflict between man and nature and between man and man—the true resolution of the strife between existence [the condition of dependence among humans under capitalism] and essence [the true nature of humans], between objectification and self-confirmation, between freedom and necessity, between the individual and the species. Communism is the riddle of history solved, and it knows itself to be this solution" (Marx 1844 [1959], Third Manuscript). My clarification in brackets.

17. Weisethaunet and Lindberg, for example, imply this distinction when they reference Simon Frith's assertion that "Keith Richards is 'only' a rock and roll star (the only rock and roll star?) but it is a life, not a pose." Richards, that is, "is taken to be 'authentic' because he *is* the rock-and-roll star that we see on stage" (Weisethaunet and Lindberg 2010, 475).

18. As a further example of this bifurcation of treatments of authenticity into objectivist and subjectivist groupings, consider Weisethaunet and Lindberg when they characterize Johan Fornas's position as following "the practice of those (academic) writers, to whom 'authenticity' is a quality *ascribed* to representations, whereas to most others it is taken literally, as an essence *inherent in* the object" (Weisethaunet and Lindberg 2010, 466).

19. As Bendix expresses it: "[t]he most powerful modern political movement, nationalism, builds on the essentialist notions inherent in authenticity, and folklore in the guise of native cultural discovery and rediscovery has continually served nationalist movements since the Romantic era" (Bendix 1997, 7).

20. As Jeff Todd Titon puts it, by the end of the twentieth century, "influential studies in critical theory denied the possibility of an authentic essential, inner self. Identity, it was argued, was multiple, contextual, and constructed by ideologies" (Titon 2012, 229). To offer a little further flavor of this trend, consider also Weisethaunet and Lindberg's comment that "[i]n literary theory, authorship—in particular, the value of authorial and biographical interpretations of literary works—has been under debate for a great deal of the 20th century. This development has complicated notions of authorship, but far from severed the strong ties between work and author—not even for Foucault . . . , to whom the author is certainly an ideological projection but, as a *name*, marks a presence that fulfils a significant function in discourse: one becomes an author by force of the works that bear one's signature" (Weisethaunet and Lindberg 2010, 468).

21. Accordingly, it might be conceptually surprising to discover the meager degree to which such a "subjective turn" has sometimes been appealed to in assessments of "authentic" folk music, since one criterion historically peddled for determining the authenticity of folk music was that its etiology must involve anonymity, that is, the very absence of an identifiable, perhaps unified, "self" from which the music is presumed to emanate. Indeed, as Regina Bendix comments about folklore generally: "[f]olklorists, in a peculiar reversal, for a long time located authenticity within the anonymity of entire social groups, or the 'folk.' Lack of identifiable authorship, multiple existence over time and space, variation of the items, and the social and economic circumstances of the 'bearers of tradition' served, instead, as ways of testing folklore's authenticity" (Bendix 1997, 15).

22. This putatively dual characteristic of authenticity, being subjective ontologically speaking while nevertheless objectively intended, might what Moore hopes to reference when he quotes Michael Pickering saying "'authenticity' is a relative concept which is generally used in absolutist terms" (Moore 2002, 210).

23. Recall, for example, that certain musicians may have attempted some such thing when they tried to re-create the success they experienced from earlier releases of recorded material in their careers.

24. For example, according to Bill Malone, country songwriter, Fred Rose, once remarked that "he never truly understood the real meaning of country music until he stood backstage one night at the Grand Ole Opry and watched Roy Acuff, with tears streaming from his eyes, sing a tragic song about a dying child, 'Don't Make Me Go to Bed, and I'll Be Good'" (Malone 1968, 207). On this occasion, I venture to speculate that Roy's intentions at that moment may have involved something other than merely putting on a show to make a buck.

Chapter 8

Conclusion

I began the foregoing on the assumption that the efficacy of social protest music is dependent on the degree of its exposure to the public. With limited exposure, a social protest song may well exist, but its social efficacy will remain limited because the breadth of awareness of its substance, be it discursive or nondiscursive, will also remain limited. Based on this assumption, I then proceeded to explore how exposure of music to the public has, at least during the last couple of centuries or so, depended on a wider commercial infrastructure that worked to vet, produce, and disseminate music for profit. This exploration involved considering who and what had a role in controlling the means of music exposure to the wider public, from composers, musicians, bandleaders and theater managers to music publishers, professional societies, record producers, promoters, distributors, broadcasters, radio programmers, government agencies, and others seeking to make a profit from its exposure at any specific point in time.

That such constituencies with vested interests in music exposure influenced what music was ultimately heard by the public has certainly been well-documented for some time. At least as music exposure is considered in relation to making a profit from it, consider, for example, the following excerpt from a memorandum that was sent from the Trade Practices Board to the Federal Trade Commission (FTC) in June of 1937 regarding an application that had been submitted by the Music Publishers' Protective Association (MPPA) to institute trade rules to govern illegal means of promoting exposure:

> [t]he products of the [popular music] industry consist of popular songs, orchestrations and musical compositions. To induce members of the public to buy it is necessary to afford them the means of hearing the tune of the musical composition, for it is only when they are attracted by the tune that they are induced to buy. Thus in promoting the sale of their products *the members' of the industry constantly strive* to have their songs and musical compositions accepted by those providing public entertainment and played or performed over the radio,

in theaters or by orchestras or singers in hotels, restaurants, and other place of public amusement. (Coase 1979, 282; my italics)[1]

Indeed, an appreciation of the connection between the exposure of music to the wider public and the influence of the interlocking constituencies that comprise the music industry has been repeatedly characterized in varying ways. For example, Richard Peterson and David Berger, among others, have made reference to this connection when they claimed that from about 1750 to the early 1970s, there existed a "close association between the nature of the [music] industry and the message contained in lyrics" (Peterson and Berger 1972, 282–83) and, therefore, that one should be hesitant to assume that changes in the lyrics of popular music, particularly those that occurred between 1948 and 1968, are solely due to a widespread change in consciousness. As Peterson and Berger less obtusely articulated the point:

> [m]ost explanations of this difference [in lyrics] are rooted in the assumption that there has been a rapid change in public consciousness, but this is, at best, a partial explanation. It does not take into the account either the long-term trends in popular music or the ways it has been influenced by changes in the technology of disseminating popular culture, the music industry structure, and the market of popular songs. (Peterson and Berger 1972, 282)

Furthermore, this connection between music exposure and particular moving parts of the music industry is also found referenced in the work of Denisoff and Levine, who, though bifurcating the influence of the record producers from the broadcasters, noted that "[w]hether the public 'hears' a record is determined greatly by the cultural gatekeepers over whom the [record] industry has little control" (Denisoff and Levine 1972a, 243). Moreover, the seemingly insurmountable control the music industry consistently appeared to wield over any public dissemination of music was often on the minds of various musicians themselves. This was arguably true, for example, of those artists who had a passion for launching programs to unleash the efficacy of social protest music, such as Pete Seeger and his associates. For it was precisely because of the nature of the relationship of the music industry to music exposure that Seeger and others presumably established People's Songs in the first place. In his own words, Seeger asserted, "[t]he important thing about People's Songs is: we have set up a new technique and organization for getting people's songs spread, and circumventing the music monopoly of Broadway and Hollywood" (Seeger 1946, 88).

My specific interest in focusing on the conditions and circumstances that influenced music exposure, particularly in the United States, was informed by a few factors. First, unlike most other genres of music, I assumed that social protest music, because of its nature, could not survive being feigned, imitated, simulated or counterfeited. For to feign, imitate or counterfeit it was, in essence, to strip it of any social protest quality it might otherwise possess. This, it seemed to me, was because social protest, whatever else it might be, principally consisted of a resistance to servitude, and resistance to servitude, I assumed, could not remain resistance when it was merely imitated, simulated, "inauthentic," or feigned. Second, I surmised that whatever music managed to enter the public consciousness to any great extent could only do so provided it traveled through the music industry labyrinth, understood to include the technological machinery operative when it did, and that, in so doing, it had to conform to the pressures and interests of that labyrinth, where these pressures and interests were primarily informed by an intent to produce profit above all else. Accordingly, I came to believe that any social protest song that was fortunate enough to enjoy widespread dissemination must have been shaped, at least to some notable degree, by these pressures and interests into a mere imitation of social protest. This, I believed, was conspicuously the case with rock and roll and whatever social protest aspirations it may have possessed at times. Thus, any clear understanding of the degree to which rock and roll could ever retain a social protest quality, consequent to its public exposure, would need to address the commercial fetters the industry had placed on its production and dissemination, within the context, of course, of other relevant social, technological, and economic events that occurred before and throughout its development.

What I found was that even the putative sources of rock and roll, though they appeared to contain traces of some kind of an original, had previously been commercially influenced in significant ways, whether one considers the threads of styles that were eventually woven into Presley's music and rockabilly generally, the music of specific signature bands such as the Beatles or the Rolling Stones, the genres of the folk-revival of the 1960s, or the folk and psychedelic rock that followed. Accordingly, this "tradition" of commercializing music for profit certainly did not begin, but merely continued with rock and roll. As Bill Graham, the somewhat late coming but nevertheless influential promoter, appropriately underscored in his notoriously harsh reminders to his acts, given their ongoing proclivities "to party," what the bands were doing was putting on a professional "show," a performance, and people were spending their hard-earned money to see it. From the Doors to the Rolling Stones, from Janis Joplin to Jimi Hendrix, from Bob Dylan to Joan Baez, the performances were, from start to finish, always a show, a sort of fantasy that the acts were putting on, not unlike going to the movies. Even something as countercultural as the Acid Tests themselves (and it is hard to imagine much more countercultural than them) almost immediately developed show-like qualities once they headed out from La Honda, despite the ongoing emphasis on the value of "being real" or "authentic" with one another, to paraphrase former Digger Peter Coyote or draw from Tom Wolfe's characterizations in *The Electric Kool-Aid Acid Test*. Even the opening run of the Acid Test "tour," if it is fair to call it that, namely the three-day 1966 Trips Festival, was, by all accounts, the first foray into commercializing the Acid Tests for profit, and eventually led to the establishment of the two Filmore venues (West and East), and the use of the Carousel Ballroom. As Fred Turner points out,

> [t]he festival grossed $12,500 within three days and had spent very little in the way of overhead. Two weeks later, Bill Graham could be found staging a trips festival every weekend at the Fillmore. Within a year, teenagers from across America would be streaming into Haight-Ashbury, looking for the sort of bohemian utopia Graham was marketing. Reporters for *Time* and *Life* were not far behind. (Turner 2006, 66)

Certainly the Monterey Pop Festival and Woodstock, which soon followed, were certainly shows. Even for the Grateful Dead, that arguably resisted a variety of commercial influences throughout its career, the performances were always considered shows. Deadheads certainly called them "shows," and "going on tour" was often related to running away with the circus or carnival, which were in many ways shows. In fact, "going on tour," along with the evolution of "Shakedown Street," soon adopted, be it in fictionalized ways, imagined trappings of entertainment drawn from bygone days, such as traveling medicine shows and vaudeville.

What I also began to take note of during this investigation was that the poster "But the Man Can't Bust Our Music" was, perhaps, emblematic of something far more reaching than the nature and authenticity of rock and roll and social protest music specifically, namely a sort of hypocrisy that appeared to saturate nearly all corners of advanced industrial society. This hypocrisy, I speculated, issued from a kind of duplicitous existence individuals found themselves needing to adopt to effectively manage their lives within the social structure in which they found themselves, while they, nonetheless, persisted to yearn and seek out the very absence of such duplicity. From this perspective, their quest for authenticity was, in effect, a quest for a kind of freedom they might enjoy if they could only manage to circumvent the need for the duplicity that their functionality within their world required. On the one hand, in other words, individuals yearned for a unity with themselves that this freedom would afford—being "as they are"; on the other hand, they found themselves pressured to cultivate a secondary, split and schizophrenic, personality to "appear" in a way that hopefully would be of interest and, thus, of use to others. While some persons have vaguely attributed this duality and hypocrisy to the advent of the "modern" world, to "modernity," or to civilization as such as Rousseau at times seems to imply, I came to see it as more directly related to any system, including capitalism, the nature of which inevitably entails turning human beings into servants and slaves.

Naturally rock and roll was certainly no more immune to manifesting this sort of hypocrisy than anything else. Rock and roll expressed, I believe, a yearning for authenticity, for being and being real, as opposed to a mimicry of or "lies" about being, and so a desire for an unfettered freedom from the corporate infrastructure that nonetheless gave birth to its many manifestations and the mainstream society to which it stood as an emotive objection, be that only in the form of a persistent but gnawing ambivalence. In this very quali-fied respect, I think rock and roll was protest music. After all, was not this emotive objection not conspicuously present in rock and roll's manifestations of white "covers" of historically black tunes that rock and roll appreciated and in which it took pleasure? Meanwhile, however, these tunes were co-opted, glossed, and only eventually saw the light of day because they were profitable. Rock and roll, in this sense, was, quite in "deed," an emblem of a contradiction, or of a persona that is at odds with itself, that is arguably indicative of the sort of *zeitgeist* that permeates the contemporary world of advanced industrial society. Rock and roll, accordingly, was merely one more symptom of the fact that, as Ralph Gleason put it perhaps best, "in order to make money, corporate American enterprise will, in a kind of autolysis, allow its own destruction to be preached via a product that is profitable" (Gleason 1969, 144). But what other flavor of countercultural activity should one really expect to maintain traction in a society principally governed by capitalism?

In any event, it seems unrealistic to suppose that rock and roll could have maintained much genuine social protest quality, emanating as it did from commercial fetters that otherwise molded its manifestation as a mere prod-uct for purchase and consumption. Instead, from a quasi-Marxist if no less Hegelian lens,[2] it seems certain "material" conditions of the music business incidentally coincided with other contemporaneous events to give rise to rock and roll, such as it was, with whatever limited semblance of social protest quality remaining, most often because it was profitable. That said, it may be somewhat ironic that, in its wake, various subsequent and sometimes unan-ticipated social and musical manifestations that its advent may have triggered continued to shape, in turn, additional social and material realities, some of which embodied social protest qualities. On the one hand, the emergence and evolution of rock and roll, including whatever social protest residue it may have contained, was primarily motivated and facilitated by a unique confluence of events that at their core were, perhaps paradoxically, driven by capitalistic forces. Here, what is material largely determines what is ideal or conceptual. On the other hand, the product that resulted from these material conditions, the rock and roll itself, often proceeded to influence in varying ways the nature of the material conditions that originally gave rise to it, as well as other social protest and countercultural realities that followed.

Fox and Williams once raised the questions: "Is music simply a cultural reflection of underlying social structures, or may it register at least some independent impact upon these structures? To what extent do changes in music foreshadow or lag behind societal changes?" (Fox and Williams 1974, 354). To answer in the case of rock and roll, I vaguely propose that it was both an effect as well as a cause of the underlying social, economic, technological conditions that preceded, were concurrent with, and that followed its development. Accordingly, I hope that the foregoing has given some reasons for thinking that changes in music can reflect as well as shape social structures, and thus foreshadow and lag various "societal changes," both materially and ideally considered.[3]

NOTES

1. From "U.S. Federal Trade Commission, Materials on the Popular Music Industry Used in Preparation of R. H. Coase's Payola in Radio and Television Broadcasting (available at University of Chicago Law School Library)" (Coase 1979, 282, footnote 57). My italics.

2. One should not construe my appeal to Marx, Hegel, Plato, or Rousseau, among others, as expressing a general adherence to or endorsement of their philosophical outlook. Rather, I merely invoke their thinking throughout to serve as instruments of philosophical reflection to help generate or further clarify a fruitful perspective to understand the nature of rock and roll as social protest music and its impact on the contemporary society in which it emerged.

3. In a vein akin to Fox and Williams, Judith McCulloh considered the question about the relationship between the "material" and the "ideal" when she asked "Professor Wilgus to speculate, if he would, on where he might draw the line on a causal relationship between the development of country-western music and the industrialization of the South, or the Urbanization of the United States. Suppose we set up a kind of scale from one extreme of determinism to the other, with some of the steps along the way reading as follows: 'Music, like language, changes naturally and by itself. Music changes when culture changes. Music changes because culture changes. Music changes to a particular form when culture changes in a particular way. Music changes to a particular form because culture changes in a particular way.' Would any of these statements obtain, with or without modification? Could we have had country music as we know it today without the industrialization and urbanization just mentioned? Is that urbanization both a necessary and a sufficient condition for the growth of country-western music?" (McClulloh 1970, 181–82). In his response, Wilgus asserted: "If Mrs. McCulloh thinks I'm going to try to answer those questions, she is greatly mistaken . . . The questions are so good, there are no answers at this point" (Wilgus et al. 1970, 182).

References

Allen, Gary. 1969. "More Subversion than Meets the Ear." *American Popular Opinion* 12, reprinted in *The Sounds of Social Change*: 151–66.

Allen, Michael. 2015. "'Just a Half a Mile from the Mississippi Bridge': The Mississippi River Valley Origins of Rock and Roll." *Southern Quarterly* 52, 3: 99–120.

Barnouw, Erik. 1968. *The Golden Web.* New York: Oxford.

Baskerville, David. 1979. *Music Business Handbook and Career Guide*. Los Angeles: Sherwood Company.

Belz, Carl I. 1967. "Popular Music and the Folk Tradition." *The Journal of American Folklore* 80, 316: 130–42.

———. 1972. *The Story of Rock*. Second Edition. New York: Oxford University Press.

Bendix, Regina. 1997. *In Search of Authenticity: The Formation of Folklore Studies*. Madison: University of Wisconsin Press.

Benjamin, Walter. 1936 [2019]. "The Work of Art in the Age of Mechanical Reproduction." In *A Museum Approach to Heritage* 16: 226–43.

Berman, Marshall. 1970. *The Politics of Authenticity: Radical Individualism and the Emergence of Modern Society*. New York: Atheneum.

Bindas, Kenneth J. and Houston, Craig. 1989. "'Takin' Care of Business': Rock Music, Vietnam and the Protest Myth." *The Historian* 52: 1–23.

Born, Georgina and Hesmondhalgh, David. 2000. *Western Music and Its Others: Difference, Representation, and Appropriation in Music*. Berkeley: University of California Press.

Boyes, Georgina. 1993. *The Imagined Village: Culture, Ideology, and the English Folk Revival*. Manchester: Manchester University Press.

Chapple, Steve, and Garofalo, Reebee. 1977. *Rock 'n' Roll Is Here to Pay: The History and Politics of the Music Industry*. Chicago: Nelson-Hall.

Clark, T. J. 1985. *The Painting of Modern Life: Paris in the Art of Manet and his Followers*. Princeton, NJ: Princeton University Press.

Coase, R. H. 1979. "Payola in Radio and Television Broadcasting." *The Journal of Law and Economics* 22, 2: 269–328.

Cohen, Anne. 1977. "Folks and Hillbilly Music: Further Thoughts on Their Relation." *John Edwards Memorial Foundation Quarterly* 13: 50–57.

Cohen, John. 1967. "The Folk Music Interchange: Negro and White." *Sing Out: The Folk Song Magazine, Vol. 14, No. 6* (January, 1964): 42–49. Reprinted in *The American Folk Scene: Dimensions of the Folksong Revival*: 59–66.

Cohen, Norman. 1970. "Tin Pan Alley's Contribution to Folk Music." *Western Folklore* 29, 1: 9–20.

Cohen, Ronald D. and Capaldi, James (eds.). 2014. *The Pete Seeger Reader*. New York: Oxford University Press.

Cole, Richard R. 1971. "Top Songs in the Sixties: A Content Analysis of Popular Lyrics." *American Behavioral Scientist* 14: 389–99.

Conroy, Stephen S. 1983. "Popular Technology and Youth Rebellion in America." *Journal of Popular Culture* 16, 4: 123–33.

Denisoff, Serge. 1968. "Class Consciousness and the Song of Persuasion." *Sociological Quarterly* 11: 228–47. Reprinted in *Sing a Song of Social Significance*: 58–79.

Denisoff, R. Serge. 1969. "Folk-Rock: Folk Music, Protest, or Commercialism?" *Journal of Popular Culture* 3: 214–30.

———. 1970. "Protest Songs: Those on the Top Forty and Those of the Streets." *American Quarterly* 22, 4: 807–23.

———. 1972. "The Evolution of the American Protest Song." *The Sounds of Social Change: Studies in Popular Culture*, R. Serge Denisoff, Richard A Peterson (eds.), Rand McNally College Publishing Company: 15–25.

———. 1973. "The Evolution of Popular Music Broadcasting: 1920–1972." *Popular Music and Society* 2: 202–26.

———. 1983. *Sing a Song of Social Significance*. Bowling Green University Popular Press.

Denisoff, R. Serge, and Levine, Mark H. 1970. "Generations and Counter-Culture: A Study in the Ideology of Music." *Youth and Society* 2, 1: 33–58.

———. 1971. "The Popular Protest Song: The Case of 'Eve of Destruction.'" *Public Opinion Quarterly* 35, 1: 117–22.

———. 1972a. "Youth and Popular Music: A Test of the Taste Culture Hypothesis." *Youth and Society* 4, 2: 237–55.

———. 1972b. "Brain Washing or Background Noise: The Popular Protest Song." *The Sounds of Social Change: Studies in Popular Culture*. R. Serge Denisoff, Richard A Peterson (eds.). Rand McNally College Publishing Company: 213–21.

Denisoff, Serge and Peterson, Richard A.(eds.). 1972. *The Sounds of Social Change: Studies in Popular Culture*. Rand McNally College Publishing Company.

Denzin, Norman K. 1970. "Problems in Analyzing Elements of Mass Culture. Notes on the Popular Song and Other Artistic Productions." *American Journal of Sociology*, 75, 6: 1035–38.

DeWhitt, Bennie Lee. 1977. *The American Society of Composers, Authors and Publishers, 1914–1938*. Unpublished dissertation, Emory University.

Dixon, Richard D. 1979. "Music in the Community: A Survey of Who Is Paying Attention." *Popular Music and Society* 7, 1: 37–56.

Eisen, Jonathan (ed.) 1969. *The Age of Rock: Sounds of the American Cultural Revolution*. New York: Random House.

Elliot, Robert. 1987. *Faking Nature: The Ethics of Environmental Restoration*. London: Routledge.

Erdelyi, Michael. 1940. "The Relation between 'Radio Plugs' and Sheet Sales of Popular Music." *Journal of Applied Psychology* 24, 6: 696–702.

Ferrandino, Joe. 1969. "Rock Culture and the Development of Social Consciousness." *Radical America*. Reprinted in *Side Saddle on the Golden Calf*, edited by George H. Lewis. Pacific Palisades, CA: Goodyear Publishing Company, Inc.: 263–90.

Flood, Marilyn J. 1991. "Lyrics and the Law: Censorship of Rock-and-Roll in the United States and Great Britain." *New York Law School Journal of International and Comparative Law* 12, 3: 399–445.

Fornas, Johan. 1995. *Cultural Theory and Late Modernity*. London: Sage Publishing.

Fortune. 1979 (April 23). "The Record Business: Rocking to the Big-Money Beat": 58–68.

Fox, Kathryn Joan. 1987. "Real Punks and Pretenders: The Social Organization of a Counterculture." *Journal of Contemporary Ethnography* 16, 3: 344–70.

Fox, William S. and Williams, James D. 1974. "Political Orientation and Music Preferences among College Students." *Public Opinion Quarterly* 38, 3: 352–71.

Gleason, Ralph J. 1967. "Like a Rolling Stone." *American Scholar*. Reprinted in *The Age of Rock*: 61–76.

———. 1969. "The Greater Sound." *The Drama Review* 13, No. 4: 160–167. Reprinted under the title "A Cultural Revolution" in *The Sounds of Social Change: Studies in Popular Culture*: 137–46.

Gonczy, Daniel J. 1985. "The Folk Music Movement of the 1960s: Its Rise and Fall." *Popular Music and Society* 10, 1: 15–31.

Gordon, Robert Winslow. 1938. *Folk Songs of America*. New York.

Grazian, David. 2003. *Blue Chicago: The Search for Authenticity in Urban Blues Clubs*. Chicago: University of Chicago Press.

Green, Archie. 1959. "A Discographic Appraisal of *American Balladry from British Broadsides: A Guide for Students and Collectors of Traditional Song*, G. Malcolm Laws, Jr. Philadelphia, American Folklore Society, 1957." *Caravan* 15: 7–13.

———. 1965. "Hillbilly Music: Source and Symbol." *The Journal of American Folklore* 78, No. 309: 204–28.

———. 1972. *Only a Miner: Studies in Recorded Coal-Mining Songs*. Urbana: University of Illinois Press.

Greenway, John. 1953. *American Folksongs of Protest*. Philadelphia: University of Pennsylvania Press.

Grendysa, Peter. 1978 (February). "The Forty Year War: The Story of the Music Licensing Societies." *Goldmine*: 22–23.

———. 1986 (January). "Origin of the Species: The Microgroove Revolution." *Goldmine*.

Grossberg, Lawrence. 1992. *We Gotta Get Out of This Place: Popular Conservativism and Postmodern Culture*. New York: Routledge.

References

Guralnick, Peter. 1994. *Last Train to Memphis: The Rise of Elvis Presley*. Boston: Little, Brown.

Harris, Charles K. 1926. *After the Ball*. New York: Frank-Maurice.

Hentoff, Nat. 1961. "The Rise of Folkum Music." *The Commonweal* 75, 4: 99–100.

———. 1962. "Folk Finds a Voice." *The Reporter* 26, 1: 39–42.

Hirsch, Paul Morris. 1963. *The Structure of the Popular Music Industry: An Examination of the Filtering Process by Which Records Are Preselected for Public Consumption*, Survey Research Center, Institute for Social Research, The University of Michigan. Reprinted 1973.

Hirsch, Paul M. 1971. "Sociological Approaches to the Pop Music Phenomenon." *American Behavioral Scientist* 14, 3: 371–88.

Hirsch, Paul M., Robinson, John, Taylor, Elizabeth Keogh, and Withey, Stephen B. 1972. "The Changing Popular Song: An Historical Overview." *Popular Music and Society* 1: 83–93.

Hoeptner, Fred. 1959 (April). "Folk and Hillbilly Music: The Background of Their Relation, Part 1." *Caravan* 16: 8, 16–17, 42.

———. 1959 (June). "Folk and Hillbilly Music: The Background of Their Relation, Part 2." *Caravan* 17: 20–23, 26–28.

Hugunin, Marc. 1979. "ASCAP, BMI and the Democratization of American Popular Music." *Popular Music and Society* 7, 1: 8–17.

Jarnow, Jesse. 2018. *Wasn't That a Time: The Weavers, the Blacklist, and the Battle for the Soul of America*. New York: Da Capo Press.

Keil, Charles. 1966. *Urban Blues*. Chicago: University of Chicago Press.

Lair, John. 1935 (March 16). "No Hill Billies in Radio." *WLS Weekly*: 7, 12.

Larson, B. 1970. *Rock and Roll: The Devil's Diversion*, 3rd ed. (McCook, Bob Larson).

Lewis, George H. 1970. "Pop Artist and His Product: Mixed Up Confusion." *The Journal of Popular Culture* 4: 327–38. Reprinted in *Side Saddle on the Golden Calf*: 305–313.

———. (ed.). 1972. *Side Saddle on the Golden Calf: Social Structure and Popular Culture in America*. Pacific Palisades, CA: Goodyear Publishing Company, Inc.

———. 1983. "The Meanings in the Music and the Music's in Me: Popular Music as Symbolic Communication." *Theory, Culture and Society* 1, 3: 133–41.

Linden, Paul. 2012. "Race, Hegemony, and the Birth of Rock and Roll." *The Journal of the Music and Entertainment Industry Educators Association* 12, 1: 43–67.

Lund, Jens and Denisoff, R. Serge. 1971. "The Folk Music Revival and the Counter Culture: Contributions and Contradictions." *The Journal of American Folklore* 84, 334: 394–405.

Lydon, Susan. 1968, November. "Would You Want your Sister to Marry a Beatle?" *Ramparts* 30: 66.

Lydon, Michael. 1969. "Rock for Sale." *Ramparts* (December). Reprinted in *Side Saddle on the Golden Calf*: 313–20.

Mabry, Donald J. 1990. "The Rise and Fall of Ace Records: A Case Study in the Independent Record Business." *The Business History Review* 64, 3: 411–50.

MacDougald, Duncan Jr. 1941. "The Popular Music Industry" in Paul F. Lazarsfeld and Frank N. Stanton (eds.) *Radio Research 1941*: 65–109.

Maddock, Shane. 1996. "'Whole Lotta Shakin' Goin' On': Racism and Early Opposition to Rock Music." *Mid-America: An Historical Review* 78, 2: 181–202.

Mailer, Norman. 1957. "The White Negro: Superficial Reflections on the Hipster." *Dissent* 4.

Malone, Bill C. 1968. *Country Music U.S.A.: A Fifty-Year History*. Published for the American Folklore Society. Austin: The University of Texas Press.

Marcus, Greil (ed.). 1969a. *Rock and Roll Will Stand*. Boston: Beacon Press.

———. 1969b. "A Singer in a Rock and Roll Band" in *Rock and Roll Will Stand*.

———. 1972. "A New Awakening." *The Sounds of Social Change: Studies in Popular Culture*, [Serge Denisoff and Richard A. Peterson (eds.). Rand McNally College Publishing Company:]: 127–36.

———. 1995. "The Old, Weird America." *Common Knowledge* 4, 3: 35–47.

Marx, Karl. 1959. *Economic and Philosophic Manuscripts of 1844*. Martin Milligan (trans. 1932). Moscow: Progress Publishers.

McCulloh, Judith. 1967. "Hillbilly Records and Tune Transcription." *Western Folklore* 26, 4: 225–44.

——— —. 1970. "Prepared Comments" on "Country-Western Music and the Urban Hillbilly" by D. K. Wilgus. *The Journal of American Folklore: The Urban Experience and Folk Tradition* 83, 328: 180–82.

McDonald, James R. 1988a. "Censoring Rock Lyrics: A Historical Analysis of the Debate." *Youth and Society* 19, 3: 294–313.

———. 1988b. "Politics Revisited: Metatextual Implications of Rock and Roll Criticism." *Youth and Society* 19, 4: 485–504.

McLeod, Kembrew. 1999. "Authenticity within Hip-Hop and Other Cultures Threatened with Assimilation." *Journal of Communication* 49: 134–60.

Middleton, Richard. 2006. *Voicing the Popular: On the Subjects of Popular Music*. New York: Routledge.

Mol, Joeri M., and Wijnberg, Nachoem M. 2007. "Competition, Selection and Rock and Roll: The Economics of Payola and Authenticity." *Journal of Economic Issues* 41, 3: 701–14.

Monson, Ingrid. 1995. "The Problem with White Hipness: Race, Gender, and Cultural Conceptions in Jazz Historical Discourse." *Journal of the American Musicological Society* 48, 3: 396–419.

Moore, Allan. 2002. "Authenticity as Authentication." *Popular Music* 21, 2: 209–23.

Nekola, Anna. 2013. "'More than Just a Ausic': Conservative Christian Anti-rock Discourse and the U.S. Culture Wars." *Popular Music* 32, 3: 407–426.

Nevill, Richard. 1970. *Play Power: Exploring the International Underground.* New York: Random House.

Noebel, David A. 1965. *Communism, Hypnotism, and the Beatles*. Tulsa, OK: Christian Crusade Publications.

———. 1966. *Rhythm, Riots and Revolution*. Tulsa, OK: Christian Crusade Publications.

Oforlea, Aaron. 2012. "The Search for Authenticity: African American Folklore in the Age of Late Capitalism." *The Griot* 31, 1: 21–40.

Orman, John M. 1984. *The Politics of Rock Music*. Chicago: Nelson-Hall, Inc. Publishers.

Otto, John S., and Burns, Augustus M. 1974. "Black and White Cultural Interaction in the Early Twentieth Century South: Race and Hillbilly Music." *Phylon* 35, 4: 407–17.

Peterson, Richard A. 1971. "Taking Popular Music Too Seriously." *Journal of Popular Culture* 4, 3: 590–94.

———. 1990. "Why 1955? Explaining the Advent of Rock Music." *Popular Music* 9, 1: 97–116.

———. 1997. *Creating Country Music: Fabricating Authenticity*. Chicago and London: Chicago University Press.

———. 2005. "In Search of Authenticity." *Journal of Management Studies* 42, 5: 1083–98.

Peterson, Richard A. and Berger, David G. 1972. "Three Eras in the Manufacture of Popular Music Lyrics," in *Sounds of Social Change*: 282–303.

———. 1975. "Cycles in Symbol Production: The Case of Popular Music." *American Sociological Review* 40, 2: 158–73.

Peterson, Richard A. and Davis, Russell B. Jr. 1978. "The Contemporary American Radio Audience." *Popular Music and Society* 6: 169–83.

Peterson, Richard A. and DiMaggio, Paul J. 1973. "The Early Opry: Its Hillbilly Image in Fact and Fancy." *Journal of Country Music* 4: 39–51.

Platoff, John. 2005. "John Lennon, 'Revolution,' and the Politics of Musical Reception." *The Journal of Musicology* 22, 2: 241–67.

Pound, Louise. 1922. *American Ballads and Songs*, New York: C. Scribner's Sons.

Pratt, Ray. 1986. "The Politics of Authenticity in Popular Music: The Case of the Blues." *Popular Music and Society* 10, 3: 55–78.

Randle, William M. Jr. 1966. "A History of Radio Broadcasting and its Social and Economic Effect on the Entertainment Industry, 1920–1930." Unpublished PhD dissertation. Western Reserve University.

Rennhoff, Adam D. 2010. "The Consequences of 'Consideration Payments': Lessons from Radio Payola." *Review of Industrial Organization* 36, 2: 133–47.

Roberts, Michael. 2010. "A Working-Class Hero Is Something to Be: The American Musicians' Union's Attempt to Ban the Beatles, 1964." *Popular Music* 29, 1: 1–16.

Robinson, John P. and Hirsch, Paul. 1969. "It's the Sound That Does it." *Psychology Today* 3: 42–45.

———. 1972. "Teenage Response to Rock and Roll Protest Songs" in *The Sounds of Social Change*: 222–31.

Robinson, John P., Pilskaln, Robert, and Hirsch, Paul. 1976. "Protest Rock and Drugs." *Journal of Communication* 26, 4: 125–36.

Rodnitzky, Jerome L. 1969. "The Evolution of the American Protest Song." *Journal of Popular Culture* 3, 1: 35–45.

———. 1971. "The Decline of Contemporary Protest Music." *Popular Music and Society* 1: 44–50.

Root, Robert L, Jr. 1986. "A Listener's Guide to the Rhetoric of Popular Music." *Journal of Popular Culture* 20: 15–26.

Rosenstone, Robert A. 1969. "'The Times They Are A-Changin': The Music of Protest." *The Annuals of the American Academy of Political and Social Science* 382: 131–44.

Roszak, Theodore. 1969. *The Making of a Counterculture*. Garden City, NY: Doubleday (reprinted in 1995. Berkeley and Los Angeles: University of California Press).

Rousseau, Jean-Jacques. 2011. *Basic Political Writings* (2nd edition). Donald A. Cress (trans). Indianapolis/Cambridge: Hackett Publishing Company.

Roy, William G. 2004. "'Race Records' and 'Hillbilly Music': Institutional Origins of Racial Categories in the American Commercial Recording Industry." *Poetics* 32: 265–79.

Russell, Ross. 1973. *Bird Lives: The High Life and Hard Times of Charlie Parker*. New York: Charterhouse.

Ryan, John. 1985. *The Production of Culture in the Music Industry: The ASCAP-BMI Controversy*. Lanham, MD: University Press of America.

Sanjek, David. 1991. *American Popular Music Business in the 20th Century*. New York: Oxford University Press.

Seeger, Pete. 1946 (July 16). "People's Songs and Singers." *New Masses*: 7–9. Reprinted in *The Pete Seeger Reader*. 2014.

Taylor, Charles. 1991. *The Ethics of Authenticity*. Cambridge: Harvard University Press.

Taylor, Timothy Dean. 1997. *Global Pop: World Musics, World Markets*. New York: Routledge.

Time Magazine. 1941 (January 27). "No Letup": 48.

Titon, Jeff Todd. 2012. "Authenticity and Authentication: Mike Seeger, the New Lost City Ramblers, and the Old Time Music Revival." *Journal of Folklore Research* 49, 2: 227–45.

Trilling, Lionel. 1974. *Sincerity and Authenticity*. London: Oxford University Press.

Turner, Fred. 2006. *From Counterculture to Cyberculture: Stewart Brand, the Whole Earth Network, and the Rise of Digital Utopianism*. Chicago: University of Chicago Press.

Warner, Harry P. 1953. *Radio and Television Rights, the Law of Copyright, Trade-Marks and Unfair Competition in the Broadcasting Industry*. New York: Matthew Bender and Company.

Watson, Sheila. 2019. *A Museum Studies Approach to Heritage*. Abingdon, Oxon; New York: Routledge.

Weisethaunet, Hans and Lindberg, Ulf. 2010. "Authenticity Revisited: The Rock Critic and the Changing Real." *Popular Music and Society* 33, 4: 465–85.

Wilentz, Sean. 1998. "Dylan's Old Weird America." *Dissent* 45, 2: 100–6.

Wilgus, D. K. 1970. "Country-Western Music and the Urban Hillbilly." *The Journal of American Folklore: The Urban Experience and Folk Tradition* 83, 328: 157–79.

Wilgus, D. K., McMahon, George, Tremain, Robert, Pilling, Arnold, Shepard, Leslie, Fowke, Edith, and Johnson, Aili. 1970. "[Country-Western Music and the Urban

Hillbilly]: Discussion from the Floor." *The Journal of American Folklore: The Urban Experience and Folk Tradition* 83, 328: 182–84.

Willis, Ellen. 1969, February 1. "Records: Rock, Etc.: The Big Ones." *New Yorker*: 61, 63.

Wolfe, Charles. 1978. "Columbia Record and Old-Time Music." *John Edwards Memorial Foundation Quarterly* 14: 118–25.

Wolfe, Charles K. 1993. "The White Man Blues, 1922–40." *Journal of Country Music* 15, 3: 38–44.

Index

About the Author

Kurt Torell is associate professor of philosophy at Pennsylvania State University. In conjunction with enjoying multiple academic and administrative appointments over the arc of his career, he has taught courses in political theory, philosophy of art, ethics, modern philosophy, and the 1960s counterculture. In addition, he has delivered national and international talks, and published on a variety of topics, ranging from Thomas Hobbes and Native American myth to issues in the *Philosophy of Science* and the Grateful Dead.